# Finding Our Indian Blood

## Vance Hawkins

Published by:
Bluewater Publications
1812 CR 111
Killen, Alabama 35645
www.BluewaterPublications.com

# INTRODUCTION

I've tried to look through the telescope of time, and hope there is no mirror at the end looking back, telling me what I want to hear. I've done my best not to see what I wanted to see, but to be objective.

I remember as a child going to a pow-wow and dad saying we had some Indian blood. I first thought we were part Comanche because we lived in Southwestern Oklahoma. I remember someone telling me "You look like a White Indian." One day someone asked me "What tribe?" and I had no idea. I said "Comanche" because I had no idea, and since they lived here, well maybe that was it. Later I learned there was a family story that we were related to Sequoyah. However I never researched these things at that time. I just remembered them, but let them be.

I was probably 40 years old before I really started looking into our heritage. I'm 60 now (as of late December 2012). I remember Uncle Andrew when asked about our heritage, replied, "I'd be careful about looking into that, if I were you. You might not like what you find." What on earth did he mean by that? Dad bought a book by "Dub" West in 1976 entitled "The Mysteries of Sequoyah" so he must have been looking into it, too. After he passed on in 1992, I got more serious about looking into our heritage. Dad only had 2 sisters left. That generation was going fast. As a child I knew some of my great uncles and aunts, grandma's generation. I had never asked any of them anything about our heritage. Now that generation was gone, and the generation after theirs was almost gone, too. Then one of the two remaining Aunts passed on. Time was short. I sent off a letter to Aunt Lorena, the last of her generation and I have included that. Now she too, is gone.

If you look at old family photos, one branch of the family goes from looking mostly Indian not so long ago, to mostly Caucasian today. The generations of my ancestors that knew our true heritage have gone now.

Gradually, this research has consumed me. I thought it would be easier to find our Indian heritage – it has not been. I literally looked into EVERY Guess/Guest/Gist/Gess surname in just about EVERY state I thought relevant – Oklahoma/Indian Territory, Arkansas, Texas, Louisiana, Mississippi, Alabama, Tennessee and elsewhere. One by one, just about every hopeful candidate was laid to rest. Then one day, magic! We found our Gist's! That came after 20 years of complete confusion and frustration. I hope one day to be able to say the same about our Brown's. I literally researched EVERY Indian Tribe found in

Oklahoma, both the indigenous and emigrant tribes and their migration routes. I've looked into remnant groups remaining in the East.

I have tried to be sensitive to American Indian concerns. I've learned to keep quiet and low key at home. I just "wanna-learn" about a part of my family that is hard to track down. I say as did my father, "I have a little American Indian blood, not much though." Then after saying that there is always someone in the group; someone mostly White, who blurts out, "I'm half-Cherokee!" – you don't have any idea how many times I've heard that – dozens, literally! This person really means to say either his father or mother had family stories of having Indian blood on one side of the family, but not the other. That gets the full bloods or enrolled people laughing again, thinking we are all full of hot air, and lump us all together, and then they forget about us as worthy of serious consideration. My quiet voice is either forgotten, or gets lumped in with those who make crazy statements. I have really tried to follow the middle ground. I strongly believe many of the people who say they have Cherokee blood really have Eastern Siouan – Catawba, Saponi, Saura/Cheraw/Xualla. There is a record of the Sizemore's who had 200 rejected applicants to the Guion Miller or Dawes Rolls who says they heard an ancestor mention moving away from the *Catawba Reservation!* I suspect that was true of many others as well. As I thought maybe my family was Comanche because we lived in Southwestern Oklahoma, perhaps those on the rejected rolls thought they were Cherokee for the same reason.

I have heard people say, "Why are all these White people claiming they are Cherokee? And why do they all have to claim to be descended from FAMOUS Cherokees? Why can't they say they descend from some average Joe?" So in many ways I wish our stories of a Cherokee heritage hadn't included Sequoyah or the Brown's. This research project has taken many turns and twists I hadn't foreseen. When my great uncle wrote in IPP (Indian Pioneer Papers) we lived near Fort Smith and either Sequoyah or Leflore Counties, I thought it would be easy – that's just a short distance to where Sequoyah lived. Little did I know there would be no possible connection to Sequoyah for a hundred years further into the past, and that connection would be discovered in East Tennessee. Although discouraged, we eventually went full circle, and found a possible connection. Maybe that's all we will ever find. We will need help confirming it, and will keep looking.

Although I have researched all the genealogies of all my ancestor's surnames, this report is just about our Indian blood. Surprisingly, we had contact with some interesting characters in history, and we can prove it. If that character had contact with American Indians of his region and time, I might have included a page or two about it. If I write only about my family, this would be full of nothing but census records and that would bore the reader to death. I do include a generous portion of census records, but I also have some interesting stories about several historical figures.

We have both saints and sinners, one of us was hung as a horsethief and another was a Methodist circuit-riding Minister. We've known famous Indian Chiefs and one relative knew George Washington personally. My ancestors have fought in just about every American War, and several have been killed in those wars, from the American Revolution to World War Two and beyond. At least one cousin had a son in Iraq a couple of years back, so the tradition continues. We were always (with one exception) enlisted, not officers.

There are so many people to thank that it would take several pages to name them all. My sisters, Linda Haltom and Carol Milson. My nephew Brad Haltom. Cousin Page [Beagle] Dull, granddaughter of Uncle Cecil. A second cousin Carla Davenport, wife of the grandson of grandma's sister, Aunt Ettie, and other relatives. Off the top of my head, Dr. Thomas Blucher, famous researcher of the Catawba. When I showed him our family stories he got excited and told me about a group of Catawba who were said to have moved to the Fort Smith, Arkansas area, and told me about them. Jerri Chasteen, former registrar of the Cherokee Elder's Society. She was one of the catalysts that helped put me on the right track. I vowed to NOT be lured by fake histories, but to rather make sure of my information and check everything out. Donna Sutliff, a descendant of the Bull family, provided a great deal of help in discovering more information about Tarleton Bull.

Sticher and Jim Sanders, genealogical researchers of the Gist/Guess/Guess surname. Don was similar to Jerri, in that he didn't let me get away with fake or "maybe history – I had to check everything out, seek primary sources. Numerous others were helpful and I appreciate them all.

# Contents

# FINDING OUR INDIAN BLOOD, PART 1

## CHAPTER 1: FAMILY STORIES

My birth certificate says I am Vance Hawkins, born December 28th, 1952 in Okmulgee, Okmulgee County, Oklahoma. It also says Alpha Omega Hawkins is my father. Dad's birth certificate says he was born August 15th, 1915 in Manitou, Tillman County, Oklahoma. Dad said however, he was born on their farm with his grandma, Josephine [Brown] Richey being the midwife who delivered him. Their farm was near Manitou, Tillman County, Oklahoma. His birth certificate says his mother was Lona (Loney) Clementine Richey. Her birth certificate (delayed) says her parents were Jeffrey Hoten Richey and Josephine Brown. It is through my paternal grandma, Loney, that we have stories of having some Indian ancestry. I have spent a great many years trying to document or disprove these stories.

In 1940, the Oahu, Hawaii census, Schoefield Barracks, 13th Field Artillery census mentions my dad, Alpha O. Hawkins, 24 years old, Private (he was a corporal by the time of the Pearl Harbor attack twenty months later), single, from Oklahoma. Census records in 1910, 1920 and 1930 have us living in Holton Township, Tillman County, Oklahoma. The 1900 census has my Richey's living in the Pickens District of the Chickasaw Nation. Below is a 1909-1910 school photo in shows two of grandma's brothers, Otho and Hoten. Otho and Hoten are blown up in the next two photos. Otho, Hoten and grandma Loney are brothers and sister.

SOUTH DEEP RED SCHOOL (first location), 1909-10. Back row, from left: Walter McPherson teacher, Annie Montgomery, Fannie Roten, Montgomery, Herbert Butcher, T. E. Hall, Other Little, Otho Richey, Bill Perry, Belle Fryer, Mary Wyatt, Tom Fryer, Mary Lizzie Perry, Perry with Beulah Perry in front of her, Maggie Lee Butcher, Ollie Montgomery, Iona Wade, Ruth Bryan, Jossie Ayers, and Maude gomery. Center row: Marion Butcher, Blanche Roten, Maude Bryan, Eva Roten, Roe Hall, David Bryan, Jim Wade, Estelle Bryan, Schmidt, Reba Montgomery, Henry Schmidt, Opal Priest, Sallie Perry, Fred Spille, Zula Hall, Sula Hall, and Fannie Wade. Front row: Wiggins, Hugh Turner, Floyd Dickerson, Penn Butcher, Luther Hall peeking over True Hall, Ballard Stanford, Paul Wyatt peeking ar Raymond Harper, Rex Roten behind Jim Fryer, Andrew Wyatt, Reuben Wilson peeking over Don Butcher, Bertha Wyatt, Ida Mae W behind Holton Richey, Reecie Wade (blurred) behind Tom Stanford, Cora Wade behind John Schmidt, and Clifton Overton.

Above is an old school photo, 1909-1910. I have blown up the photos of the two Richey boys, 2 of grandma's brothers, Uncle Hoten on the left and Uncle Otho on the right. They clearly have American Indian blood [1.].

## A. The Search for Sequoyah

We've always had a family story that we were somehow related to Sequoyah. It was supposedly great Aunt Ettie that had more of this information than the rest of the kids.

My family leased land from the Chickasaw. I haven't found the original leases and I don't even know where to look for them. On a trip to Oklahoma City, to the Oklahoma Historical Society building diagonally across from the state capital building, I did find the 3x5 inch index card (to the lower right). My great grandpa did lease land from the Kiowa Agency to be used for cattle grazing. When I asked to see the file indexed however, I was told they couldn't find it any more. Well, I'll keep looking for it, that and many other things I can't find.

**Great Aunt Ettie's Letter to Grandma**

For some reason for many years, an old letter from Aunt Ettie to grandma was kept. It must have been written in the early 1950s and has been Xeroxed many times, so many it can barely been read anymore. Here

```
RICHEY, JEFFREY H., Lease of. Kiowa Reservation

        See
        Kiowa - Cattle & Pastures
        Oct. 31, 1905
        Mar. 31, 1906
        Oct. 18, 1906
```

is a transcription of it (she was a poor speller). Originally there also was a small piece of paper that mentioned David Brown and Harriet Guess but I have lost it. I have tried to retain her original spelling and grammar:

*Lona, here is the copy of our family history I can't send the old original it to old it would come to pieces this is all of us childrens and their death.*

### Family Births

*Jeffrey H. Richey was Borned May 1st AD 1851. Josey Feen Brown was Borned March 24 1854. Joseph David Richey was Borned March 4th AD 1873. Charlotte Richey was Borned January 17 AD 1875. Ettie Elizabeth Richey was Borned February 15th AD 1877. Swany Adow Richey was Borned March the 8th AD 1879. Oscar Taylor Richey was borned September 10th AD 1881. Loney Clementine Richey was Borned December AD 21 1883. Beatrice Pearl Richey was Borned March 23 AD 1886. William Franklin Richey was Borned Dec AD 9th 1889. Otho Ewell Richey was Borned September 20 AD 1892. Jeffrey Hotten Richey was borned October 18th AD 1894.*

*Lona, Joseph was borned in Ark. Me and Swanie and Charlotte was Borned in Ark. You and Taylor were Borned in Denton Co Texas. Bea was Borned in Montague [Co], Texas. The others were borned In the Indian Territory.*

*Marriage of the family of Richey's*

*Jeffrey H. Richey and Josey Feen Brown was married March the 10th AD 1872. Etta E Richey and Charley T Davenport married June 17 AD 1896. Swanie Adow Richey and Zora Vanscoder were married March AD 1900. Oscar Taylor Richey Emma Price were married Sept 10, 1905. Lona Clementine Richey married Noah Hawkins*

*Records of Deaths*

*Our brother Joseph was 18 months old when he died. Our sister Charlotte was 9 month old when she died. Joseph was buried in Ark. Charlotte was buried down here in Chocktow Nation. I give you this so you will no where all is Burred. Joseph David Richey died Oct 27 AD 1874. Charlotte Richey died November 1st 1875. Otho Ewell Richey died August 17th 1917. Jeffrey H Richey died June 2 sec 1926. Josey Feen Richey died July 24th 1932. William Richey died Dec 10 1950. Swaney Adow Richey died Aug 4th 1940. Oscar Taylor Richey died July 17 1952.*

*Lona, I've wrote till I'm nervous.*

*From your sis, Ettie*


**Dad's Sequoyah Story**

I once heard a cousin say "we descend from Sequoyah". But I know that is not exactly what Dad said. Below is how I remember his story went.

Dad used to tell me the following story. He said he often walked to school barefoot. I used to have access to a photo of him barefoot at a one room school, but when mama died it vanished, and I have asked for a copy but no one seems to know what became of it. He also said his grandparents lived between his house and the school, and said sometimes on the way home from school, he'd stop by their house for a time. He said on occasion, his grandma looked through his Oklahoma History book, and said she pointed to a picture of an Indian in the book, and said, "Do you know you are related to him?" Dad always said he didn't remember which Indian it was. Now since Dad's grandma's maiden name was Josephine Brown, and Josephine's mother's maiden name was Harriet Guess, well many of us suspected maybe it was Sequoyah.

Well Dad and I used to argue over petty things when I was young — I was rebellious. Him being born in 1915 and me in 1952, there was a generation gap. As a child he went to town in a mule driven wagon, and a 20 mile trip to town and back took all day and half the night. It was so different from how things are now. He was penniless as a child and I never lacked much. He was a very good man. Now I understand why he was as he was, but he's not here to tell him. I didn't get interested enough in those stories until Dad was older. I finally showed him that photo of that famous King painting of Sequoyah from an old Oklahoma history text book and ask him if that was the photo he'd shown his grandma and she'd referenced. But all Dad would ever reply was "I just don't remember." Too bad. So I wished I'd asked him before, and I'd wished I'd been more curious about this when I was younger, and that we hadn't argued so much. He was a lifelong Democrat and practically worshipped Roosevelt, saying his policies saved the family "from starving to death" (his words), during the Dust Bowl. The children of the Dust Bowl are probably rolling over in their graves, looking at their grandkids attitudes towards Roosevelt's reforms.

On the left is grandma, Lona [Richey] Hawkins – called Loney. That is a honey suckle vine behind her, and that mark on her left arm is the shadow of that honey suckle. I remember very well when I was a small child her walking up to me and pulling off a honey suckle bloom from that vine she is standing by, and showing me how to suck out the "honey" from it. On the right is a copy of a very old tin-type of, I was told, my great great-grandma, Harriet [Gist/Guess] Brown. It was sent to me by a relative, Carla Davenport. She emailed me how she received it. A copy of that email is below. I don't know who the child is. I suspect it might be her granddaughter, my great Aunt Ettie. It was her descendants that preserved that old tin-type.

**Correspondence with Carla Davenport**

I received a lot of help from Carla Davenport. She was wife to the grandson of my great Aunt Etta, grandma's sister. Now Aunt Ettie (that is what we called her even though technically, she was a great aunt) was a sort of family historian, and had old records, all of which were lost when she passed on in the 1960s.

I asked Carla about our Indian blood, and she had been researching it longer than I. Here is something I received from her on that topic, and how she came to have that old tin-type, above. I asked her about how she obtained that tin-type. Here is her response:

*This is very sad. When I went to visit Ettie in 1965, she showed me many pictures and then took out the Bible, but would not let me read it for myself or even hold it. I asked her why and she said because their spelling was not correct. Even though I told her I could still read it she refused to let me. She said she would read it to me. So she did, read the "parts" I asked about. Then when she died, my mother-in-law found the center section of the Bible ripped out and thrown in the trash. She was only able to salvage 1 page for me, that was all that was left to my knowledge. Apparently someone wanted the Bible and did not care about anything else. Then she found the oldest photos and tintypes we had gone through in another trash basket, and she brought those to me. Makes me sick to think of the callous disregard for her things.*

*It seems the entry for David B. Brown and Harriet Guess was exactly that and she insisted that her name was Guest. This was very confusing to me as the marriage record as recorded from the marriage index by B. Sistler was Harriet Guess. (Thank goodness, your sister Carol had a copy of the original from the Memphis courthouse. Now we know it was Guess.)*

*When I told Ettie that J. L. (her son) had told me about her Indian heritage, she was furious, and said she did NOT HAVE ANY INDIAN. Of course, we all know that is not true from what she has told so many of the kids, even J.L. knew. Unfortunately, my baby had developed an earache on the trip and she was very disruptive until we found a doctor. When I came to different photos, she would tell me who they were, we did not get through the entire box because I had to cook dinner and after I had cleaned up I found she had put the box and Bible away and wanted to go to bed and would NOT get them out again. The next morning we left early so I was really elated that I "inherited" what little I did.*

*Later,*

*Carla*

It was from Carla that we got a copy of the tin-type of Harriet.

**Aunt Lorena's Story about Sequoyah**

After Dad and Aunt Lula passed away, I realized if I wanted to have any other stories about our Indian blood, I'd have to ask Aunt Lorena, the last of her generation. So I wrote her and asked her if she ever heard any family stories about us being related to Sequoyah. Below is what she replied. Now there was originally a fifth page in which (I'm paraphrasing) she said she was "quite sure" her mother had said that Harriet (Lona Richey, Aunt Lorena's mother, was the daughter of Josephine Brown, and Josie's mother was Harriet Guess/Gist) was Sequoyah's "niece or great niece". Now there were only 4 or 5 lines on that fifth page, but what it said was important. I don't know what became of it. I have transcribed the majority of her letter, and I had part of page five transcribed on my computer before I lost it. Here is that transcription:

*Dear Vance and wife,*

*I am sorry I have been so slow answering your letter. I have no idea what I could tell you that you don't already know.*

*The reason I am so late answering is I had an accident at a dinner theater here in town during intermission. I have no idea how it happened unless I tripped on a man's coat lying on the floor or someone may have pushed me. I fractured my shoulder and hip on the left side. Have spent almost two months in rehab hospitals. I walked the first time last week. I'm home now and will have rehab at home. I tire easily.*

***I remember more about what our mother told us than grandmother Richey. We had a wonderful grandmother and I suppose she talked more about Sequoyah to the boys than to us girls. Alpha was almost 6 years older than I. She was a Brown before she married grandfather Richey. Her mother was a Guess before she married great grandfather Brown. I think mama said she was a niece of George Guess, "Sequoyah".*** *He was known as a Cherokee intellect. I have some literature on him. He was never a Cherokee chief but was called upon to deal with the U. S. Government. He did live in Indian Territory as well as Arkansas. He had a home in Sallisaw, Ok. I don't know if it still exists. He was born in 1778 in a small Cherokee village of Tuscegee in Tennessee. He is known for inventing the Cherokee alphabet. I remember a lot about him in our Oklahoma History.*

*Our mother looked a lot like some Indian trait, as well as her sister Aunt Bea, Uncle Hoten, Uncle Will, and Uncle Swan. I saw a picture of Uncle Hoten and Uncle Otho (he died in 1917 or 1918). A school picture of the old Holton school just about a mile and ½ from where we were raised South and East of Manitou. They definitely showed Indian blood, very nice looking, though. The Cherokee were the most civilized of the "Five Civilized Tribes."*

*Grandpa and Grandma Richey came to Indian Territory before Oklahoma became a state. They lived in covered wagons when Mama and Aunt Bea were little girls. I used to love to hear her talk and tell when they were children. Aunt Etta drove a team of oxen while grandpa and I suppose Uncle Swan drove the others/horses. Sage grass was taller than mama and Aunt Bea. Grandmother made little red caps for them to wear when they went out to play. Both Andrew and Raymond were born before Oklahoma became a state. They and Cecil were born in a half dugout. Our Aunt Zora (Uncle Swan's wife) was the mid-wife to the three boys. Grandmother Richey delivered Lula. They were having a snow storm and the doctor couldn't get there until she was three days old. I think Doctor Comp delivered the rest of us kids. He lived in Manitou.*

*I know you didn't ask for –*

[Note: And I no longer have the last page. But I did save in one place on my computer some excerpts of her letter. The following was on page five.]

*I know you didn't ask for a lot of the things I have written. I'm proud of them and still love to think about their early lives, so different from today . . .*

*I'm quite sure it was Great-grandmother Brown who was a Guess and was a niece or great niece of George Guess.*

*With love and best wishes,*
*Aunt Lorena*

May 30, 2000

Dear Vance and Wife,

I am sorry I've been so slow answering your letters. I have no idea what I could tell you that you don't already know. I'll try.

The reason I'm so late answering is I had an accident at a Dinner Theatre here in town during intermission. I have no idea how it happened unless I tripped on a man's coat lying on the floor or someone may have pushed me. I fractured my shoulder and hip on the left side. Was apart almost 2 months in rehab hospitals. I worked the first time last week. I'm home now and will have rehab at home. I tire easily.

I remember more when our mother told us that Grandmother

He is known for inventing the Cherokee Alphabet. I remember a lot about him in our Oklahoma history.

Our mother looked a lot like some Indians, as well as her sister Aunt Bea, Uncle Walter, Uncle Will and Uncle Swan. I saw a picture of Uncle Walter and Uncle Otho (he died in 1917 or 1918) A school picture of an old Walter Grade School just about a mile and 1/2 from where we were raised south and East of Manitou. They definitely showed Indian blood. very nice looking tho. The Cherokee's were the most civilized of our "5 Civilized Tribes."

Grandpa and Grandma Richey came over to Indian Territory before Oklahoma became a state. They lived in covered wagons. When Mama and Aunt Bea were

Richey. We had a wonderful great-mother and I suppose she talked more about Sequoyah to the boys than to us girls. Bepha was almost 6 yrs. older than I. She was a Brown before she married Grandfather Richey. Her mother was a Guess before she married Great Grandfather Brown. I think Mama said she was a niece of George Guess "Sequoyah." he was well known as a Cherokee Intellect. I have some literature on him. He was never a Cherokee Chief but was called upon to deal with the U.S. Government. He did live in Indian Territory as well as in Arkansas. He had a home in Sallisaw, Ok. I don't know if it still exists. He was born in 1778 in a small Cherokee Village of Tuskigee in Tennessee.

little girls. I used to love to hear them talk and tell when they were children. Aunt Ella drove a team of oxen while Grandpa and I suppose Uncle Swan drove the others. Sage Grass was taller than Mama and Aunt Bea. Grandmother made little red caps for them to wear when they went out to play.

Both Andrew and Raymond were born before Oklahoma was a state. They and Cecil were born in a 1/2 dug out. Our Aunt Zora (Uncle Swan's wife) was the mid wife to the 3 boys. Grandmother Richey delivered Beula. They were having a snow storm and the doctor couldn't get there until she was 3 days old. I think Dr. Comp delivered the rest of us kids. He lived in Manitou.

I know you didn't ask for

9

## B. Indian Pioneer Papers

There is a historical record of some early settlers of Indian Territory called IPP, or Indian Pioneer Papers. This was a Dust Bowl Era project to get Old Times of all races and mixes to tell their family story of how they came to live in Oklahoma when it was known as "Indian Territory". There were thousands of such interviews.

### About the Collection

In 1936, the [Oklahoma Historical] society teamed with the history department at the University of Oklahoma to get a Works Progress Administration (WPA) writers' project grant for an interview program. The project employed more than 100 writers scattered across the state, with headquarters in Muskogee, where Grant Foreman served as project director. Asked to "call upon early settlers and (record) the story of the migration to Oklahoma and their early life here" the writers conducted more than 11,000 interviews, edited the accounts into written form, and sent them to the project director who completed the editorial process and had them typed into more than 45,000 pages. When assembled, the Indian-Pioneer Papers consisted of 112 volumes, with one set at the university, the other at the society. There are only two complete bound sets of originals.

These interviews can be found online (along with other documents) here – http://digital.libraries.ou.edu/whc/

My great Uncle Oscar and his wife Emma both responded to this request. [2] Here is a record of the transcription of their contribution:

### Oscar Taylor Richey

Oscar was grandma's brother. Both he and his wife were interviewed for this project. Here are those accounts.

*Date: August 23, 1937*

*Name: Oscar T. Richey*

*Post Office: Lone Wolf, Kiowa County, Oklahoma*

*My parents were natives of Arkansas and grew up near Fort Smith which is just across the line from Indian Territory. Both come from pioneer families.*

*After they were married in the year 1872, they moved into Indian Territory and settled in either the present Sequoyah or Leflore Counties. I do not know on which side of the Arkansas River they lived, but I remember very clearly hearing my mother say that the territory was like a wilderness and that they had to go back to Fort Smith for everything they* had to buy and that when they needed protection all the officers of the law had to come from Fort Smith.

Mother never ceased to tell us children of an experience which she had while living at that place. Two White men and Two Negroes committed some kind of a crime in the Indian Territory, were taken to Fort Smith tried and convicted and were sentenced to be hanged.

When the day of the hanging came, she and Father like everybody else in the country started early for the hanging was to be a public affair, and they traveled all day through the woods and across the streams and when they reached Fort Smith there were literally a thousand people which was a great number at that time, gathered as if at a picnic to witness the hanging. Mother watched the hanging and it was so horrible to her that she regretted attending such a thing all the remainder of her life.

My parents then moved to Texas where there was more settlement and I was born in Denton County, September 10, 1881.

In 1889 we came back to Indian Territory and Father bought a 10 year lease, from a Squaw-man named Clint Murcus. Our lease was east of the present town of Duncan in Stephens County, on Mud Creek.

Living was pretty hard for us as we were poor and the land had to be cleared and broken before we could plant or grow any crops. Everything had to be hauled by wagon from Nocona, in Montague County, Texas and the roads were only wagon tracks with no bridges on the streams to amount to anything and the bridges which were built would wash away every time there was a flood on the river or creek.

At first we depended for our food mostly on rabbits, squirrel, fish and other small game. These animals furnished us with meat and we raised a little corn on land which we were able to clear out. The brush had to be cut by hand or with ax and burned. The larger trees had to be girdled or out all round and left to die, so the tree could be gotten off the land and if they would not burn they had to be dragged off the land.

For plowing we used a Georgia Stock which is a walking plow drawn by one horse and in the stumps that was slow work. As we cleared more land and got it into a state of cultivation we planted other things, vegetables, some cotton, and some feed for our stock. In that way we lived much better and built more log houses and sheds and fenced in more lots.

After the Rock Island Railroad came through the country living conditions improved for we could buy our necessities and sell our produce at Duncan instead of being forced to go to Nocona, Texas.

*People settled in communities and built small school houses at their own expense and all teachers from one dollar and a half to two dollars per month for each pupil and the school ?year? would last from two to three ?months? a year.*

*The little school houses were __?__ and for churches. The first minister I remember was the Reverend Mr. White. When the Comanche Reservation was ???, Mr. White drew a claim west of the town of Comanche and built a dugout on it. The dugout was not built well and fell in killing him and his family.*

*I remember a Holiness Minister, we called him Stammering John. His name was John Fry. As the years passed I continued to farm using the improved machinery. I later moved into the Kiowa Country, settling North of Lone Wolf, where my family and I now live.*

*Transcribed in August 2003, by me, Vance Hawkins, great-nephew of Oscar.*

## Emma

Emma Price married my great Uncle Oscar Richey. Although we are related to her family only through marriage, her story tells another story of what life was like in Indian Territory.

*Indian Pioneer History Project for Oklahoma*
*Date: August 23, 1937*
*Name: Emma Price Richey*
*Post Office: Lone Wolf, Kiowa County, Oklahoma*
*Field Worker: Ethel B. Tackitt*
*Interview #:*

*My parents moved to Indian Territory in 1890 and settled 12 miles northeast of the present town of Duncan. in Stephens County.*

*My father was very fortunate as he bought a lease from a Chickasaw Indian named Belton Colbert* [Vance's note: I suspect this was Benton Colbert. I found no "Belton" Colbert, but there was a Benton Colbert. She was writing in the 1937 about what happened when she was a child in 1890. The Colbert's were a powerful/well known Chickasaw family] *which was rather well improved. He also bought a lease from an Indian woman by the name of Leewright and at last a lease from an Indian named Hahan.*

*Leases could be purchased very cheaply from these Indians for the white people would come in and take a ten year lease and stay as long as they wanted to or until they grew tired of the hardships of the country and then they would sell out for anything they could get. Sometimes they would sell out for a cow, horse, or wagon and then if they could not find a buyer for their claims they would simply move out and leave what improvements they had put on the land*

*If a person bought a lease he or she would finish out the remainder of the ten years of residence which were required. Father bought this Hahen lease and it only had two years on it. The house was a good boxed two rooms in front with a shed room running the full length. We were proud of this house for it was the best in the country and had a shingle roof. Almost everybody else lived in a log house or in a dugout.*

*We then lived near Harrisburg about 12 miles southeast of Duncan. Harrisburg had a store and a post office. And the community built a little boxed school house.*

*The school was paid by subscription at the rate of a dollar and a half per month for each pupil. The term was usually two or three months and never more than four months. As a general thing, if it was grammar school it was a two months term and if it was taught in the winter, it was a three months term.*

*The first teacher I remember was Charley Davenport* [Vance's note: This is the same Charles Davenport that married Oscar's sister, my great Aunt Ettie. Many ex-Confederate political and military officials moved into the Choctaw and Chickasaw Nations after the Civil War, so many that parts of southeastern Oklahoma are called "Little Dixie" to this day. The Davenport's were one of these families.] *and later Will Metcalf taught us. A school teacher in those days did not have to have any certificate for teaching and reading, writing and spelling were about the only subjects taught unless the teacher wanted to teach arithmetic and geography too.*

*Later, there were camp meetings where the people would build brush arbors at some convenient place and would come and bring their families. The people would put up tents or would put up smaller brush arbors and make themselves camps where all who came for miles around were welcome and these meeting would continue two, three and four weeks. The ministers would take turns at preaching and nobody thought of its costing anything for everybody brought vegetables, fruits, chickens, and meats or anything they had to eat and nobody thought of imposing on anybody else.*

*I remember one summer when Father and Mother took our whole family to Sunset, in Montague County, Texas to attend a camp meeting held by the Hudson brothers.*

*I married Oscar Richey and when the Kiowa Country, opened up we moved to Lone Wolf community and have continued to farm and live on our claim. Here we have reared our family and have taken part in all the activities of the community. ??? enjoy the rural mail delivery, the telephone, the highways and consolidated school districts with the busses which take the children to school.*

*Transcribed in August 2003, by Vance Hawkins, great-nephew of Oscar and Emma.*

## James Harvey Gist

J. M. Gist was the son of James Harvey Gist. DNA test results and genealogical data say that my family is closely related to James Harvey Gist. His descendants also have family stories of having Indian ancestors, by the way. A descendant of his also was interviewed for IPP, Indian Pioneer Papers. Here is a transcription of his interview:

*Interview #9000*
*Field Worker: John F. Daugherty*
*Date: October 23, 1937*
*Name: J. M. Gist*
*Residence: Route 1, Mill Creek, Oklahoma*
*Date of Birth: August 24, 1868*
*Place of Birth: Missouri*
*Father: James Gist, born in Kentucky*
*Mother: Annie Meek, born in Texas*
*My parents were James H. Gist and Annie Meek Gist, born in* Kentucky [Vance's note: These Gist's were in the Whitley, Wayne, Pulaski County area of Kentucky before they moved to Northwestern Alabama] *and Texas. Father was a farmer. There were two children. I was born August 24, 1868, in Missouri*

*I came to the Indian Territory in 1887. I had an uncle living at Berwyn and I came to see him. Father and Mother lived in Arkansas in the swamps and Father was in very poor health. I decided that Indian Territory was the ideal place for him. He enjoyed hunting and fishing so I saddled a horse and went home to move them here.*

*We moved in a covered wagon. We came through Sulphur and there was nothing there but an old log ranch house and the old Gum Springs. We camped at this spring. We had no bread and the man (Col. Froman?) who lived in the log house had his wife bake us some corn bread.*

*When we got to Berwyn we had no house to move into, so we camped under a large cottonwood tree until we could cut poles to make a log house. We built our house on the bank of the Washita River and drank river water. I went to the Creek Nation a short time after we moved here and went to work on the Bar-B-Q Campbell Ranch east of Okmulgee.*

14

I was working here when the Buck Gang stole several steers and burned their brand on them. This was done by a group of six Indians and one Negro headed by Rufus Buck, a Creek Indian. They were very wicked. Human life meant nothing to them and they killed several women before they were captured.

They took these cattle near the F. S. Ranch. A posse of cowboys and ranchmen were searching for this gang when they found these steers from the Bar-B-Q Ranch and knew that the gang was not far away. They found their hiding place and a lively shooting fray ensued, without the loss of life.

Just as both sides were about out of ammunition, the Creek Light horsemen arrived on the scene and some United States Marshals arrived shortly afterwards. The Buck Gang saw that they were caught so they surrendered peaceably.

Two of the gang escaped, however. One was wounded and was hidden in the brush and couldn't be found and the other ran away. They were chained together and loaded into the prisoners' wagon and taken to Okmulgee. When they arrived everybody began shooting to signal all the parties hunting for the desperadoes to come in as the desperadoes were captured and the team hitched to the prisoners' wagon became frightened and ran away. Then there was some more excitement. But the team was stopped without the loss of a prisoner and the Buck Gang was put in jail at Okmulgee.

The next day before the officers started to Muskogee with the prisoners an old squaw brought one of the escaped members of the gang in. She had him rolled up in a feather bed in a wagon and he was nearly frightened to death. It was a number of days before they found the wounded outlaw. He finally came in and gave himself up. These men were taken to Fort Smith and tried. They were hung according to law and thus ended one of the worst gangs of cattle thieves in the history of territorial days.

One night a crowd of our boys went to a Creek Stomp Dance. They heard that the Buck Gang was coming so they left to avoid trouble. The cowboys hated the Buck Gang and there was always shooting when they encountered each other. I was just a boy and I stayed to see what would happen. When the Buck Gang rode up, they began shooting and tried to frighten the Indians, but the dancers paid no attention to them. They soon became tired of their sport and rode away.

When our boys started across Elk Creek there was only a small cow trail down the bank to the creek and when one started down he must go on as there was a thicket on each side and it was impossible to turn around.

*Just as the leader got to the bed of the Creek he saw Rufus Buck on his buckskin horse. He couldn't turn around and he couldn't warn the boys behind him, so the cowboys proceeded across the creek without giving any sign of recognition to the Buck Gang, who stood and watched our boys ride away.*

*After Buck and his gang were captured he was asked why he didn't kill the Bar-B-Q boys that night and he said the gang had used all their ammunition at the dance or they would have fired at the cowboys.*

*The cattle on our range were very wild. If a person went across their range walking instead of riding, the whole herd would get after him. They paid no attention to anyone riding but they certainly permitted no walking on their range. Some of the cattle had horns four feet long.*

**One day I was in Checotah when a very funny incident occurred.  An Indian man named Gentry had a store there and his brother, Bill,** *drank a great deal. Bill would sit on the porch of this store and his favorite pastime was shooting between the feet of cowboys and making them dance. On this day a cowboy stepped up on the porch where Bill was asleep. He suddenly awoke and began shooting at the cowboy's feet, commanding him to dance. The cowboy said that he couldn't dance, but Bill told him he would kill him if he didn't dance. So the cowboy danced until he was almost exhausted. He went into the store and purchased what he wanted. When he got ready to go home, he came out of the store and Bill was asleep again. He stepped over to his saddle, got his gun and shot between Bill's feet. Bill sat up in astonishment, asking what he meant. The cowboy took his gun and told him to dance. Bill said, "I can't".  The cowboy told him that he would kill him if he didn't.  Bill began to dance and the cowboy continued to shoot. He made Bill lie down and roll over like a pet dog. Then the cowboy made Bill dance some more. He had him doing all sorts of tricks with the townspeople looking on. When the cowboy got through putting Bill through these antics he had him a sober man. The cowboy got on his horse and rode away amid the cheers and whoops of the onlookers.  That cured Bill of making cowboys dance. He decided it wasn't much fun when he had to do the dancing instead of the cowboys.*

*Bill enjoyed playing jokes. One day a drummer came into the store and Bill was drunk as usual.  He had a very fine buggy and mare. He asked the traveling man to go riding with him. The man unsuspectingly climbed into the buggy and away they went up and down the street and around the town.  The traveling man thought he was seeing the town. There was a lake southwest of town which covered about four acres of ground. The mare would do anything Bill told her to do. He started to the lake.  Just before they reached it he gave the*

16

*mare a cut with the buggy whip and commanded her to go to the lake. Then Bill rolled out of the buggy and dropped the lines on the ground. The mare jumped into the lake with the buggy and the drummer. The drummer couldn't get the lines and the water came up into the buggy and almost drowned him before he could get out.*

*I was married to Georgia Ray, near Center, in 1893. We have two children. I have lived in Johnston County since 1918.*

There is some information online about Bill/William Gentry. Mrs. Caroline Everett was also interviewed in the same "Indian Pioneer Papers" – she was daughter of William E. Gentry – the same "Bill Gentry" mentioned in the above account, the same man who ordered the cowboys to "dance". She also mentions same city of Checotah. As you might expect, her description of her father was far different that my relatives story about him. At the beginning of the interview it says in parentheses:

*Mrs. Caroline Everett, informant Council Hill Oklahoma (daughter of Wm. E. Gentry). Interview as given to Jas. S. Buchanan, Indian Research Worker.*

Mrs. Everett is recorded as saying:

*By ancestry, he [note: meaning William/Bill Gentry] was a Catawba Indian adopted into the Creek Tribe . . .*

*His business interests, however, were not confined to the cattle business, as he owned a large share in the Gentry hotel in Checotah . . .* I will have more about the Catawba Indians in Indian Territory, later. The Creek Council House still stands and is in Okmulgee, Okmulgee County, Oklahoma – which is also the town where I was born.

## C. Tarleton Bull

Dad was a natural born story teller, and as a child I remember him talking about meeting his uncle (actually a great uncle by marriage only), named Tarleton Bull. According to Dad's stories, he was a kind of a "bigger than life" character who dad said "was a great big man, nearly seven feet tall." The more that I looked into him the more interesting he became. So I am including quite a bit about him.

### Lizzie

Lizzie Bull was Tarleton Bull's older sister. They moved from Wisconsin to Texas going through Indian Territory (Oklahoma) on the way where the entire family got sick, and Tarleton's father died. A Denton, Texas newspaper found an old letter Lizzie had written and published parts of it.

17

These excerpts are from an article that was published in the Denton Record-Chronicle, on Wednesday, January 3, 2007, by Nita Thurman / Denton County [3]

### Pioneer letters attest to tough times on the frontier

*Lizzie Bull dated her letter Nov. 2, 1859, Denton, Denton County, Texas:*
*She traveled for 10 weeks after leaving Iowa, a trip she describes as the "hardest time I ever expect to have." The trip might have been pleasant, she wrote, except for an unidentified illness that apparently struck down most of her family in Indian Territory.*

*She apparently nursed her father, mother and at least one relative, Tarleton, probably a brother, as well as the doctor who was traveling with them and succumbed to the same illness. A heavy September storm raging around their tent added to the misery.*

*Her father died Sept. 28 on Horse Creek in the Cherokee Nation, Lizzie wrote, and asked her sister to put a notice in the Herald, a local newspaper.*

*"Think of my feeling when father was a corpse and Mother and Tarleton so low that they didn't know anything of it," she wrote, "and not a woman to come in to see me."*

*After burying her father, she sat all night with her critically ill mother. The doctor traveling with them had "given up" on mother, Lizzie continued, and by now was also very ill. A man named George — probably a relative — went about 15 miles for a half-Indian doctor to treat the gravely ill travelers.*

*"It was coming up a storm, and I think we had as hard a storm that night as I ever saw," she continued. She sat in the tent that night with her mother, Tarleton and the first doctor, who was so sick that he could not sit up. The doctor died four days later.*

*After giving all the bad news, Lizzie changed subjects without even a comma or a period:*

*"This is a very pretty country," she continued, "but not what we call good watered country at all." Her mother was still weak from the illness, but was "on the mend" and hopefully would soon be well.*

*Lizzie ended her letter with a request that word of her father's death also be sent on to "the boys" and sent her love to all her friends.*

*So what happened to the Bull family? In his History and Reminiscences of Denton County, Ed Bates gave a roll call of the pioneers in each of the early settlements. He lists George and Tarleton Bull as two of the first people in the Denton Settlement.*

Lizzie was Tarleton's sister. His father died in the Cherokee Nation while the family was migrating from Wisconsin to Texas. Tarleton was a child at the time.

**From "Genealogy of the Jackson Family" © 1890, by Hugh Park Jackson, Hugh Hogue Thompson, and James R. Jackson**

Tarleton's mother was a Jackson. Someone took time to write a genealogical record of them. A part of that record that mentioning Tarleton is below. [4] Oh, these Jackson's were somehow related to Andrew.

*P 114-115*

*8. Tarleton D. Bull, born March 1, 1845, in Wisconsin; married first April 29th, 1869 in Denton County, Texas to Mary Montgomery, She was a member of the M. E. Church, and died January 27th, 1871 leaving an infant; Sarah A, Bull born January 11th, 1871 in Eastland, Texas, and resides at home with her father,*

*T. D. Bull married second time, Feb, 2. 1879 to Sarah A. Brown* [Vance's note — she is sister to my great grandma Josey (Brown) Richey]. *He is engaged in the livery business in Desdemona, Eastland County, Texas; he is a non-church member and a Democrat. He was a Confederate soldier for three years and nine months. He enlisted first in the 18th Texas Cavalry, March 17th 1861, and was dismounted at Little Rock, Arkansas. At Pine Bluff Arkansas, his unit was nearly all captured.*

*And afterwards was transferred to the 29th Texas Cavalry Regiment, Company E, Colonel Demorse, Gano's Brigade, Maxey's Division, General Price's Army of Cavalry, and remained in that regiment til the close of the war, west of the Mississippi River. He was in 37 engagements, and was not wounded or captured. The following are some of the battles in which he took part: In Arkansas, Pine Bluff, Elk Horne, Saline River and Poison River. In Louisiana; Mansfield. In Indian Territory; Cherokee Nation. While engaged in this last named cavalry conflict his horse stood on his father's grave. There his brother George was captured and was a prisoner two years. His company went into war with one hundred eleven men, and came out of the war with seventeen men. T. D. Bull rode the same horse all through the war, and brought him home with him. When he arrived at home he was penniless, having suffered untold hardships and privations.*

*They have four children:*

*1. Walter T. Bull born May 19th, 1880, died May 14th 1882.*

*2. Nancy A. Bull, born February 11, 1883.*

*3. Alta D. Bull, born May 5th, 1886.*

*4. William Cleveland Bull, born November 19th, 1888.*

Vance's note — on 1920 census they are living in Murray County, Oklahoma. I don't know where this Jackson researcher got his information, but since it was written in 1890 Tarleton was still living — perhaps he got it from Tarleton himself. I thought it interesting that Tarleton's horse survived the war, and also that his horse stood in Tarleton's father's grave, as well. I suspect it is an unmarked grave, and I wonder if it could still be found — probably not. Also does this conflict described match a known historic battle? I think it is Cabin Creek or Honey Creek — maybe Honey Creek as he mentions his brother was POW for 2 years and it was in 1863.

## From Tarleton Bull's Confederate Pension Application

Here are excerpts from Tarleton Bull's Civil War Pension Application from Texas. Texas rejected his pension application. Later, he applied in Oklahoma for a pension and we accepted his application. However his Oklahoma application gave very little personal information, while his Texas application provided more details as to what he did in the Texas Confederate Cavalry.

*Disapproved — applicant is under 60 years of age and does not connect his disability with service. I hear by disapprove the within application this 23 Sept AD 1899. Co-Judge fee paid.*

*What is your name? T D Bull*

*What is your age? 54*

*In what county do you reside? Eastland*

*Who long have you resided in said county? 20 years.*

*Post Office? Desdemona*

*What is your occupation? Livery business*

*What is your physical condition? Bad*

*If your physical condition is such that you are unable by your own labor to earn a support, state what caused your disability. Piles and hemorage of the lungs, while in the Army contracture.*

*State I what company and regiment you enlisted in the Confederate Army, and the time of your service. Company G, 18th Texas Cavalry. About 3 years. Enlisted in 1861 or 1862.*

*[Have you] received any other pension . . . No sir.*

*What real and personal property do you own, and what is the present value of such property.*

*One small house and lot in Desdemona, Texas worth about $100.00, 2 horses worth about $50, and 2 cows worth about $40.*

*What property, and what was the value thereof, have you sold within the last 2 years . . . 1 cow and 1 calf worth $50*

*What income, if any do you receive? None at all. I have a small mail contract but it barely pays expenses.*

*Are you in indigent circumstances? Yes I am.*

*Are you unable by your labor to earn a living? Yes. My health is such that I will have to give [?up?] the mail contract.*

### Affidavit of witnesses

*There must be at least 2 witnesses.*

*The State of Texas, county of Eastland. Before me, GW Darkan, county judge of Eastland County, Texas, on this day personally appeared GW Bull and JM Huddleston. JM Huddleston only swears to the applicants inability to support himself by labor of any sort who are personally known to me to be credible citizens, who being by me duly sworn on oath, state that they personally know T D Bull, the above named applicant for a pension, and that they personally know that the said T D Bull enlisted in the service of the Confederacy and performed the services of a soldier . . . . Sworn to and subscribed to me this 12th day of August, 1899.*

*Before me, GW Darkan, county judge of Eastland County, state of Texas, appeared Dr. L. C. Downtain, who is a practicing reputable physician of this county, who . . . States that he has thoroughly and completely examined TD Bull, applicant for a pension, and finds his laboring under the following disabilities which render him unable to labor at any work sufficient to earn a support for himself: suffering from Piles, Hemorage of the lungs.*

*. . . I find the said applicant is lawfully entitled to the pension provided by the Confederate Pension law of this state, and hear by approve said applicant. . . . GW Darkan*

*. . .*

*. . . We, the undersigned members of the Commissioners Court, of Eastland County, Texas, find the said applicant is lawfully entitled to the pension . . . This 15th day of August, 1899. . .*

*John ?Levelor/Lovdder?*

*What is your age? 55 years old.*

*Residence. Gunsight, Stephens County, Texas.*

*I am acquainted with T. D. Bull. I have known him for 37 years.* **I first saw him at Camp Jeff Davis in Red River County, Texas,** *in camps when I first got acquainted with him. He lives in Eastland County at Desdemona.*

*He was in the Confederate Army. I do not know where he enlisted. He served 2 ½ years, Company E, 29th Texas Cavalry.* **I was in a fight with him at Elk Creek Ind Nation and another place called Cabin Creek. As far as I know he was a good soldier.**

*If he ever deserted I never heard anything of it. I do not believe he did.*

*I messed with T. D. Bull. Sometimes he served in Texas and Indian Territory and Arkansas about 2 & ½ years. He is 5 ft. 10 in height, weighs about 120 pounds. Tall slender, very spare made, 55 years old. John (his "x" mark) Levdder.*

*Tal Murphey.*

*My age — 59 years old, Gunsight, Stephens Co., Texas.*

*I have known him 37 years. I got acquainted with him in the Army at Camp Jeff Davis, in Red River County, Texas. He now lives in Desdemona, Eastland Co., Tx.*

*He was in the Confederate Army.*

*Can not state when or where he enlisted.*

*Company E 29th Texas Cavalry. About 2 and ½ years. I was ????? With him every day and saw him every day. H made a good soldier I am ?sertain?* [Vance's note: probably should be "certain"]

*I never heard any complaint to that effect.*

*By soldering with him in Confederate Army.*

*He served 2½ years.*

*About 5 ft. 10 in height, weight 120 pounds, age 55, Tall and slender, very spare made. Joe Murphy —* [Vance's note: here it definitely says JOE, as a given name]


## 1868 Indian Raid

The next is a story about Tarleton, from 1868, 3 years after the Civil War.

Colonists of Navarro and Denton Counties fight Indians. by A. J. Sewell, in San Antonio Light. [5]

*The first settlements made in what is known as Denton county were on Hickory and Prairie creeks, from 1842 to 1845 by the WAGNERS, CLARYSES, KINGS and others. In*

*June 1845, there were seventeen families in all. In the latter part of 1845 came MURPHY, the HARMASONS, the HOLFORDS, WELDERS, FRENCHES and others, and in the early part of 1846, the CARTERS, S. A. VENTERS and the YOCKHOMISES settled on Clear creek and the STRICKLINS on Isle de Bois.*

*Denton County was organized in July 1846, and named for Captain John B. DENTON, who was killed in a fight with Indians on the Trinity. The Indians were numerous and hostile, and often bloody encounters took place between them and the pioneers.*

*In 1868, a party of Indians, supposed to be about twenty in number, made a raid into Wise and Denton counties. Crossing Denton Creek near the overland road and meeting no opposition, the savages at 12 o'clock at night dashed into the town of Denton and drove out about thirty head of horses without the inhabitants being aware of their presence. Next morning horses were missed from lots and pastures and Indian trails were discovered in the fields. Scouts were sent out in several directions and it was discovered by them that the Indians had gone out by the Gainesville road to the crossing on Clear Creek, gathering all on the horses on the route.*

*No attempt had been made by them to kill any of the citizens on the route. When crossing Clear Creek they attempted to capture two of Mr. ROLL's little boys, who happened to be some distance from the house. Their main object seemed to be to get as many horses as possible. They gathered all the horses in the way until the rove amounted to fifty or sixty, then left the settlements beyond Clear creek and started in the direction of Cook County. Capt. R. H. HOPKINS, Stephen CURLEY and three other men who ranches on Clear creek were swept of a good deal of valuable stock, mounted fleet horses and started in pursuit. Another force of ten men also joined in the chase farther in the rear, not being able to keep pace with the Indians, all of whom were now mounted on fresh horses.*

*The pursuit continued for many miles over the prairie, the party keeping in sight of the Indians all the time until the squad under Captain HOPKINS made a flank movement for the purpose of getting reinforcements from some of the ranches on the right. This move so confused the Indians, who thought this was some strategem, that they turned into the brakes and briers on Clear creek, where they were charged upon by Hopkins and his men and nearly all of the stolen horses recaptured. The Indians escaped with the horses they were riding and went off in the direction of Montague County.*

*Soon after this rain a runner hastened to the town of Denton and reported Indians in force gathering between the ranches of Thomas EAGAN and George McCormick. About twenty-five of the citizens immediately armed themselves, mounted horses and started in pursuit. About ten miles from town the scouts discovered two Indians on Hickory Creek driving about fifteen head of horses to the main herd. They raised a yell and charged them and recaptured the horses.* **Tarleton Bull was in the lead** *and fired first at close range, wounding an Indian in the spine. The Indian turned and fired at Bull but missed him. He then raised his bow to discharge an arrow but was fired on by the others of the party and hit with three more balls and fell from his horse dead, without shooting the arrow. Mr. Bull secured his horse and E. ALLEN got the gun and bow and the quiver of arrows. The other Indian escaped.*

*The scouts then pushed on closely after the main body of the Indians up the North Hickory, but did not come up with them until they halted at Chisholm's Ranch* [Vance's note: Is this talking about Jesse Chisholm, the man for whom the Chisholm Trail was named? He was mixed with Cherokee, descended from John Chisholm and a Cherokee woman. I had thought he was a son until I read Ricky Butch Walker's "Doublehead", where Jesse is a grandson, not a son, of John D. Chisholm. I looked into it and he's right. His grandfather is the same John Chisholm who knew and befriended Chief Doublehead]. *Here the Indians formed for battle, the chief blowing a shrill whistle. Hearing the whistle, a dog belonging to one of the settlers ran over to the Indians and was at once killed by them. The number of white men by this time had increased to forty-three men and the Indians numbered about one hundred and fifty. Firing commenced on both sides and the Indians, seeing the small force of the settlers as compared with their own number, raised the war whoop and charged.*

*As is often the case in battles with Indians some white men cannot stand the charge and yell of an Indian, and so in this case some broke away and then others followed and all soon became scattered in a disorganized fight. Encouraged by the braver men, the retreating ones rallied and a stand was finally made, but in the flight Sevier WHARTENBURG was killed and then scalped and stripped of his clothing. William EAVES was wounded and George McCormick's horse was killed, but he succeeded in making his escape across the creek. The stand that the white men made was not of long duration, but they succeeded in checking the Indians and then retreating more slowly in a body. The Indians succeeded in getting away with about three hundred head of horses. The body of the slain man was afterwards recovered and carried to his home and buried. [7]*

Left to right: Present Occupant, Tarlton Bull, Occupant's Wife, and William Lee McCormick. Scenes near White's Creek where a pile of rocks marks the spot where Sevier Fortenberry was laid after being killed by Indians in the Raid of October 29, 1868. Kodaks by Mrs. Annie (Bull) DaLee (Mrs. H. L. DaLee of Denton, Texas)

## Pioneer Resident Visits in Denton

Tarleton Bull, pioneer resident of Denton County, is here from Sulphur, Okla., the guest of relatives and friends. Bull lived in Denton in the early days of the town, joining the first company of Confederate soldiers that went out from Denton and serving throughout the war, and later took part in Indian fights in this section. He recalls distinctly the events of the early days, and tells some interesting stories of the strenuous life in Denton County before and following the Civil War.

In the year 1879, Tarleton D. Bull married Sarah A. Brown, great-grandma's sister. *Texas Marriage Collection, 1814-1909 and 1966-2002; Name: T. D. Bull Gender: Male Marriage Date: 6 Feb 1879 Spouse: Sarah Brown Marriage city: Denton Marriage State: Texas Source: Texas Marriages, 1851-1900*

Now I remember vividly Dad saying "Tarleton was a great big man, nearly seven feet tall." Per his pension application, he was 5 ft. 10 inches. And from the photo below, he doesn't look like *a great big man,* either. Oh well . . .

The second man from the left, with a cane in one hand and a stetson in the other, is Tarleton Bull. [6]. From the way Dad talked about him, you got the feeling he was the kind of a man whose grandkids would sit on his lap and say, "grandpa, tell us a story." And he'd be off to the races, standin' high in the saddle on his favorite pinto. Well, age changes us. But apparently, he had once been a formidable warrior himself, and I want him remembered. While the other two men stare off into space, Tarleton stares right at the camera. That newspaper article was dated 1929 and I suspect the photo probably dates to the same timeframe.

## D. Dad, Uncle Eual Lee, and other Stories

I am proud of my Dad. I never really told him, but I was. He was a humble man. Below is a WW2 photo of my father, Alpha Omega Hawkins (1915-1992). After spending so

much time on Tarleton, I feel I ought to mention Dad. Dad was like Tarleton, only his stories were about the Dust Bowl, having no food except pintos and corn bread. If they wanted meat, they grabbed a shotgun or a fishing pole, maybe both, some home-made jerky, a slice of corn bread or a couple of biscuits, and came back with a cat fish or two, or a couple of cotton tails or squirrels. He told stories of walking to school a mile and a half away, barefoot as he had no shoes at times. All the young boys wore bandanas around their necks, so when they saw the black clouds of dust coming they'd turn them around and wore them like the outlaws in old westerns, covering their noses so they could breathe better in the dust.

His job was looking after the one or two dozen head of cattle they had. When he'd see what he called "black dust clouds" in the distance, he'd take off in a hurry. He'd make sure the cattle got back in the barn before the black dust clouds arrived. He had a dog he called "Ol' Coalie" because he was black as coal. Dad said the dog helped him with the cattle. He'd also talk of World War Two, specifically about Pearl Harbor or the Battle of the Bulge. One story he told just before he died, about freezing in a little pup tent. When the snow thawed they realized they'd camped over the bodied of six frozen German soldiers. He'd speak with both wonder in his voice and a sadness in his eyes. Oh, dad had many stories that he only told, never wrote down. But he had a hundred of them. Dad and Tarleton may have been kindred spirits. I loved those old stories dad told, and I suppose maybe that's why I am researching these stories, today.

One of Dad's stories dealt with something funny that he was told as a boy. His grandma and uncles and aunts were raised in the Chickasaw Nation. As a child on the farm, his Aunt Ettie came running into the house one day hysterical, saying, "Wild Indians are coming! I saw their feathers crawling through the tall grass!" Well, dad said his grandpa, Jeffrey Hoten Richey, calmly, not saying a word, walked over to where they kept the shot gun, picked it up, loaded it, and walked outside. He started walking over to where Aunt Ettie (his daughter) said she'd seen these "Indian feathers". The family waited in the house, a little worried I suppose. Now this was in the early 1890s, and the last Comanche/Kiowa War, known as the Red River War, had ended in 1875, a decade and a half earlier. That was fresh enough in their minds to think it possible, but far enough back in time to have some doubts. The great Comanche War Chief Quanah Parker was still living, and his home was in what is now the town of Cache, maybe 20 or 30 miles or so from where my great-grandparents called their home. But now it was known that he had accepted the need for a change in lifestyle if the Comanche were to survive into the future. Still what about the young bucks? They had traditionally been a society of warriors. The younger men might want to gain a reputation. Thinking about these things, great-grandpa Richey slowly disappeared from view of his family.

The family heard that shot gun go off. Being rural people, they knew the difference between a shotgun and a rifle, and they knew their papa, Jeffrey, had fired that shot gun at something or someone. Well, some anxious moments passed, as they all wondered what was going on outside. After a few minutes, he returned. He had with him a wild turkey gobbler. Those feathers great aunt Ettie had seen belonged to a turkey! When I was a child they told that story at family reunions, all my great uncles and aunts had a big laugh – everyone except Aunt Ettie, that is.

Later I told this story to a Chickasaw who also had a good laugh. I asked about the usage of the term "Wild Indians". And he said yes, they called the Plains Tribes "Wild Indians". He also said the Comanche and Kiowa often came and stole horses and cattle from their Chickasaw farms and ranches and this was a great concern. Above is a photo my father as a young man, and beneath that is a photo of him as an old man, taken from his last driver's license, that expired in 1993, the year after he died. He was 77.

I was told a funny story about Quanah Parker. He last surrendered in 1875. He lived until 1912, so half of his life was spent living as the White's lived. Quanah Parker's house still exists but it is really run down and falling apart. There is this little store just off highway 62 near Cache, Oklahoma. If you catch his descendants there, they might take you on a tour of his house, and you can give a donation. One day I happened to be there at the right time, and was given a tour. I forget who it was, a grandson or a great grandson maybe. Anyhow I was told the following story. Quanah's house had 5 stars on the roof. He wanted all the Army officers at Fort Sill who might come calling on him to know that he out-ranked them.

Here's the story his descendant told me. Well, one day this preacher saw Quanah in the streets of Cache. Now Quanah had 5 wives (or was it seven?). This preacher told him it was a sin to have more than one wife and he had to get rid of all of them except one to get right in the eyes of God. Quanah paused and pondered those words. Then after a short time, said to the preacher. "Tell ya what. *You* go over to my place, stay a while, observe them. Then you decide which one can stay. Then you tell the others they have to get out." That was the last time the preacher brought this subject up.

As I write this, it is December 8th, and I apologize for being so long winded. But I can't quit without telling Dad's Pearl Harbor story. He used to start this story by saying that on Friday, they went on some kind of an alert. He had joined the Artillery he said, so he could get stationed close to home, as Fort Sill near Lawton, Oklahoma was the Army's Artillery School. He was raised about 25 miles from Fort Sill. Well, instead of being stationed near the fort, they shipped him to Schoefield Barracks on Oahu, Hawaii, then a territory.

Well part of going on alert involved moving their big Artillery guns to the beaches. To get to the beach, they had to go over these mountains. Now the roads were muddy, and their trucks kept getting stuck in the mud. Dad said they had Army mules and had to use them to get their trucks out of the mud. I think he said they did this in the rain, but maybe it

28

was just in the mud. I am pretty sure he said it was raining. I just don't remember exactly. Anyhow, by the time they got their howitzers in place, they were exhausted and muddy themselves. Now Saturday they moved those same big guns back where they'd been before, back over the mountains, through the same mud, with the same mules again saving the day. I think dad liked using those mules more than the trucks. He seemed to get a kick out of telling this part of his story. Again, he was very exhausted by the end of the day. When Sunday morning finally came, he seriously thought about not getting up and getting in the chow line to be served breakfast. He was so tired. But dad was a Corporal, and the Mess Sargent was a good friend of his, so he finally decided to go down and get a bite to eat. Well, since the Mess Sargent was his buddy, he didn't have to wait in line. He just started talking to him standing near him, and as they talked he casually got his plate and filled it up.

About this time they saw many planes off in the distance. Well some of the guys in the chow line started acting up, joking around. They were pretending to shoot at the planes, now a little closer to them, some pretending to be shot, themselves. Well the closer they got they noticed they didn't have our markings on them, and when they looked at the ground those who were "pretending to be shot", actually had been shot! Well, Dad said he and a few others ran to the supply building, broke the door in (it was locked) and started getting rifles (I suppose m-1s, although I recall him mentioning B. A. R.'s) and ammunition, and started shooting at those planes. He said he didn't think they hit anything, though. Later, when it was all over, he said when he saw his own bunk, the window over his bed was broken in, with broken glass on his bunk. For as long as he lived, I never knew dad to sleep in – he was always up way before dawn.

Later he came back stateside, as cadre to train others, and then off to Europe, where he joined up with **Patton's 3rd Army** about the same time and same place where his baby brother was killed.

**Uncle Eual Lee**

Well since I have gone this far, I might as well include a memorial photo of Dad's younger brother, Eual Lee Hawkins. He was in the infantry, **First Army. He was killed near St. Lo in Normandy, France on 18 Jul 1944.** He is buried in the American cemetery in Normandy. There is a pdf file online that is about this cemetery and battle. I have tried to find it again but without success. Excerpts from it say:

*Rapidly, the Allied armies increased in size and strength. On 26 June, Americans freed Cherbourg; on 9 July, British and Canadians fought their way into Caen; and on 18 July Americans took St. Lo. Proceeded by a paralyzing air bombardment on 25 July, the U.S. First Army stormed out of the beachhead area. Coutances was liberated three days later and, within a week, the recently activated U.S. Third Army cleared Avranches and was advancing toward Paris on a broad front. To the right is the only photo I have ever seen of him.*

Late in his life Dad said he was sad that his brother was buried overseas, saying no one wanted to be buried overseas.

## Mandy (Amanda Brown) Knight

Now about Amanda "Mandy" J. Brown. She, along with Sarah, Tarleton's wife, and great grandma Josephine wife of Jeff Richey, were the three Brown girls who left Indian Territory and moved to Denton County Texas with their mother Harriet, David Brown their father, having passed on in May, 1865. John Henry their brother, also seems to have gone to Texas. David's brother Alfred (Alph) seems to have stayed in IndianTerritory.1880 Census - 18 years old, living with sister's family, Josephine (Brown) Richey, in Denton Co., TX. pg. 98, Mandy (Amanda Brown) Knight, so she is already married to John, but he is not listed in the census.

According to the Knight family, her husband was John W. Knight, 1850 census - 4

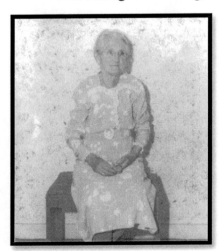

years old, living in Denton Co., Texas. pg. 107 B. In 1860 he is 13 years old, living in Denton Co., Texas. pg. 427 A. In 1870, John W. Knight is 22 years old, living with his first wife, next door to his father, in Lewisville, Denton Co., Texas. pg. 182 B.

Texas Land Abstracts: District: Fannin County: Denton Grantee: John Knight Patentee: John Knight Patent Date: 29 Aug 1871 Patent #: 82 Patent Volume: 39 Acres: 138.50 Class: Fan. 3rd. File: 4253. 1880 Census - John is not listed, but his second wife, Mandy, is 18 years old, living with her sister's family, Josephine (Brown) Richey, in Denton Co., TX. pg. 98. John W. Knight

[Parents] was born in 1845/1847 in Denton Co., Texas. He married Amanda "Mandy" J. Brown sometime before 1880. Amanda "Mandy" J. Brown was born in Lawrence Co., Arkansas. She died about 1890. She married John W. Knight before 1880. They had the following child:

## Amie Lee Knight

One of Amie's descendants sent me a file about her grandma, including a photograph (above) of her as an elderly lady. The photo is of Amie [Knight] Goldsbury, b. Apr 19, 1880, d. October 4th, 1956, at the age of 75. Her delayed birth certificate said she was born in Arkansas, but her obituary said she was born in Oklahoma.

Her obituary mentions 3 sons, Olen, Marvin, and Henry Goldsberry, and a daughter Mrs. Beulah Lane. She had 2 brothers, Jim and George Knight, and a sister, Mrs. Ruth Foster.

### John Henry Brown
1870 Black River, Lawrence Co. Ar, census

| | | | | |
|---|---|---|---|---|
| Harriet Brown | 53 | F | keeping house | Tn |
| John H | 18 | M | | Ar |
| Josephine | 16 | F | | Ar |
| Sarah A | 13 | F | | Ar |
| Amanda | 11 | F | | Ar |
| James D McNutt | 12 | M | | Ar |

1880 El Monte, Ca, LA, dist 34 —

| | | | | | | |
|---|---|---|---|---|---|---|
| John H Brown | M | 28 | laborer | Ar | Al | Al |
| Cariane | F | 23 | keeping house | Tx | Mo | Al |
| Emma | F | 3 | | Tx | Ar | Tx |
| Ida | F | 1 | | Tx | Ar | Tx |
| Minnie Bailey | F | 8/12 | ?unreadable? | Az | Fl | Tx |

I wish I had more on John H Brown, Josephine's brother. Notice in California, that John was born in Arkansas and his parents were born in Alabama. Also his wife was born in Texas. Two of his 3 sisters married after the family moved to Denton County, Texas, so perhaps he did as well. Notice the McNutt name – it will become a prominent surname in the second half of this report. I do not know what became of him or his descendants.

31

## E. Oh, and Just Who Is Alph Brown?

In Arkansas, we first find our ancestor, David Brown, on the 1848 tax records for Lawrence County. David is on a tax list in 1847 in Walker County, Alabama, so we know pretty much the exact year he went to Arkansas. He is found in 1861 as joining the 8th Arkansas, Confederate. In 1862 he is taken POW at the battle of Corinth, Mississippi, and was paroled 8 days later. We have had difficulty after that, as there were so many men named David Brown, in the Civil War, on both sides.

We have the following record of the death of David Brown, Josephine's father:

*In the Probate Court Lawrence County before the clerk [?]*

*I Aaron M. Sawyers here app[?] for [?] of administration upon [?] estate of David B. Brown, deceased, do swear that the value of said estate will not exceed about six hundred and [?] dollars, that said deceased died on or about the day of 1 May AD 1865 without a will as it is said that he left surviving him a widow Harriet Brown and four children. John Henry, Josephine, Sarah Ann, and Amanda Brown, All of Lawrence County. That I will, if appointed administrator, make a perfect inventory of and faithfully administer all [?] the goods and chattels rights and [?] which [?] of the deceased and pay his debts as far as his assets which come to my [?] or possession [?] [?] and the law direct, and that [?] will account for all pay over according to law, all assets that may count to any [?] or possession so help me God.*

*M. Sawyers.*

*Sworn to and subscribed before [?] [?] this 30 day of September A D 1865*

*C W Harlow clerk*

*J W T[?]eau D C*

David had died on 1 May 1865 so it took a few months before they got around to his Probate Court being settled.

Per the 1850 and 1860 census records of Lawrence County, Arkansas, the same children listed above were their children. There are also three others in the household we have always heard were orphans. Per census records — Nancy I. Joiner, Thomas McNutt, and Nancy A. Loony, who is recorded as Nancy A. Brown on the 1860 census. Who were they? We will find out, later.

A record of the marriage of my great grandparents exists and says –

*Jeffrey H. Richey, Josephine Brown, marriage. This is to certify that I, Hugh Rainwater did on the 10th day of March, 1872 the rights of matrimony between Jeffrey Richey age 21 and Josephine Brown age 18 in the residence of Alph Brown in the state of Arks. In the county of Lawrence my credentials being recorded in the clerk's office in Powhatan this 14th day of March 1872. Hugh Rainwater.*

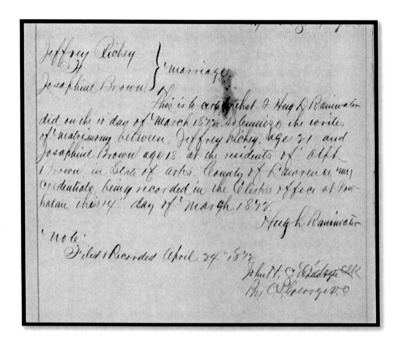

Now remember we have a record of my great grandparents moving to Indian Territory, near Fort Smith, Arkansas. Recall my great grandma's statement about attending a public hanging at Fort Smith, and there being mention of needing protection from the law.

Well, we also have the following:

*THE UNITED STATES OF AMERICA, the Western District of Arkansas. The United States of America to the Marshall of the Western District of the state of Arkansas – greeting: Whereas complaint under oath has been brought before me charging that Alph Brown, Elias Jeffries, and Eli Beavers did on or about the 15th day of July A. D. 1884 in the Indian Country Western District of Arkansas, commit the crime of assault with intent to kill contrary to the form of the statute in such cases made and provided, and against the peace and dignity of the United States to apprehend the said Alph Brown, Elias Jeffries, and Eli Beavers and bring their bodies forthwith before James Brizzolara, Commissioner appointed by the United States District Court, for said district, whenever they may be found, that they may then and there dealt with, according to law for said offense.*

*Given under my hand, this 2nd day of August, A. D. 1884, in the 109th year of our Independence.*

*James Brizzolara, Commissioner, U. S. Courts, Western District of Arkansas*

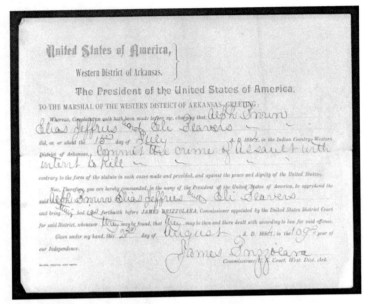

So my great-grand-parents were married in the home of "Alph Brown" in 1872, moved to the vicinity of Fort Smith shortly thereafter. Well, a decade after that "Alph Brown" becomes a wanted man for the crime of "assault with intent to kill" in Indian Territory somewhere near Fort Smith. Just who is Alph Brown? We will have more on him later. Also note the "Jeffries" surname – it was a common Catawba surname, as was Brown.

Here is my great-grandma, Josephine [Brown] Richey (b. Ar 1854 — d. Ok 1932). To her right is my Uncle Andrew. The person who sent me this photo just wanted a picture of Josey, and didn't know who the young man was standing near her, so they cut him partially out. Uncle Andrew is the uncle who heard I was interested in researching the family, and responded "You might not like what you find." However he was probably in his 60s or 70s at least, when he said this to me. Great-grandma Josephine [Brown] Richey was sister to Tarlton Bull's wife Sarah Ann [Brown] Bull. She is the one who said she regretted attending that public hanging at Fort Smith, Arkansas all the remainder of her life, the infamous Judge Roy Parker, known to history as "The Hanging Judge", presiding.

34

# CHAPTER 2 OUR ARKANSAS FAMILIES

Our Indian heritage seems to have come through Arkansas. When I started researching my family, I only thought our Indian blood came from the Brown's and Guess/Gist's, and that they were Cherokee. But the more I looked into it and the more evidence that arose, I started thinking we had found Indian ancestry with the Wayland's as well. There is a strong possibility they were Catawba. Now our Joseph Richey married Mary Wayland, and their son Jeffrey married Josephine Brown. For this reason I thought it important to talk a little about the Richey's, even though we don't think they had any Indian blood. The part of the family we had originally thought were Indian-mixed and had intended to research because of family stories – were our Brown's/Gist's. So before actually getting back East of the Mississippi and finding the documentation of an Indian ancestry, I need to talk a little about our Arkansas heritage.

## A. The Story of the Wayland's

The Wayland's came from England to Ireland, with our bunch arriving in South Carolina about the time of the American Revolution. Nevil Wayland, the progenitor of our branch of the Wayland's in America, moved to Virginia about 1797. He died in 1806. It is thought he married a Catawba Indian woman. Her surname seems to have been Gibson. This will be brought out over time. When you read stories about the first families or the first settlers in Arkansas, the name "Wayland" usually pops up.

These Wayland's are part of my family.

### The Arrival of the Wayland's in Arkansas

The earliest documentation I have found of our Wayland's in Arkansas mention my ancestor, William Wayland:

### Early Lawrence County, Arkansas Records

*William Wayland, 1/2 appraised value*

*P 5 — Tuesday, November 23, 1819 — Thomas Griffith is authorized to keep a ferry at White River where James Akins now lives . . . He is allowed to charge the same rates . . .*

*Friday, November 26, 1819 — **William Wayland** is appointed overseer of the second road of said township [Spring River Township]*

*P 10 — Wednesday, third day of term, June 6, 1821 — Jacob Flannery is appointed overseer of the first division in the place of **William Wayland***

*Before Tuesday, January 15th, 1822 — P 13 — Samuel Crow is appointed overseer of the road leading from Davidsonville to White River, in the first road division of Strawberry Township in the place of* **William Wayland**

*P 21 — Tuesday, the second day of term, 5 July 1825 — Ordered that the following named persons be commissioned judges at the ensuing August election, to wit: Jesse Jeffrey, Henry Wayland, and Samuel D Gibson for Strawberry Township, and that the election, and that the election be held in the house of Jesse Jeffrey.* [Vance's note: Jeffrey and Gibson are both well-known Catawba surnames, and our Wayland's lived with Gibson's in the first known Melungeon community in Scott County, Virginia. Also note my ancestor, William Wayland, was at one time (until Jan 1822) overseer of a road from Davidsonville to White River. White River was the dividing line between the Arkansas Cherokee and the White settlers until sometime after 1828.]

*P 23 — Tuesday, February 28, 1826 — Henry Wayland, Esquire, is appointed to apportion the hands to work on the lower road from Jacob Fortenberry's to the Independence County line.*

*P 24 — Monday, June 26, 1826 — Peyton R Pitman, Esquire, Rubin Richardson, and Henry Wayland and James Sloan, are appointed to apportion the hands to work on various road divisions in Lawrence County.*

*P 25 — Monday, February 25, 1827 — Henry Wayland is appointed an overseer of a road, and Joseph Ware of another road.*

*P 26 — After Feb 27, 1827 and before June 25, 1827 — The court now proceeds to settle with the sheriff, James M Kuykendall*

So William is first mentioned in 1819, Henry in 1825, and Nevil not until about 1827. However while most researchers claim Nevil was in Arkansas first, documentation first mentions William, my ancestor. Notice the mention of a Jeffrey and a Gibson family. Both these surnames could be Catawba or Piedmont Catawba. As we'll see, the Wayland surname pops up in Virginia living with these same known Catawba Indian families.

**The Abraham Ruddell Story**

You might wonder why I mention Abraham Ruddell, as we are not related to him. We have a tale of Abraham Ruddell. The author writes in flowery words about a man who was captured while still a small child, by the Shawnee and spent 16 years with them. He knew Tecumseh personally. I add this portion because at the end of this of this section of the book it casually mentions that Nevil Wayland came to Arkansas with him. I wish it had mentioned

36

William as well, my ancestor, but it doesn't. Since Lawrence County documentation mentions William before it mentions Nevil, I am hoping it can be implied William came with Abraham and Nevil Jr., also. [7]

## REMARKABLE LIFE OF ABRAHAM RUDDELL

*Abraham Ruddell, of Independence County, had a career, which the pen of J. Fennimore Cooper might have depicted as it deserved, but which my pen in the space allotted cannot adequately express. He was born as far west as white people at that time had found permanent homes. Far down on the Holstein in Virginia in a log house on August 3, 1774, he first saw the light of day. He never knew much about this home nor his parents, for on June 22, 1780, the Indians fell upon the little settlement and with savage ferocity tomahawked its residents, carrying off as a prisoner the little curley-headed Abraham Ruddell. They carried him over into Kentucky and the same something that prompted his savage captors to spare his life, whatever that may have been, prompted the great Tecumseh to not only further spare him, but to take him into his family as an adopted son. Strange fortune was this! Strange mutation of the little child's life. He grew up under Tecumseh's eye and was trained by that renowned warrior in all the arts of Indian life and Indian warfare. He learned the language of the tribe, played the Indian boyhood games, and took part in all the Indian wars. He was an adept in the use of a tomahawk, though his white blood restrained him from its more barbarous uses. He was skilled with the bow and could contest favorably with all his dusky comrades. In the use of the rifle he had no superior and Tecumseh awarded him many happy encomiums. When the tribe fought other Indian tribes Ruddell fought at Tecumseh's side and fought well. He had no particle of cowardice in his system and was far more venturesome than even his savage friends. He was trained, however, to know that he was white, and Tecumseh always held out to him the fact that at some time he would go back to the whites to live the white man's life. So gentle was Tecumseh to him that he grew to love him and throughout his life had a warm vein of affection for the great warrior. When Tecumseh died there was one white man. at least, that sincerely mourned his death. Logan, the Mingo, stood alone in his absolute lack of mournful friends; Tecumseh was mourned by his tribe and by Abraham Ruddell. For Tecumseh's brother, the prophet, Ruddell had a supreme contempt, and it was only his love for Tecumseh that kept him from openly showing his dislike.*

## LIVED SIXTEEN YEARS WITH INDIANS.

*After sixteen years of captivity under the provisions of Mad Anthony Wayne's treaty, he returned to the whites. His parting with Tecumseh was grievous, and each shook the hand of the other in proud good faith as they separated. Ruddell went back to his own people, a stranger in their midst. In Kentucky he started a new life, the white man's life with an added Indian education. His counsels were sought by the border woodsmen, and his Indian craft was used to circumvent the craft of the Indians. In 1811 he became a soldier of the United States and with the backwoodsmen of Virginia and Kentucky, with unerring rifles and forest tactics, marched with the brave and gallant Winchester into Canada. He was in the ever memorable fight of the Raisin and with others felt all the mortification of defeat. All day long his eye swept the field of savage faces hunting for the familiar face of Tecumseh. At the risk of his life he would have tried to shake Tecumseh's hand again. He had bullets for the Indians, but none for Tecumseh. But he saw not his friend, nor did he see that other, the Prophet, for whom he had saved a special bullet, and whom he would gladly have shot. Ruddell always attributed the prevalence of the Indian atrocities to the evil eye of the Prophet.*

## MOVED TO ARKANSAS.

*In battle after battle the defeat was retrieved and the war cry "Remember the Raisin," became the rallying cry of all future combats. Ruddell served through the war and went back to his forest home to ever afterwards live a peaceful life. In 1816 the Western fever attacked his neighborhood and with one accord they pulled up stakes and began a journey into the greater and newer West. Crossing the Mississippi below St. Genevieve they took the old St. Louis and Washita road and turned South. One by one they found their Canaan and blazed their claims. Ruddell found his in the fairest part of what is now Independence County, in that township which will forever carry his name. Grand old Abraham Ruddell! Was there ever a man more respected in the county?*

## UNIVERSALLY RESPECTED.

*Fent Noland, who knew him well, who gleaned the fore-going story from his lips, said, "No. He was a man of his word, honest and clean. He was never asked for a bond, and hated a liar. He was not only respected, but loved, and at his death, February 25, 1841, the whole county grieved. He loved the forest and spent the greater part of his time in its depths.*

He knew all the trees and communed with them; he knew the habits of all the birds and loved to imitate their music. Every flower of the county was known to him, not by its Latin, but by its loving backwoods name. Such a man had in him all the fire of a poet linked to the soul of a scientist. He never injured any man and all men were his friends. He could lie down in the forest, draw the drapery of a couch around him, and in the presence of the stars sleep that sleep which abounds only in pleasant dreams." Fent Noland was a clean man — a man of lofty, poetic ideals, and his testimonial to the character of Abraham Ruddell is one of the brightest parts of old Independence County history. He had several children, but at his death had but one son and one daughter living, who with his wife shed genuine tears of regret. He never sought office, and but one of the name, John Ruddell, is enrolled on the county's official roll. George Ruddell was a citizen of Batesville in 1821. Abraham Ruddell's name marks the township in which Batesville stands, and that is a most signal honor. There on the hallowed ground where James Boswell, Richard Peel, Richard Searcy, Thomas Curran, J. Redmon, Charles H. Pelham, Charles Kelly, J. Egner, John Read, Colonel Miller, J. L. Daniels, Robert Bruce, John and James Trimble, Colonel and Fent Noland, James Denton, Townsend Dickinson, William Moore, and other choice spirits of the earliest times met with him and lived with him — there was he buried amidst the most profound grief of his fellows. No more romantic character ever lived on Arkansas soil, and some rising Arkansas Octave Thanet will do credit to her name by writing a characteristic romance with Abraham Ruddell as its central figure. He was "The Last of the Mohicans," as it were, but his life story ought not to die.


## OTHER PIONEERS.

**In the same year that Ruddell passed away, in the last days of August another settler who came in with Ruddell in 1816, but who settled in what is now Lawrence County, died and was buried, not with his fathers, but in a new graveyard in the west. His name was Nevill Wayland and he left children to perpetuate his name.** In October of 1840, at Spring Hill, Hempstead County, died Aquilla Davis in his sixtieth year, having lived in Arkansas twenty-four years. He left a large family and a most excellent name. His house was headquarters for all the young people and his hospitality knew no bounds. He was said to entertain a poor man equally as lavishly and with the same spirit that he entertained richer people. His cheerfulness was his main characteristic and with this he made troops of friends.

The treaty mentioned was after the Battle of Fallen Timbers in 1794. Admittedly the Author spices up this account a great deal. I am not sure the details are accurate. Other authors mention his brother Stephen Ruddle and say Stephen was treated well by the Shawnee and Abraham was treated as a slave. Whatever the truth, when my family meets interesting figures, I want a record of it so others of later generations can know of it. My Wayland's travelled to Arkansas with Abraham Ruddell, and Abe knew Tecumseh.

On pages 113-114 of the same book we have the following:

*What shall we say of Lawrence County in early days? In 1830 a census was taken, which showed some remarkable instances of long life. The rules of the United States Census Bureau in 1830, although not so systematic as today, required nevertheless that the ages should be classified.*

*Between sixty and seventy years of age at the date of the enumeration were the following Lawrence County pioneers: William Hix, Sr., Henry Murrey, Arthur Murphy, Colonel Stephen Byrd, Thomas Lewis, John Pierce, Mary Welch, Mrs. Nathaniel McCarroll, Ananias Erwin, William McKnight, Isaac Flahery and James Davis.*

***Between seventy and eighty years: Nathan Luttrell, Sr., James Boyd, Mrs. Wayland, Peter Taylor, James S. Fortenberry, Daniel Williams, Martin Van Zant and Mrs. Joseph Killett.***

*Eighty years and upward: John Shaver: Twenty-one persons were in Lawrence County sixty years of age and upward in 1830.*

On that 1830 census that one "Mrs. Wayland" was living in the household of my direct ancestor, William Wayland. Her name is not given. She could be Kezziah, William's mother, but she might be his wife's mother. Kezziah, William's mother, is the one who we think has Catawba blood. We believe William's wife to have been a Stuart, but we can't prove it. One of William's daughters was named Mary Stuart Wayland. At any rate, an elderly woman is recorded living in William's household.

## First Church in both Arkansas and Indian Territory

Our Wayland's were some of the earliest settlers in Arkansas. There is a record of our family helping organize the First Methodist Church in Arkansas, which it turns out was also the first church in Indian Territory as it was defined at the time. Below is some of the documentation to back that up. If fact most histories say the First Church was at Dwight Mission. It wasn't established until 1818. Well, when they showed up, we were already there.

Our church was on the White River in north-central Arkansas while the far better known Dwight's Mission was on the Arkansas River in the west-central part of that state.

From "The History of Methodism in Arkansas", we have [8]:

In the Tennessee Conference which met at Bethlehem, Wilson County, Tennessee, October 20th, 1815, Spring River Circuit was made a part of the Missouri District. This was the first regular work laid off by the Conference in the Territory of Arkansas. . . **As the work was left to be supplied, this was done by Eli Lindsay, a local preacher who lived on the Strawberry River,** near the mouth of Big Creek.

*Rev. John M. Steele, from whose manuscript I am indebted for this information, says: "Col. Magnus stated to me that their first preacher was named Lindsay, and that he preached on White River and Little Red River, and thence to Strawberry and Spring River."*

*In 1818* [note: should be 1828] *the tribes of Indians, began, according to treaty stipulation, to remove to the West, but as they were not hurried by the influx of the Whites into the territory, they did not all remove for a number of years.*

*From this date, as the original inhabitants began to decline in numbers, and the White population to increase . . .*

From "The Story of Methodism in Oklahoma" [9]:

*In recording the activities of Methodism in what is now the State of Oklahoma, we necessarily have to commence with Methodism as it functioned in what is now the State of Arkansas.*

*At one time the western boundary of Arkansas was a line beginning near Fulton, on the Red River, Hempstead County, thence in a northeasterly direction to the mouth of Point Remove Creek, on the Arkansas River, Conway County, thence to a place on White River near Batesville, Independence County, thence northwest up the White River to Missouri line, all west of this line belonging to Indian Territory. Roughly estimated, this line gave twenty-seven counties, or about one-third of the present State of Arkansas to Indian Territory. It must also be remembered that at one time Indian Territory was Arkansas Territory . . .*

## Chronicles of Oklahoma Article
### Volume 7, No. 4, December, 1929 [10]

*From history of Methodism in Arkansas, by Horace Jewell we learn that the Tennessee conference which was held in Wilson County, Tennessee, October 20, 1815, Spring River Circuit, which is in Arkansas, was made a part of the Missouri District and left to be supplied. This was the first regular circuit in the Territory of Arkansas. Sometime during the conference year, a local preacher by the name of Eli Lindsay was placed on the new circuit as a supply. Spring River, from which the circuit was named, has its source in the Mammoth Springs located in Fulton County, the southwest corner of said county being about ten miles distant from the White River, which was at one time, as stated above, the dividing line between the Indian and Arkansas territories.* **From Jewell's history, we are informed that the local preacher, Eli Lindsay, while on the Spring River Circuit, preached at points on White River, Little Red River, Strawberry River and Spring River. The point we are making here is that, Little Red River is south and west of White River, and therefore in the Indian Territory, when the White River was the dividing line between Arkansas and Indian country.** *At the close of the conference year, Mr. Lindsay reported a membership of ninety-five, which was a good report for such a new and sparsely settled country.*

So the parts of this first Methodist circuit that were west of White River were in Indian Territory at the time.

From "Lawrence County, Arkansas Historical Journal", [11] Summer 1982 – Volume 4 – Number 3, History of Methodism in Walnut Ridge:

*Here it should be noted that Walnut Ridge Methodist Church has drawn some if its most staunch Methodists and strongest leaders from pioneer families in the western district of Lawrence County.* **It will be remembered that the Spring River Circuit, which includes part of Western Lawrence County, was the first pastoral charge organized in Arkansas in 1815 by the Rev. Eli Lindsey. It was this same year that Nevil Wayland came to Arkansas and his son, Jonathan Wayland. They, with Hugh Rainwater and Terra Stuart and their families, organized a Church on Flat Creek. Jonathan Wayland became a local preacher and so did Hugh Rainwater.**

**To the present generation of Waylands and Rainwaters (many of whom have held membership in Walnut Ridge) belong the distinctions of being descendants of the first Methodist Church organized in Arkansas.**

On page 66 of "A Centennial History of Methodism in Arkansas, 1815-1935" under the chapter title "1836-1843" we have the following [12]:

*Jonathan Wayland was grandfather to E. T. Wayland of North Arkansas Conference. He had in 1815 cooperated with Eli Lindsay in organizing Flat Creek Church, possibly the first Protestant Congregation ever organized in Arkansas, and certainly one of the first churches of the first circuit organized.*

REV. JONATHAN WAYLAND

The above is in error. It was Jonathan's father who helped create the first church in Arkansas territory, as Jonathan wasn't even born yet. This photo of Jonathan was taken from the same page as the above named book. His grandfather was White, but we have substantial evidence that Jonathen's paternal grandmother was Melungeon, from a community of people proven to be tri-racial in Southwestern Virginia and Northeastern Tennessee. Wild claims that they were Gypsies or Portuguese or even Turks is ridiculous. Sorry, but evidence of that is based on people who were afraid to say in a court of law that they had any Negro blood, at a dark time in history when Negroes were slaves. I use the Occam's Razor approach and claim them only tri-racial, White, Black, and Indian, with the Indian component probably Saura (also Cheraw), with Upper and Lower Saura Towns found nearby. These were a band of the Catawba. They were not Cherokee.

## Military Service at Fort Gibson with Bean's Ranger's

In "A Tour on the Prairies" [12] by Washington Irving, we have a first-hand account of the First Dragoon Expedition. In 1832, Washington Irving, the creator of Rip Van Winkle and Ichabod Crane, travelled to Indian Territory and Fort Gibson. He mentions travelling to the "Cross Timbers" (central Oklahoma) with the Army, of meeting the various Indian tribes. One tribe called "Pawnee Picts" in his account and other accounts was actually the Wichita who are not related to the Pawnee at all. Again why bring this up?

According to Fort Gibson records, Jarrett and James Wayland served at Fort Gibson from its founding from at least, around 1832 to about 1836. Jarrett and James were first cousins to my great-great grandma, Sarah Ann [Wayland] Richey. They were also first cousins of each other, With Sarah descending from William, Jarrett descending from Nevil

43

Jr. (as did Jonathan pictured about – they were brothers), and James being a son of Henry, the oldest son of Nevil Sr.

## Roster of Bean's Rangers

[13] "*Act of Congress approved June 15, 1832, authorized the President to raise a battalion of 600 mounted rangers to serve on the frontiers.*" *Rangers were to be* "*Active men, under 40 years of age, capable of enduring all the fatigues of arduous service.*" **The following list from the National Archives was made from the first muster rolls at Fort Gibson, Oklahoma. Most of the men were enlisted by Jesse Bean from his own Batesville, Independence Co., Arkansas area. Possibly many were future Oklahomans.**

OFFICERS: **Jesse Bean**, *Capt., Joseph Pentecost, 1st Lt., Robert King, 2nd Lt., George Caldwell, 3rd Lt. John W. Patrick, 1st Corp. Annanias Erwin, 2nd Corp. James Elms, 3rd Corps.* **Jarrett Wayland**, *4th Corp. John England, 5th Corp. Edward W. Scruggs, 1st Sgt. Robert A. Gibson, 2nd Sgt. Morfet E. Trimble, 3rd Sgt. Isaac Bean, 4th Sgt. Furgus S. Morrison, 5th Sgt.*

BUGLERS: *Elijah G. Shrum, Musician Alexander C. Childers, Musician*

PRIVATES: *Aikin, Eli V.; Allen, Washington; Archer, Andrew B.; Alston, James; Allen, Westly; Bennett, James H.; Barr, James; Baird, Benjamin; Brounts, Joshua; Bayles, Caleb; Compton, John B.; Clements, Jeremiah; C. Caldwell, James; Caldwell, Abiram; Dupuy, David; Davis, Abner; Dudley, William; Darter, Hezekiah; Davis, Johnson; Dennis, John; Dillard, John; Elms, Garrett; Elms, David M.; Fulbright, William; Gill, Addison; Guist, Isaac; Griggs, Samuel; Garner, John C.; Hammon, John; Hammon, James M.; Hulsey, William B.; Hogan, John W.; Hyles, David; Hyde, Ezekial; Howell, Harvey B.; Ivy, Thomas G.; Johnson, Samuel; Johnson, Marbree; King, Drury; Kister, John (also spelled Kester. Died 30 Oct 1832); Kellet, William; Kavanaugh, John; Litchfield, Samuel; Labass, John; Logan, Massa; Logan, Bennett T.; Lee, John; McClenden, Willis; McKinney, Clark S.; McCloud, Neil; Meacham, James A.; Meacham, Christopher; Murphy, Mark; Markham, Thomas Sr.; Markham, Thomas Jr.; Manson, William; Martin, James; Nipper, Solomon; Newcomb, Thomas; Newman, John; Nelson, Charles; Osburn, James; O'neal, John; Powers, Simmeon; Palmer, David M.; Palmer, King L;. Penter, Martin; Peel, Richard; Peel, John; Peel, William; Pool, Washington; Palmer, John J.; (Died 27 Sept 1832); Price, Jacob; Peryhouse (?), Nelson; Ryan, John; Russell, Samuel; Raney, David J.; Ryan, William; Stokes, James; Shaddon, Lewis; Sawyers, William; Turley, Thomas S.; Tate, William C.; Turney, Isham; Taylor, Wiley; Vickers, William; Wilson, John S.; Wilson, Absolom; Wilson,*

*Edward; Wilson, Daniel; Wilson, Joseph; Wyatt, Joseph S.; Wilson, William;* **Wayland, James***; Welborne, Melton [Vance's note: was he related to the Alabama Melton's?]; Young, Harvey K.; Zeachsa, Burr H. Replacements for the two deaths were Dolson Howell and Phillip Howell. Their origin is not noted.*

http://www.angelfire.com/il/oaparchives/cd072499.html

These military units first organized at Fort Gibson, Indian Territory were first called the First Dragoons, a name changed to the First Cavalry during the American Civil War. Below is a record of their military unit, the First Cavalry. The image to the left is an old historical marker about 16 miles north of Altus, my home town, in Southwestern Oklahoma. It says:

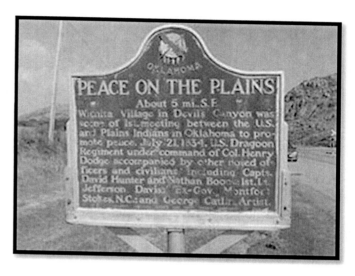

*OKLAHOMA — Peace on the Plains. About 5 mi. S. E. Wichita Village in Devils Canyon was scene of first meeting between U. S. and Plains Indians in Oklahoma to promote peace, July 21, 1834. U. S. Dragoon Regiment under command of Col. Henry Dodge accompanied by other officers and civilians including Capts. David Hunter and Nathan Boone, 1ˢᵗ. Lt. Jefferson Davis, Ex-Gov. Montford Stokes, N. C. and George Catlin, artist.*

## THE FIRST REGIMENT OF CAVALRY
### *by APT. R. P. PAGE WAINWRIGHT, 1ST U. S. CAVALRY.* [15]

*The "United States Regiment of Dragoons" was organized by Act of Congress approved March 2, 1833, becoming the "First Regiment of Dragoons" when the Second Dragoons were raised in 1836. Its designation was changed to "First Regiment of Cavalry" by the Act of August 3, 1861. The first order announcing appointments in the regiment was dated March 5, 1833, and gave the names of the colonel, lieutenant-colonel, major, four captains and four lieutenants, stating that the organization of the regiment would be*

45

*perfected by the selection of officers from the "Battalion of Rangers." Headquarters were established at Jefferson Barracks.*

*The organization of the regiment does not appear to have been completed until June, 1834, the regimental return for that month naming the following officers:*

*Colonel Henry Dodge.*

*Lieutenant-Colonel Stephen W. Kearny.*

*Major Richard B. Mason.*

*Captains Clifton Wharton, E. V. Sumner, Eustace Trenor, David Hunter, Lemuel Ford, Nathan Boone* [Vance's note: son of Daniel Boone], *J. B. Browne,* **_Jesse Bean_** [Vance's note: roster of Bean's Rangers is listed above and included 2 of our Wayland's. This tells us that Jesse and Jarrett Wayland's unit, Bean's Rangers, went along on this expedition], *Matthew Duncan and David Perkins.*

*First Lieutenants P. St. G. Cooke, S. W. Moore, A. Van Buren, J. F. Izard, Jefferson Davis, L. P. Lupton, Thomas Swords, T. B. Wheelock, J. W. Hamilton (adjutant), B. D. Moore, and C. F. M. Noland.*

*Second Lieutenants James Allen, T. H. Holmes, J. H. K. Burgwin, J. S. Van Derveer, J. W. Shaumburg, Enoch Steen, James Clyman, J. L. Watson, and B. A. Terrett.*

*Brevet Second Lieutenants William Eustis, G. W. McClure, L. B. Northrop, G. P. Kingsbury, J. M. Bowman, Asbury Ury, A. G. Edwards and T. J. McKean.*

*Lieutenant Jefferson Davis was the first adjutant but resigned the staff position February 4, 1834, and was assigned to Company A.*

*In October, 1833, the five companies first organized were sent under Colonel Dodge to winter in the vicinity of Fort Gibson, Arkansas Territory, where they remained until June, 1834.*

*In June, 1834, the regiment was sent on the "Pawnee Expedition,"* [Vance's note: these were mistakenly called Pawnee – in reality they were Wichita Tribe] *during which, although it ended in September of the same year, one fourth of the officers and men of the command died of fevers. On the 6th of August, Colonel Dodge writes to Lieutenant-Colonel Kearny: "I have on my sick report 36 men, four of whom have to be carried in litters. My horses are all much jaded, and would be unable to return by the mouth of the Wishitaw and reach their point of destination this winter season. This has been a hard campaign on all; we have been for the last fifteen days living almost on meat alone. The state of the health of this detachment of the regiment makes it absolutely necessary that I should arrive at Fort Gibson as early as possible, as well as the difficulty of providing grain for the horses. I am well aware you are placed in a most unpleasant situation, encumbered as you must be with sick men, baggage and horses, and regret exceedingly that it is not in my power to help you."*

*The third effort to make contact with these Western Indians was successfully carried out in 1834, by what became known as the famous Dragoon Expedition. General Henry Leavenworth arrived at Fort Gibson April 28 of that year and assumed command of the post, which he held until June 12 when he departed in command of the expedition. This expedition included also Colonel Henry Dodge, Colonel Stephen Watts Kearney, and Major R. B. Mason. Jefferson Davis, a lieutenant a few years out of West Point, was in command of one company. This train of five hundred mounted troops, a large number of white-covered baggage wagons, and seventy head of beeves made an imposing procession. It was accompanied by eleven Osage, eight Cherokee, six Delaware, and seven Seneca Indians who went along to serve as guides, hunters, interpreters, and as representatives of their respective nations. They crossed the Arkansas River below the mouth of Grand River, passed over the prairies near the site of the future Muskogee, traveled southwest to the mouth of the Washita River, then northwest, where they visited the site of a Comanche village at the western end of the Wichita Mountains* [Vance's note: this was NOT a Comanche Village – it was Wichita and the historic marker (above) tells of the same event.].

*This was a disastrous expedition which resulted in the deaths of nearly 150 men from disease and the effects of excessive hot weather and poor water upon the unseasoned and undisciplined soldiers lately recruited from private life in the North and East. Included among the casualties of this expedition was that of General Leavenworth, who died July 21 near the Washita River.*

*However, they did succeed in bringing back to Fort Gibson representatives of the Kiowa, Wichita, and Waco tribes, and after their return invitations were extended to all the Indians within reach to attend a grand council at the post—Choctaws, Cherokees, Creeks, Senecas, Osages, Delawares, and others. Here, on September 2, 1834, began one of the most interesting and important Indian councils ever held in the country.* [Vance's note: the above is not 100 percent true – only 2 or 3 years earlier the Osage had massacred an entire Kiowa Village at a place and event called "Cutthroat Gap Massacre," so-called because the Osage cut their throats, and placed the severed heads in cooking pots. Therefore the Kiowa did not attend. They did not want peace until they had gained revenge on the Osage. More on this in Appendix 6 at the end of this report.] *On this occasion every effort was made to impress the wild Indians who had never made a treaty with the United States and make them understand the changed political condition of the country. There were 150 Indians participating in the council, & with their numerous women & children, tepees & tents, they made one of the most picturesque scenes ever witnessed at any army post.*

*Governor Stokes and the army officers who attended did not have authority at this time to enter into a treaty, but, with the potent influence of Colonel A. P. Chouteau, who participated in the council, the commissioners secured an agreement with the wild Indians to meet in treaty council the following year. And so the plans which were launched and carried out at Fort Gibson resulted in a treaty council begun August 24, 1835, at Fort Mason on the Canadian River near the present Purcell, Oklahoma, where was negotiated the first treaty ever entered into by a number of these western tribes.*

*In 1837 members of the Kiowa, Apache, and Tawakoni tribes were induced to send representatives to Fort Gibson, where on May 26 another important treaty, the first with these Indians, was negotiated. These treaties gave assurance of peace on the part of the Indians and guarantees of safe passage for the traders over the Santa Fe route. And two of my Wayland's were there, too.*

## B. Our Richey's go to Arkansas

**Goodspeed Biography**

Hamilton Richey was interviewed for the Goodspeed Biography and said the following about his father, John Richey:

*John Richey, of Virginia, who moved to Indiana in his younger days, and married Miss Polly Woods, of that State, locating in Gibson County, where Hamilton was born December 29, 1829. John Richey followed his occupation of farming in Indiana until the year 1844, when he removed to Arkansas, and settled in Lawrence County. He resided in that place, and reared his*

*family, until the time of his death, in the fall of 1861, when he passed away, regretted by all who knew him. Up to the time of his decease Mr. Richey had been a survivor of the War of 1812, and was at Mobile, Ala., when the battle of New Orleans was fought. He was also a captain of militia during his residence in Indiana.*

About the above claim that John was a "Captain of Militia" – I contacted an Indiana historian about this claim. I told him I had my doubts about this because he would have so young, more a boy than a man. Census records put his birth about 1797. He said this was an honorary title, only. He said some units designated a new "Captain of Militia" weekly or monthly. Also boys as young as he was were allowed to enlist in those days.

## War of 1812 Service Record for John Richey

On John Richey's grave is a veteran's tombstone. On it is recorded: John Richey; PVT, PEYTON'S MTD RANGER; WAR OF 1812; 1797-1861.

On a website marking the veterans of the War of 1812 [16] the following is found —

*Name:*
*JOHN RICHEY*
*COMPANY: CAPT. PEYTON'S CO., MOUNTED RANGERS, INDIANA MILITIA.*
*Rank - Induction: PRIVATE*
*Rank - Discharge: PRIVATE*
*Roll Box: 174 Roll Exct: 602*

Although John's son wrote that he was in Mobile, Alabama when the Battle of New Orleans was fought, the Indiana militia's also fought against Tecumseh. In 1812, John would have been 15 years old.

## Joseph Richey

Joseph E. Richey was John's eldest son. He was born 19 Oct 1821 in Gibson County, Indiana, and died 15 Feb 1852 in Lawrence County, Arkansas. He married Sarah Ann Wayland 03 Feb 1848 in Lawrence County, Arkansas. She was born about 1829 in Lawrence County, Arkansas, and died 1857 in Lawrence County, Arkansas. She was the daughter of William Wayland and Elizabeth [Stuart] Wayland. They had two children – Alfred H. Richey, b. 1849, and last appears in the 1860 census. No one knows what happened to him. I descend from the other brother Jeffrey Hoten Richey. Jeffrey was born 1

May 1851. Joseph Richey died in 1852, and his younger brother Hamilton, married his widow.

**Mexican War – Joseph Richey's Time at Fort Smith and Fort Gibson**

In a book entitled "Arkansas Mexican War Soldiers" we have the following: *Historical Highlights by Jay Brent Tipton.* [17]

*The Arkansas Gazette on June 25, 1846 [18] reported that a company of volunteers (mounted gunmen) from Lawrence County led by Capt. J. S. Ficklin arrived at Little Rock and took the road to Fort Smith where they are destined for service on the Arkansas frontier. The Lawrence County troops, Company C, Arkansas Battalion Infantry and Mounted Rifles were officially mustered into U. S. service at Fort Smith on July 6th, 1846, and were sent to Fort Gibson in the Indian Territory. . . Company C, along with the other companies of the Battalion, was mustered out of service on April 20th, 1847 at Fort Gibson. Even though they did not face the Mexican Army, these men served Lawrence County, Arkansas and ultimately the nation by volunteering and remaining at their station.*

Two men in this company are Richey's and are brothers, including my direct ancestor, Joseph E. Richey. The other is David L. Richey. David's wife was also a Wayland girl, by the way. They were mustered in and out at the dates and places mentioned in the previous paragraph. Later I hope to mention a Catawba migration to the vicinity of Fort Smith, Arkansas. A son of Joseph Richey and Sarah Wayland, Jeff Richey, married Josephine Brown, a daughter of David Brown and Harriet Guess/Gist, in 1872. I descend from that union. This seems to be the origin of our Indian blood.

## C. Our Brown's Arrive in Arkansas in 1848

David Brown last appears in Alabama on a tax list dated 1847. He first appears in Lawrence County, Arkansas the next year, in 1848, a year after Joseph Richey returned from military service in Indian Territory. A daughter of David Brown will later marry a son of Joseph Richey, and become my ancestors.

**The 1850 census lists David's family:**

| | | | |
|---|---|---|---|
| David B. Brown | 29 | farmer | Ala |
| Harriet Brown | 33 | | Ala |
| Nancy I. Brown | 7 | | Tenn |

50

| Thomas McNutt | 16 | farmer | Ala |
|---|---|---|---|
| Nancy A. Loony | 6 | | Ala |
| Thomas Opdych | 61 | physician | Ohio |

**1860 Census, Lawrence County Arkansas:**
Thomas McNutt 26 laborer Ala
Orlena McNutt 25 Ala
James McNutt 21 Arkansas
Betsy A. McNutt 3/12 Ark
" — next door is – "
David B. Brown 37 Al
Harriet Brown 43 Tn
Nancy I. Brown 17 Tn
Nancy A. Brown 15 Al
John Brown 8 Ar
Josephine Brown 6 Ar
Sarah A. Brown 3 Ar
Amanda Brown 1 Ar

Notice "Nancy A. Loony" in 1850 has become "Nancy A. Brown" in 1860. Oh before I forget, other records say Nancy I. Brown's real name was Nancy I. Joiner. Where do these McNutt's, Joiner's, and Loony's come from? More on these things later.

I find the Wayland's and Richey's – my direct line of Wayland's – and a Gibson (most likely related to my Wayland's) – all living next door to one another. There is another interesting family of Brown's living in Lawrence County, Arkansas that wasn't there in 1850, listed below.

**1860 census, Lawrence County, Arkansas:**
| Mary Brown | 59 NC |
|---|---|
| Nancy J Brown | 19 Ala |
| Martha L. Brown | 16 Ala |
| (next door) | |
| Malinda JOHNSON | 34 AL Laborer |
| Nancy " | 13 AL |
| Levi " | 12 AL |

David      "      10 AL
Thomas      "      1 AR

Malinda Johnson was living next door to Mary Brown (her mother) for this census, 1860.  Ten years earlier for the 1850 Walker County, AL census, Malinda is Linday, and the children Nancy, Levi and David, were living in the Mary Brown household.

I was able to get in contact with one of these Johnson's and she said she was told they had Indian blood on the Johnson side. At the time, she was unaware that Malinda Johnson was a "Brown".

I found this same family in 1850 in Walker County, Alabama:

**1850 Walker County, Alabama census**
Mary Brown 49 NC
Linday Brown 25 Ala
Elizabeth Brown 16 Ala
Orleny Brown 15 Ala
Alfred Brown 13 Ala
Nancy Brown 10 Ala
Martha Brown 8 Ala
Syntha Brown 4 Ala
Nancy Brown (inmate) 5 Ala
Levy Brown (inmate) 3 Ala
David Brown (inmate) 1/12 Ala

**1870 Lawrence Co., AR census, Marion Township, page 278, household #35**
David Johnson      21 MS      Farm Laborer
Malinda JOHNSON    45 AL      Keeping House
Levi Johnson      22 AL      Farm Laborer
Rufus Johnson      15 MS
Thomas Johnson      11 AR
Mathew Johnson      08 AR
Sarah Harvey   18 AR

Malinda Johnson is a daughter of Mary Brown.  Malinda was living with Mary Brown (her mother) for the 1850 Walker County, AL census.  In 1860 Malinda lived next door to Mary Brown in Lawrence County, AR.

**1880 Campbell, Lawrence Co, Ar census**
Rufus Johnson 25 M W farmer Ms Al Al
Amanda 52 F W kpn hs Al Al Al
Madison 16 M W frm lbr Ar Al Al

**Marriages Found**
Name: RUFUS JOHNSON
Spouse: BETTIE A. RANEY
Marriage Date: 26 Dec 1877
County: Lawrence
State: AR
Name: DAVID JOHNSON
Spouse: ELVINA RANEY
Marriage Date: 2 Mar 1871
County: Lawrence
State: AR
This is all we know at present, about the Johnson branch of our Brown's.

## Alfred Brown

This is the same family that is in Lawrence County, Arkansas in 1860. Are they David's family? Also note that "Malinda" Johnson is "Linday" Brown in 1850. They 3 youngest children in the Brown household in 1850 in Alabama are her children in 1860, and they are all Johnson's. They are living next door to Mary Brown, her mother. We have found Alfred Brown in Hopkins County, Texas in the 1860 census, is 22 years old, and says he was born in Alabama. He then appears in Lawrence County, Arkansas again in 1870, and is married. Notice "Orleny" Brown, 15 years old in Alabama in 1850 is 25 years old and is married to Thomas McNutt, who was living in David's household in 1850 and they are next door to him in 1860.

**1870 Census Lawrence County, Ar**
Alfred Brown 33 laborer Al
Nancy I. Brown 25 keeping house Tn
Mary J Brown 5 Ar
Louisa Brown 3 Ark

Alice Brown 2/12 Ark

Is this Alfred Brown the same "Alph Brown" in whose house my great grandparents were married in 1872? Well, one more census record will clinch it.

### 1880 Census, Denton County, Texas

Jeffrey H. Richey, age 28, Ar, In, Ar

Josephine, 26, Ar, Al, Al.

Etta E., 2, Tx, Ar, Ar.

Swaney, 1, Tx, Ar, Ar.

Mandy Knight, 18, sister-in-law, Ar, Al, Al.

Mary J. Brown, 16, cousin, Ar, Al, Al.

"Mandy Knight" is "Amanda Brown" in previous census records, sister to Josephine [Brown] Richey, Jeff's wife. Mary J Brown is a "cousin". The 1870 census of Alfred Brown – he had a daughter named Mary J Brown, 5 years old. Mary J Brown is a cousin IF Josephine's father David Brown and Alfred Brown are brothers! Mary J. Brown lists her parents born in Alabama. Since this census lists Mary as a cousin — David and Alfred *are* brothers! Hence David is a son of Mary, also.

It has taken a lot just to get this background material in place. I could have made it three times longer had I included more census records, so be thankful. I have a lot more information than I will ever be able to organize. I have painstaking verified all the relationships so far mentioned and they are correct.

I'd like to learn more about Alph/Alfred Brown. That one document said he is wanted for *"Assault with intent to kill"* in Indian Territory. Also there are a lot of Catawba Jeffries and Brown's. Maybe that's concidence, I don't know. But in the 1890s there was a big movement to organize the Catawba in Arkansas and Eastern Oklahoma/Indian Territory. The warrant for Alph Brown's arrest was in 1884, only a few years before and these Catawba were being organized near Fort Smith.

We have also found descendants of our Nancy Loony on the 1850 census. A fellow researcher sent us a death certificate for a Nancy Owens, who was their ancestor. It marks her death as March 3rd, 1922, in Barton County, Missouri, stating she was 77 years, 6 months, and 6 days old. For her father's name, all it says is "Loney". For her mother, she says "Mary Monday." It states that she was born in Tennessee, same as ours. This would put her time of birth about 1844, same as ours per 1850 census. Unfortunately, we still don't know who her father was, or anything about the Monday's, or why our family raised her.

**Conclusion:**

I have heard stories that we were somehow related to a famous Indian, whom we believe to be Sequoyah, for most of my life. That is the main reason I have done this research. I have tried to be both pragmatic and objective, but also I know I have a personal bias, and am trying my best not to let it get the best of me. I think I have succeeded.

My family has spent quite some time in Oklahoma, first arriving here about 1830 serving in the military at Fort Gibson for the first half of that decade., We helped organize the first church in Indian Territory, and our church predates Dwight Mission by about three years. It was at a location on the White River now in central Arkansas, the western bank of which was in Indian Territory until the Old Settler Treaty of 1828. My great-great-grandpa also served at Fort Smith and Fort Gibson during the Mexican War of 1846-1847. We were in and out of Indian Territory in the 1830s and 1840s, then came to stay (except for a stint in Denton County, Texas in the 1880s) in the 1870s. Of course this is not proof of Indian ancestry, but it does say we were comfortable amongst Indian peoples.

I researched literally every Gist/Guess/Guest family found first in Indian Territory and Arkansas. Then I had to keep going east – Mississippi and Alabama. The further east I went the more I thought maye the family stories of being related to Sequoyah might not be true. Research was taking us back to alocation in North Carolina, and a hundred or more years further back in time! Are we wrong? But we've some so far from where we were, I must keep looking. If anyone will help me, I'll gratefully accept that help! There was no way I could do this alone. Gradually a possible connection to Sequoyah emerged in a place I hadn't expected. PART TWO will provide more information. Absolute proof is very difficult to run across, but it is worth aiming for nontheless.

# FINDING OUR INDIAN BLOOD PART TWO

## CHAPTER 3 THE WAYLAND'S

Now that we have the background material, we can delve more deeply into the more distant, documents concerning our family. We know we have both Richey's and Wayland's who had served in the military at Fort Gibson in Indian Territory. The Wayland's had arrived in Arkansas about 1815 while the Richey's came to Arkansas in 1844 and the Brown's in 1848.

I am indebted to Frances Davies, a New Zealander who had researched the Wayland family, and discovered a "Nevil Wayland" born in Ireland in the 1700s. Also I am indebted to many others, including Don Sticher, who knocked down my every effort to find our Gist connection, that is, all but one.

### A. The Wayland Files per Frances Davey

Frances Davies wrote a very comprehensive book entitled the "Wayland Files" [19]. Since I am writing this down to show my Indian blood, I will go over this information quickly, perhaps be more thorough at some later time. According to Ms. Davies, Robert Wayland bought Pinner House about 1611. This was in London, England. His son, Henry, had a son named Henry. This younger Henry was also born at Pinner in 1695. He married Ann Rea/Rhea. By 1724 they had moved to Co. Tipperary, Ireland.

Her book has the following about this family, p 21:

*Wayland, Henry (3), son of Henry and Ann Keeble. Chr. 1795, Pinner, England, Married (1) _____ (2) Anne Rea abt 1723 (see R Austin-Cooper's book) Emigrated to Co. Cavan, Ireland by 1724, and to Co. Tipperary by 1728, buried 9 May 1785, St. John's (on the Rock?) Cashel.*

*Father of . . .*
*Anne, b. 1725*
*Henry (4), b. 1726*
*Francis, b. 1727*
*Jane, b. May 1728*

*Elizabeth, b. 25 July 1731*
*John, b. 17 Dec. 1732*
*Alice, b. 17 Jan. 1733*
*William, b. 2 Jun 1735 – went abroad*
*Elinor, b. 24 Sep. 1738*
*Rebecca, b. 1742, d. 1742*
*Dorothea, b. 17 Mar, 1744*
*Neville/Nevil, b. 13 Oct. 1745 – went abroad, probably Virginia, U. S. A.*

Records of all these children whose exact date of birth are recorded, were from records of St. John's Church of birth christenings, in Cashel, Co. Tipperary, Ireland. St. John's was affiliated with the Church of Ireland, which is the Irish equivalent to the same denomination as the Church of England. Notice they say two of these children went abroad but only one has been found – Nevil. And when she found Nevil in Virginia she didn't know about his service in the American Revolution, where he served in the South Carolina Militia.

## B. Nevil Wayland Sr.'s Revolutionary War File

I wrote to South Carolina Archives about Nevil, and they sent me about thirty pages, Xeroxed copies of old documents. I transcribed all of them that I could, but some of it well, I had no idea what they was saying. It just looked like nonsense. And I have no desire to put the transcriptions of all 30 pages here. But I will put a little part of it here, below:

### South Carolina

Pursuant to an act of the General Assembly passes the 16th of March, 1783. We the Commissioners of the *Treasury, have this day delivered to Mr. Navil Wayland this our indented certificate, for the sum of five pounds, fourteen shillings and three pence farthing Sterling duty done in Roebucks Regiment* [note: looks like "fs af dudites" — from henceforth I will place words I can't make out in brackets, with what it looks like inside those brackets]

*The said Navil Wayland, his Executors, Administrators or Assigns, will be entitled to receive from this office the sum of eight shillings on demand for one year's interest on the principle sum of five pounds, fourteen shillings and three pence farthing and the like interest annually.*

*The said Navil Wayland,, his executors, Administrators, or Assigns, will be entitled also to receive and shall be paid, if demanded, the sum of five pounds, fourteen shillings, and three pence shilling on the [too faint] September 1788. And the said Navil Wayland, his executioners, administrators, or assigns may make any purchases at any public sales of confiscated property (except such as shall be ordered by the Legislature for special purposes) and this indent shall be received in payment.*

*For the true performance of the several payments in manner above mentioned, the public treasury is made liable, and the faith of the state pledged by the aforesaid act.*

*Given under our hands at the treasury office in Charlestown, the twenty second day of September, one thousand seven hundred and eighty six.*

*Peter Bocquet,*

*Commisioners of the Treasury*

*No. 3770 book X. Issued the 22nd September 1786 to Mr. Nevil Wayland for five pounds fourteen Shillings for duty done in Roebucks Regiment. Account audited. Principle L 5..14..3 ¼. Interest 0.. 8.0.*

The above mentions pay for service in Roebuck's Regiment.

*No. 1274 Lib. Y. Issued 5 June 86 to Nevil Wayland L 14..17.. 1 ½ stg for waggoning provs. for the troops at the Indian Line from the commrs. interest 20 / 9.*

*I do humbly verify that Nevil Wayland was appointed by one commissary for the troops stationed on the Indian line and that the above wagoning was done for the services of the said troops. Wofford.* These documents infer he brought food to the troops. It mentions District 96 and "the troops on the Indian line". Wofford must have been his commanding officer.

*Next we have a letter written by Nevil himself:*

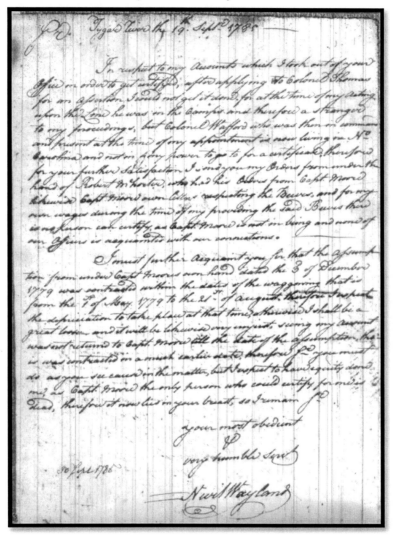

*Pd. Tyger River the 19th Sept. 1785.*

*In respect to my account which I took out of your office in order to get [?certified?] after applying to Colonel Thomas for an [?afsertion?]. I could not get it done for at the time of my acting upon the Line he was in the camps and therefore a stranger to my proceedings, but Colonel Wofford who was then in command and present at the time of my appointment is now living in Nth Carolina and not in any power to go to for a certificate. Therefore for your further satisfaction I send you my orders from under the hand of Robert McWhorter who had his orders from Capt. Moore. Over [?Cittor?] respecting the Beeves there is no person can certify, as Capt. Moore is not in [?living/being?] and none of our officers is acquainted with our connections. **I must further acquaint you Sir that the [?assump?] time from under Capt. Moores own hand dated 3rd of December 1779 was [?sontrastes?] within the dates of the waggoning that is from the first of May 1779 to the 21st of August. Therefore I repeat the depreciation to take place at that time, otherwise I shall be a great [?loo——?] and it will be likewise very unjust, [?icing?] my account was not returned to Capt. Moore till the date of the assumption. This is was contracted in a much earlier date,** but I expect to have equity done me, as Capt. Moore the only person who could certify for me is dead, therefore it now lies in your breast, so I remain your most obedient and very humble servant, Nevil Wayland. 30 Sept 1785.*

Above is taken from a Xeroxed copy of that letter.

*According to order to me given from James Moor General Commisary for the [?fonding?] provision for the use of the Frontiers in general, I do hereby appoint Nevile Wayland in my behalf to purchase provision for the said frontier and do engage the pay of debts which he shall contract on that account given under my hand this 19th day of June1779.*

The above documents are important for two reasons. ONE – It tells a time frame when and where Nevil served and TWO – one document was written I Nevil's own handwriting, showing he was well educated, but more importantly, it is a piece of my ancestor that I can see, a sort of a relic, I suppose, a family relic. I can look up battles in the summer of 1779 in South Carolina, near District 96. There are other documents that he signed, that look like receipts for animals he bought (beeves and horses) for the troops dated Nov 1779 and Feb 1780.

## His Life in South Carolina and the Melungeons

The 1790 census of Spartanburg, South Carolina has Naval Wayland 2,2,4 - the first number is males under 16, the 2nd is males over 16, and the third is females in the household. So they had 3 daughters about which we know NOTHING at all. As a result of his service in the Revolutionary War he obtained a land grant. In Spartanburg County, South Carolina. Roebuck's Regiment was also called "The Spartan Regiment" because many members came from the Spartanburg area, I suppose. He sold his lands in South Carolina and next appears in 1797 in lower Russell County, Virginia, which about 1811 or so became Scott County, Virginia.

Much has been written about the Melungeons, a tri-racial people found first in Scott County. In fact they appeared there about the same time Nevil arrived there. Now my autosomal DNA test said I am mostly Caucasian, but we do have some American Indian and sub-Sahara African autosomal DNA as well. A descendant of Francis Wayland also took the same DNA test I took and his came back with a little sub-Sahara African DNA as well, but he is mostly Caucasian. So I have been looking into this Melungeon ancestry. Who was Nevil's wife? I know the Melungeons were White, Black, and American Indian, with the American Indian component being Catawba or Piedmont Catawba. And the Catawba DID fight with the South Carolina Militias against the Cherokee. They also sold beeves to the militias to be used by the Revolutionary troops.

In "Melungeons: and Other Pioneer Families" by Jack Goins and "Melungeons, Examining an Appalachian Legend" by Pat Spurlock Elder, they say Nevil Wayland Jr. (son of the Revolutionary War Veteran) was the church clerk at Stoney Creek Primitive Baptist Church, which was in Scott County, Virginia. They say that it was in the minutes of that church that the word "Melungin" was first used in 1813. Now an earlier usage of "Lungins" has been found in Arkansas. One surname closely associated with the Melungeons is Gibson. They can be directly traced back to these eastern Siouan peoples – Catawba, Saponi, Cheraw, that have largely disappeared from history.

## C. Gibson's and Wayland's

**In Virginia – Various Documents**
*LAND ENTRY BOOK 2 [20]*
*RUSSELL CO. VA*

*PAGE 101*

*entry dated Oct 4 1805*

*Nevil Wayland Jun-r enters fifty acres of land by virtue of part of a Land Office Treasury warrant No 1855 dated March 18th 1796 lying in Russell county on both sides of Copper Creek beginning at a conditional line between John McClelan and James Gibson then running up the Creek on both sides for quantity entry dated Oct 23.* He purchased 50 aces in what became Scott County, Virginia, in 1796. Back then it was part of Russell County. James Gibson is his neighbor.

*P566 - Deposition of Margaret Lieth & Nevil Wayland, purporting the nocupative Will of Nevil Wayland, decd, ordered to be recorded. Motion of Keziah Wayland, securities: Nevil Wayland & Samuel Ritchie, adm granted on estate of Nevil Wayland, decd*

*P567 - David Cocke, Henry Cocke, John Berry & Mahal Driskil to appraise the estate of Nevil Wayland, decd.*

The last date mentioned in the records before mentioning Nevil's death is Oct. 7, 1806. So I suspect Nevil Wayland Sr. died shortly before October 7th, 1806.

*WILL BOOK 2*

*RUSSELL CO. VA PAGE 136*

*Taken 28 Sept. 2001*

*February Court 1807*

*"We being first sworn for that purpose do appraise the estate of Nevil Wayland dec'd of which the following is a true Inventory." D. cts*

*three heifers at 18*

*one cow and calf 12.50*

*seventeen head of hogs 28.75 42 25*

*one roan mare 70 1*

*black mare 30 100*

*A parcel of castings 10 58 1/2*

*A parcel of old hoes 3 8 1/2*

*Three axes and a sang hoe 3.25*

*One foot adged 4 25*

*Five bells 2*

*Two old bundles (may be sp) and curry comb-50 2 50*

*Five hackles 2.50*

*Old ploughs and Clevesas 4 6 50*

*Horse Geers and an old barrel 1*

*A parcel of Cooper ware 2*

*A parcel of Iron tools 5 7*

*One pair Steel yards 2*

*A parcel of Pewter Knives and Forks 7 33*

*One fire shovel and pot rack 1*

*One lock chain double hoe and fixings 3*

*One rifle gun 12*

*Two flax wheels 5 17*

*A razor a strap and Spectacles 1 50*

*A bottle jug and Bowls 1 25*

*A parcel of books a pair of sizzors and 3 tin cups 3*

*A big wheel and reel 1.50*

*A grind stone and tomahawk 1.25 2 75* ⇔ [Nevil NEVER lived near the Cherokee –
but he DID live near the Catawba. Also when it says "tomahawk" – it IS referring to a
tomahawk – not an axe or a hatchet.].

*Wearing apparel 12*

*a bedsled bed and furniture 20 32*

*Five bed sleds 1*

*bed and furniture 20*

*One False Cutter A chisel and four chairs 1*

*An old big coat and live bee gums 2 25*

*11 Geese 5.50 15*

*ducks 1.25 6 75*

_____ *$ 295*————

*DEED BOOK 4 1806-1843*

*RUSSELL CO. VA PAGE 486*

*This Indenture made the fifth day of May int the year of our Lord 1812, between Saml
Ewing attorney for Hugh McClung of the one part, and Keziah Weland of the other part both
of the county of Russell and State of Virginia Witnesseth That the said Saml. Ewing atty for
Hugh McClung for and in consideration for the sum of fifteen dollars lawful money of the
United States to him in hand paid the receipt whereof is hereby acknowledged hath granted
bargained and sold, and by these presents doth grant bargain and sell unto the aforesaid
Keziah Weland and her heirs forever, a certain tract or parcel of land lying and being in the*

*county of Russell on the waters of Cooper Creek including a Spring called the Pound Spring and bounded as followed to wit: Beginning on a white oak about ten poles east of the pound spring thence s45degree W. 46 poles to a White oak Nathan Mullets corner, thence s 20 degree W 14 poles to a black gum thence s 5 degree E 16 poles to a large white oak. N. 6 0 degree W 20 poles to a chestnut N. 70 degree W.10 poles to a small poplar N 40 W 20poles to two poplars near the age of a sink hole thence N. 40 degree E 36 poles to a white oak thence with a straight line to the Beginning containing fifteen acres be the same less or more. But it is to be name that there is fifteen acres excluded out of this deed for which I have already made a deed for to John Gibson dated the 7th day of November 1809.* [Vance's note: of the original 50 acres Nevil Sr. bought, 15 acres are turned over to John Gibson]. *With all the appretenances to have and to hold the aforesaid trac or parcel of land with all its apprentenances unto the said _____ Weland and her heirs, to the sole use and behoof of her the said Keziah Weland and her heirs forever. And the said Saml. Ewing atty. for Hugh Mcclung and their heirs doth covenant with the said Keziah Weland and her heirs that the said tract or parcel of land with all and singular it appuntenaces unto the said Keziah Weland and her heirs against the claim or claims of all person whatsoever shall and will forever de fend. In witness whereof the said Sam. Ewing atty. for Hugh McClung have hereunto subscribed his name and affixed his seal the day and year first above written*

    *Saml. Ewing (seal)*

    *atty. for Hugh Mcclung*

    So next door to our family was a James Gibson and a John Gibson owned a 15 acre parcel in the midst of the 50 acres purchased by Keziah Wayland, widow of Nevil Sr.

    We suspect Kezziah, Nevil's wife, was Kezziah Gibson.

*SCOTT CO. VA GATE CITY VA*

*DEED BOOK 2 PAGE 384*

*July 26, 1817*

    *Received from Francis Wayland $5.62 cents in full for the redemption of a taxed land containing thirty five and a fourth acres lying in the county of Scott on the waters of Clinch river, _____delinquent in the name of John Gibson for this non payment of the _____taxes in the year 1812 twenty nine acres of which was sold to George George of Scott County for the amount of the taxes ____ _____ remaining unpaid as appears from the statement of the there of in the year 1816 recorded in the Clerks Office of our said county court Taxes and Damages $ 0 037 Fee for publishing sheriffs exec 0 25 Executing and recording deed and ____ 2 93 Interest thereon nc 50% per acesson 3 214 93 Taxes for by* *commissioner 76 taxes charged the purchancer ¾ 4 98 ¾Clerks for and commissioner 5.62 ¾*

*wit:*

*Charles (x) More,*

*Joseph (x) Nicols,*

*William (x) More.*

Francis Wayland paid taxes on 35 acres. All the other Wayland's had gone to Arkansas. He paid it in the name of John Gibson. John must have been related in some way for him to be willing to do that. Of the other 15 acres, George George was sold 9 acres for the taxes on them.

I was told the following in an email. The person emailing me was a Melungeon Gibson researcher, and first suggested my Kezziah might be the same Keziah/Cusiah mentioned below—

*If your Kezziah is a Gibson she is likely the daughter of Thomas and Mary Gibson of Henry County, Virginia. The Champ Gibson [below] moved to Rockingham Co., NC and some of his descendants are*

*found in Hawkins Co., Tenn.*

*HENRY COUNTY, VIRGINIA*

*Will Book ? pp30-31*

*Dated 3 January 1780*

*Probated 23 March 1780*

*To my loving wife Marey Gibson and my daughter Cuzziah Gibson my whole estate.*

*Thomas (x) Gibson*

*Zackeriah King, Joel Gibson and Lambert Dotson executors. 23 March 1780. Exhibited by Joel Gibson who gave bond with Lambeth Dodson and Champain Gibson as his securities.*

*I think...but can not prove... that the Humphrey (see below) name came from Moses Humphrey who married to Frances Gibson, daughter of Thomas Gibson d. 1734 in Hanover Co., Va. Francis Gibson Humphrey was the sister of Valentine Gibson:*

*SURRY CO. NC TAX LISTS 1771 (alpha)*

*Jacob Gibson*

*William Gibson*

*Humphrey Gibson 1 [also 1772]*

*Valentine Gibson 3*

*James Shepherd 1*

*This should read, "Lewis Humphrey married to Francis Gibson". Moses Humphrey is the one that had land on Newman's Ridge Hawkins Co., TN, Deed Book 11, p. 273. James Johnson to Vardeman*

*Collins, Registered 27 May 1825. 25 February 1825. Each of Hawkins Co., TN. $400. 75 acres situated on Blackwater Creek, part of a 300-acre tract entered by said Johnson & Moses Humphreys, beg. at a white oak and hickory on Vardeman Collins' line.* end of email.

So other researchers brought this possible Melungeon Gibson connection to my attention. Notice above Frances Gibson, wife of Lewis (or Moses?) Humphrey. Also notice Frances was sister to Valentine Gibson. Notice both were son/daughter of Thomas Gibson. Also we see Humphrey Gibson living next to Valentine. This is in the 1770s. This is a known Melungeon family, known to have been descended from a band of the Catawba.

## Gibson's and Wayland's in Arkansas – Various Documents
### 1830 census, Lawrence County, Arkansas
#4, 1

James Gibson 10001, 10001 <=> 1 male, 1 female 0-5, 1 male 1 female 20-30.

Next door to James Gibson is William Wayland.

William Wayland, 020001, 30100100001 <=> 2 males 5-10, 1 male 30-40 years old. 3 females 0-5, 1 female 10-15, 1 female 30-40, 1 female 80-90 years old. The elder female would have been born about 1740-1750 – and Nevil Sr. was born in 1745. Is the elder female Keziah? William would have been born between 1790-1800.

#4, 4

Nevil Wayland Sr. 0011101, 0011001 <=> 1 son and one daughter 10-15, 1 son and one daughter 15-20, 1 son 20-30, 1 male and one female 40-50. Nevil (Jr.) would have been born between 1780 and 1790.

12 names later

Henry Wayland 01001001, 0011001 <=> 1 male 5-10, 1 female 10-15, 1 female 15-20, 1 male 20-30, 1 female 40-50, 1 male 50-60 meaning he was born between 1770 and 1780.

#4, 6

Francis Wayland 2010001, 1112001 <=> 2 males and 1 female 0-5, 1 female 5-10, 1 male and 1 female 10-15, 2 females 15-20 years old, 1 male and one female 40-50. Francis and is wife are several years, most likely, older than William.

66

#4, 9

Nevil Wayland Jr., 200001, 0001 <=> 2 males under 5, 1 female 15-20, one male 20-30. Was he a son of Nevil or Henry?

Nine names down –

Samuel D. Gibson, 0001001, 00101001 <=> 1 female 10-15, 1 male 15-20, 1 female 20-30, 1 male 40-50, 1 female 50-60.

<u>1840 census, Lawrence County, Arkansas</u>

#4, 11

Henry Wayland 201001, 00011

8 names later

Robert Gibson 00001, 20001

2 names later

William Gibson, 00001, 10001

4 names later

Humphrey Gibson 020001, 001001 (Notice this name — Humphrey Gibson, but in Arkansas living near our Waylands in 1840. Recall a couple of generations earlier, in the 1770s, we have Humphrey Gibson who was related to "Cusiah Gibson", who also was a daughter of Thomas Gibson.

#4, 16

William Wayland 10010001, 10300010001

4 names later

Sarah Wayland 0001, 00001001

2 names later

James Wayland 00001, 00001

## 1840 Census, Prairie, Washington County, Arkansas

Francis Wayland 10100001, 0110001 <=> Washington County, Arkansas borders Northeastern Oklahoma. Francis was the last of the four Wayland brothers to move west, the others being Nevil Jr., Henry and William. It is one of his descendants that took the same DNA test that I took, that showed he too, was multi-racial.

## D. The Catawba

We have established that there is a good chance that we have Catawba blood, through the people known as "Melungeons". Let us learn more about them.

The Melungeons [21]

Lewis M. Jarvis was born in 1829 and was raised in Southwestern Virginia near Northeastern Tennessee, and was raised near the known Melungeon settlers. He was interviewed, and that interview was published in the Hancock County Times, dated 17 April 1903.Below are excerpts from that interview.

*Much has been said and written about the inhabitants of Newman's Ridge and Blackwater in Hancock County, Tenn. They have been derisively dubbed with the name "Melungeons". By the local White People who have lived here with them. It is not a traditional name nor a tribe of Indians.*

*These people, not any of them were here at the time the first White hunting party came from Virginia and North Carolina in 1761 . . . [names several men] these men above named, who are called Melungeons, obtained . . . titles of the land they settled on . . . and* **they came here simultaneous with the white people not earlier than 1795. They lost their language and spoke English very well. They were originally the friendly Indians who came here with the Whites as they moved west . . . The White emigrants with the friendly Indians erected a fort on the bank of the river, and called in Fort Blackmore. . . they have married among the Whites until their race has almost become extinct. . . The old pure-blood[s] were finer featured.**

Today's researchers know the Melungeons were Eastern Siouan – the Saponi, the Saura/Cheraw, and Catawba seeming to be the main bands, but there were many others. From H. Lewis Scaife [22 ] we hear of Catawba who fought beside Americans in the Revolutionary War:

*During the Revolution, the Catawba's rendered valuable assistance to the Colonists. A company, consisting of 100 warriors of the tribe, under the command of Colonel Thompson, took part in the defense of Fort Moultrie; and besides being in a number of other battles, they were particularly useful throughout the war as guides, scouts, and runners. When Colonel Williamson marched against the hostile Cherokees, whom British emissaries had incited to commence a series of brutal massacres upon the frontiers of Carolina, a large number of Catawba warriors joined him, and in this campaign several of them were killed. Toward the close of the war, the entire tribe, except the members who were in active service in the American Army, were compelled by the British to seek refuge in Virginia, where they remained until after the battle of Guilford Court House, in which some of the tribe took part.*

If you look at the surname "Williamson" – they are found in York County, South Carolina. That is where the Catawba Reservation is located. I have emailed some

Williamson's who have family stories of being "Indian". I do not know if they are related to Col. Williamson or not. Col. Williamson was clearly White, but maybe he had a relative that married a Catawba.

Also this shows the Catawba fought side by side with the South Carolina Militias. Is this how, when and where Nevil found his wife, Keziah?

## Sizemore's

There were many people on the rejected Cherokee rolls who probably had Indian blood – it just wasn't Cherokee. For instance, there were about 200 Sizemore's on the rejected rolls. Some said that their parents never said to which tribe they belonged. In one instance we have the following:

Sizemore

No. 8584

*William H. Blevins, being first duly sworn, deposes and says:*

*I am 67 years of age. I live in Washington County, Va., I reckon. I have lived in Va. about 15 years. I was born in Ashe County, N. C. and lived there until 15 years ago, with the exception of the time of the war, when I served in the War on the side of the Confederacy. I claim through my father, Armstrong Blevins who lived and died in Ashe County. I think he was born there. He was 66 when he died. He was the son of Lydia Blevins. I do not know whether Lydia Blevins lived and died in Alleghany or Ashe County, N. C. I think it was Alleghany then. I suppose she died before I was born. Lydia Sizemore (Blevins) was a daughter of Ned Sizemore, Sr.*

*According to proof made before me in 1888 and 1896 as a Justice of the Peace of Ashe County, N. C., he was a full-blood Cherokee Indian. As a boy my father used to tell me that he was an Indian. The object of the the proof referred to was for land and money suppose to be due the Cherokees and Sizemores in the Indian Territory. The proof taken in 1888 was sent to one J. W. Mullens, of Grand View, Ark. He was an attorney employed by us to press these claims in the Indian Territory. I never saw the proof after that. I had it transferred to A. E. Ivey of Tahlequah, I. T., another attorney. I heard that Mr. Ivey died, leaving it in his office, but I do not know this to be so. The proof was to be present[ed] to the Cherokee council for our rights in the Indian Territory, but I do not know whether it was ever acted on or not. The proof taken in 1896 was from a number of old men, and was about the same kind of testimony taken in 1888. John Baldwin, J. W. Perkins, took it to put before the Cherokee counsil, but I do not know whether it was ever acted on or not. I do not know* whether it was put before the counsil and the Dawes Commission or not, but I have heard it was. If Mr. Baldwin swore that it was put before the Dawes Commission, I believe that he did.

I never heard, officially from the Dawes Commission that the claims were allowed or rejected. I never received anything from it. I never heard that my father ever received any money from the Government on account of his Indian blood. I never received any money from the Government on account of my Indian blood. I never heard whether Lydia Blevins ever received any money from the Government on account of her Indian blood. Most of my information in regard to my Indian blood came principally from my father until this proof was taken. My father spoke of it often and spoke of his uncles, Owen, George, and Ned, and his aunts Catharine Hart, Sallie Osborne, and his Aunt Sookey Stamper, and one he called Dollie, she may have been the same as Catharine. I saw his Uncle George Sizemore when I was probably ten years old, and heard him preach. This was in Ashe County, N. C. He was a son of Old Ned Sizemore. He went to what was then called the State of Virginia, before I heard him preach, and then came back. I do not know where he died, but have been informed that he died in West Virginia. I remember him well. He was tall, straight, wore his hair cut off around his shoulders, and had some gray streaks in it. He passed as a White man and Indian, and claimed to be part Indian. He was the first man I ever heard make a prayer.

They always told me that he and his brothers and sisters were related to the Cherokee Indians. I do not know if he was an ordained preacher or not. I have never heard that Owen Sizemore was a preacher, although I have heard that Hiram was a preacher.

I have never seen any but George. I never heard that Old Ned Sizemore was a preacher. I heard my father say that Old Ned Sizemore lived in what is now Alleghany County, N. C., but was then Ashe Co. at the time I was born. I think he was dead before I was ten years old, but I do not know where he died.

I have heard of Dr. Johnny Sizemore from others, but not my father. I have heard that old man Ned Sizemore's father was John Sizemore, and he lived in Stokes Co., N. C. and had a son, Dr. Johnny Gourd Sizemore, who was a brother of old Ned. That he also had a daughter by the name of Patricia. John Sizemore should have had eight children and can only name two besides Old Ned. I do not know who Patricia married.

Ned Sizemore Jr. was a son of Old Ned. I do not recollect ever hearing tell of George Sizemore ever having a son Ned. **I remember one Elisha Blevins, who said that Old Ned Sizemore came from the Catawba River, or the Catawba Reservation, as he called it.**

***Elisha Blevins has been dead some time. Wesley Blevins also testified in 1896 to the same affect.***

Stephen Hart made affidavit before me also, while I was Justice of the Peace, but I do not remember that he said where he came from. If there was any reservation there at all, I do not know anything about it, only from the testimony. I saw the affidavit of William A. Lewis of Fort Gibson, I. T., but he did not swear to where Ned Sizemore came from that I recollect. He said that he was well acquainted with the family and that he knew Catharine and Lydia and Owen, and that Ned Sizemore was a full-blood Indian, and he supposed lived and died in Ashe County. William A. Lewis went from Ashe County to the Indian Territory, as I understand it, in 1851, and died I suppose in the Indian Territory. He claimed to be part Indian

I never heard that any of the Sizemore's ever received any money from the Government on account of their Indian blood. If they did, I think I should have known it — that since I was old enough to recollect. I was not enrolled on the census of Eastern Cherokee Indians in 1885, and never heard of it before. I was not enrolled in 1851 by the Government. I did not receive any of the money paid in 1851, and none of the Sizemore family did that I know of. I have heard my father and his brothers talk something about the enrollment of 1851. They were afraid of enrollment; were afraid they would be carried to the Territory and scattered on that account. I do not think my father was enrolled in 1835, or any of the Sizemores that I know anything of. They were afraid of enrollment. I do not know anything about the removal of the Cherokees, only what I have read and heard my father say, but I think it was about 1835. He was afraid that if he was enrolled as late as 1851, he would be forced to go to the Territory. I know that there are a number of Eastern Cherokee Indians in Western North Carolina now who were enrolled in 1835 and 1851, and received money, but were not forced to go west.

The word, "Chief" in my application, means that I am chief of the White Top Band of Cherokee Indians, an organization of the principal Cherokee Indians living about White Top, and was perfected about ten years ago. We organized so as to demand our rights in a body. We thought we had not been getting them before.

In 1896, we wanted to go to Indian Territory, and organized for that purpose. When the band was first organized, there were about 2175, I believe. They were all Sizemore descendants. No one else was allowed to become a member if it was known. I have read the decree of the Supreme Court of the United States referred to in my application, and have it at

71

*home. My father, Armstrong Blevins, I do not think was a party to the treaty of 1835 and 1846(or 48?). I am putting my own interpretation on the decree.*

*Elisha Blevins, who gave testimony in 1888 and 1896 before me, was not a party to the treaty of 1835 and 1836 and did not claim to be Indian at all. I suppose Wells Blevins was living in 1835 and 1836. He lived in Ashe County, N. C. I do not know that he was a party to the Treaty of 1835-36. I do not know that any of the descendants of the Sizemores, or Old Ned himself ever live with the Cherokee Indians. I have had an affidavit before me from Mr. Wagoner that Ned Sizemore visited the Cherokee Indians. The Cherokee Indians never visited them often since I can recollect. I have seen some Cherokee Indians who claimed to be. I saw one regiment in time of War. I have seen very few living here who claimed to be Cherokee Indians except the Sizemores and the descendants of the Sizemores.*

*I have heard of Ned Hart, who lived in Ashe County, N. C. I did not understand that he was a Cherokee Indian, but he married a Cherokee Indian, and, as I understand it, the Cherokee blood of the Harts came through Catharine Sizemore.*

*The White Top Band of Cherokee Indians, of which I am Chief, has applied to share in this fund so far as I know.*

*W. H. Blevins*
*Subscribed and sworn to before me at Marion, Va., this 11th day of April, 1908.*
*J. Edward Taylor*
*Assistant to Special Commissioner Court of Claims*


After making claims of having Cherokee blood, all of a sudden in the middle of his statement, Mr. Blevins speak of someone telling him that Ned Sizemore said he came from the Catawba River, or the Catawba Reservation, as he called it. Well, that got my attention. Some on the rejected list were not rejected because they were not Indian, but because they were not Cherokee.

## Treaties [23] [24]

It is interesting that he mentions 1846 then says (or 1848?) treaty. There was a 1846 Cherokee treaty for the Cherokee in Oklahoma and some still in Arkansas. That treaty asks the Arkansas Cherokee to return to Oklahoma. But in 1848 some of the Catawba tried to come to Indian Territory per the government supplying money for that purpose at that time. Brown writes in "The Catawba Indians", p. 323 *"On July 29, 1848 the Congress* *apprppriated $5,000 to defray the expense of the move [to Indian territory]."* Chief James Kegg wrote a letter to President James Polk at that time and said there were 42 Catawba families who wanted to use that appropriation to move west. He said (p 324) *"We humbly beg his Excellency the President . . .to remove us west of the Miss[issippi] under the act of the late congress."* . Still on page 324, Brown writes, *"Whether the President ever saw the letter is problematical."* In the next paragraph Brown writes that the Cheorkee were asked if the Catawba could live amongst them and it says: *"The answer from John Ross and the Cherokee counsel was a firm NO. But before the reply was received, the Catawba themselves expressed a preference for living among the Western Chickasaws . . . [who] at one time had invited the Catawba to settle amongst them. Government representatives promptly opened up negotiations with the Chickasaws among whom – the agent was told, some of the Catawba's descendants were already settled."* It continues to say: *"The principal men of the tribe assured the agent that the Catawba would be welcome, but only the council had the right to invite them, officially. But when a Chickasaw Counsel meeting was held in February of 1849, the Catawba proposal was voted down. This change of sentiment was attributed to the sudden death of old Chief Albertson* [Vance's note: should read "Governor Albertson" – their "principal chief" is called a "Governor]", *a strong advocate of the Catawba's."* So we have a substantial number of Catawba Indians with no land base and no home. I suspect many on the rejected rolls are in reality, Catawba mixed-bloods. Were mine Catawba rather than Cherokee? Maybe both?

But before all of this was the 1840 treaty between the Catawba and the State of South Carolina. In "Catawba Nation, Treasures in History," by Thomas J. Blumer, (pp 52-53) he writes: *"The Treaty of Nations Ford is a simple document. Article One conveyed the 144,000 acre reservation to the state of South Carolina. This article was of course, carried out with the full acquiescence of the Catawba. Article Two provided the Catawba with a new tract of land far removed from White settlements. Article Two, caught in a political vacuum between North and South Carolina, was never fulfilled. Article Three regarded payment for the 144,000 acre reservation. South Carolina never made proper payment and the debt remains unsettled."*

He also talks of many Catawba who left the reservation, some to settle with the Eastern Cherokee, some just left for points unknown. No one knows how many Catawba left, or how many of these people were. People had been leaving the Catawba Reservation, assimilating, for many years, for generations in fact.

**1890s Attempt to form a "Western Catawba Association"**

Several years back, I exchanged several emails with Dr. Thomas Blumer , who was a foremost expert on the Catawba. It is my understanding that he has since passed on. I emailed him family photos and stories. He became interested in the fact that my family was Indian but not federally recognized and that we had at one time lived near Fort Smith, Arkansas. The fact that we were "Brown's" also got his attention, as Brown is one of the few known Catawba surnames. He told me of an effort to form a "Western Catawba Association" in Fort Smith, Arkansas in the 1890s. However by the 1890s we had left and were living in the Chickasaw Nation, Still, he peaked my curiosity. I wondered, was my family part-Catawba, then? I looked for more information.

Chapman Milling said in "Red Carolinians":

*By the Indian appropriation act of 1848, $5,000 was set aside to completely remove the Catawba to the Indian country west of the Mississippi. In November of 1848 the heads of forty-two families sent a petition to the Indian Office requesting to be allowed to be removed to the Chickasaw Nation. Nothing materialized because of this request, however. Eventually a few families went to live in the Choctaw Nation and in 1855 several Catawba were adopted into the Choctaw Nation.*

Muriel Hazel Wright wrote "A Guide to the Indian Tribes of Oklahoma" in 1951. In that book, she chronicled a history of all the sixty-nine tribes that either came to Oklahoma, or are indigenous to the state.

She was Choctaw herself (her father was a former Principle Chief). She said of the Catawba — *another group left the nation during the removal period. In 1897 they formed the Western Catawba Association at Fort Smith, Arkansas.* She speaks of some who received Choctaw citizenship in 1853. Ms. Wright said of the Catawba who migrated to Arkansas and Oklahoma –

*The descendants of some of the Catawba who settled in the Choctaw Nation are now absorbed into the Indian population of Haskell and Le Flore Counties. The descendants of some of those who settled in the Creek and Cherokee Nations have been reported living southeast of Checotah in McIntosh County. The main portion of the tribe live in the Eastern part of York County, South Carolina.*

*There are few Catawba in Oklahoma, and those are counted in the general Indian population of the state. They were last enumerated as a separate tribe in this region in 1896, and their total population in the Indian Territory being given as 132. The largest portion, or 78 lived in the Choctaw Nation, most of them in the region between the present cities of*

*Stigler and Spiro. Seventeen of them gave Checotah* [Vance's note: remember the Catawba Gentry family of Checotah who were adapted into the Creek Nation? We mentioned them earlier], *Creek Nation, as their post office, and 15 lived around Texanna,* [Vance's note: Texanna is also where Captain Dutch settled, as did some of Sequoyah's family] *in the Southwestern part of the Cherokee Nation, now included in McIntosh County. In the same year (1896) there were 145 Catawba living in Arkansas, most of them in and around Greenwood and Barber.*

She adds –

*In October 1848, William Morrison, chief of a band of Catawba (42 persons) living at Quallahtown,, Haywood County, North Carolina, addressed a letter to the Commissioner of Indian Affairs asking for the appointment of a superintendent to remove his people to the Indian territory . . . These people expressed their preference for settlement among the Chickasaw, but the Chickasaw council took no action on the subject.* [Vance's note: This was the head of 42 families, not individual Catawba — and we have their signatures in Brown's book. Also the Chickasaw as we have seen, did take action, and rejected the Catawba proposal in February 1848.]

In "Red Carolinians" Chapman J. Milling wrote the following –

*"The Catawba Indian Association of Fort Smith, Arkansas," an organization having a membership of 257 persons, the alleged descendants of Catawba who went West under the act of 1848. The petitioners were distributed as follows in Arkansas and Indian Territory: Arkansas—Greenwood, 44, Barber, 42, Crow, 13, Oak Bower, 6, Fort Smith, 17; Indian Territory and Oklahoma - Checotah, 17, Jackson, 15, Star, 34, Panther, 22, Oak Lodge, 10, Redland, 4, Ramville, 2, Indianola, 3, Center, 4, Ward, 3, Sacred Heart, 1, Steigler, 2.*

*It will be seen that most of those in the Indian Territory were living in the Creek and Choctaw nations. The petition sets forth that these Catawba families had removed west, some as late as 1854, "journeying at their own expense to the country west of the Mississippi River, hoping and expecting to be there furnished with new homes..." Having never been assigned lands, they were "left stranded in that Territory and the neighboring states." They therefore prayed for relief. The government took the position that the petitioners were white men with a trace of Indian blood, and therefore not entitled to relief. The memorial indicates, however, that descendants of Catawba Indians existed in considerable numbers in the Southwest only 44 years ago.* ***Although no Indians are today recorded as Catawba in the*** *state of Oklahoma, there is little reasonable doubt that an appreciable amount of Catawba blood persists in the eastern section of that commonwealth.*

Milling also says in Red Carolinians *"Having traced several distinct migrations to North Carolina, Virginia, Arkansas, Oklahoma, Utah, Colorado, we have thus seen that the Catawba Tribe is not so nearly extinct as was supposed and has been frequently asserted. It is true however that the only band having any semblance of tribal status is the remnant in South Carolina . . ."* I cannot help but think that had Congress acted, there might be a Catawba Tribe of Oklahoma, too. However, since these families have all scattered today, that is no longer possible. I suspect that, like the Sizemore's, many of these families have forgotten their tribal origins, and think their ancestors were Cherokee.

I could not help but recall what my great Uncle had written about our family living in Sequoyah or Leflore County. That is where many of these Catawba had been. Also they sought permission to live in the Chickasaw Nation. My family also lived there.

**Newspaper Articles on the Western Catawba [25]**

These three short articles about the Catawba in Arkansas were written between 1889-1895, and are found in the local newspaper, "The Fort Smith Elevator". Some people were trying to organize a group of Catawba in the late 19th century. Also found, late in the day, a few lines in an article in "The Indian Chieftain" of Vinita, Oklahoma, dated 1888, when Vinita was a part of the Cherokee Nation. Remember Oklahoma only became a state in 1907.

*August 16, 1889, The Fort Smith Elevator, Catawba Indian Association*

*The Catawba Indian Association met at Rocky Ridge on the 10th. The meeting was called to order by the President. After the reading of the minutes and the calling of the roll of the officers, transacting other business that came before the order, a call for new members was made and 90 was added to the new list, after which the meeting adjourned to meet at Ault's' Mill, three miles south of Fort Smith, the second day of the fair, the 16th day of October, where the delegates and all persons interested will please attend without further notice, as matters of interest will be considered.*

*J. Bain, President*

*G. W. Williamson, Secretary*

I obtained this material by writing to the University of Arkansas at Fort Smith library. One of their librarians wrote the following:

*Hello Mr. Hawkins,*

*Attached is a copy of the article you requested. The article mentioned another meeting held on October 16th and I found it in the October 25th edition but the film was so dark I could not get a good print to scan. The text of the article follows. Please let me know if I can be of further assistance.*

*"October 25, 1889 p. 3 col. 5, From Fort Smith Historical Society publication*


### *"Attention Catawba's*

*The Western Catawba's Indian Association met at Ault's Mill October 16, 1889, at which meeting a number of new members were added to the Association, thus making it nearly 4,000 strong. They appointed an executive committee which is empowered to transact all business and place the matter before congress. The Association adjourned to convene again at a called meeting of the president."*

*Taken originally from "The Fort Smith Elevator" (newspaper), date probably early Jan 1895.*

*All Catawba Indians by blood or otherwise are requested to meet at the County Court House in Fort Smith Arkansas on Thursday, Jan 24th, 1895 at 10 o'clock a. m. for the purpose of perfecting the census roll of the Western Catawba Indian Association and the transaction of other matters that may come before the meeting. All Catawba Indians are expected to be present or by proxy as business of importance will come before the meeting.*

*James Bain, Preset.,*

*Geo. E. Williams, Scary,*

*Western Catawba Indian Association*

Please keep the timeframe in mind. The Dawes Act (also called the Allotment Act) had just been passed in Congress meaning the Indians in Oklahoma at least would no longer own all their lands in common – each Indian family was to receive – I think it was 160 acres – I might be wrong about the number of acres. Well many more people were asking for this land than there actually were Indians living on the lands in Oklahoma. So the Indians and whites both grew suspicious some of the applicants.

We hear of all those on the rejected rolls. But we never hear of those who claimed Catawba ancestry — all we hear of are of the Cherokee rejected rolls. Apparently 4,000 people wanted to claim Catawba ancestry. The final list seems to have had only 257 names, so something happened to the rest, and we have no list of the names of those 257 persons, nor of the 4,000. I will continue to look for these lists.

Also, these 4,000 are not on any accepted or rejected roll, either, as no roll was made for the Catawba. I am hoping to discover the names of those 257 as well as those 4,000.

General opinion at the time was they were individuals who had a little Indian blood and had been living as whites. The idea of giving free land to people who had not gone through the hardships of removal, people who had left them to live as Whites, was a bitter and difficult pill to swallow, for the traditional Indians who had never left the various tribes, and who still had many full bloods. Also it was suspected that many people applying were simply full blood Whites looking to take Indian lands as had happened so many times in the past. This attitude doomed the petitioners such as these claiming a Catawba heritage, to failure. But what became of them? They seem to have vanished in the dust. Was my family a part of this movement in the late 19$^{th}$ century?

I found one more reference; from "The Indian Chieftain", a newspaper from Vinita, Cherokee Nation, and Indian Territory dated 1888, located in what is today northeastern Oklahoma.

**Indian Chieftain, March 1, 1888, Vinita, Indian Territory (Oklahoma), image 2 of 4 [26]**

*The Western Catawba Indian Association, with headquarters in Fort Smith, proposes to petition congress to set aside for the use of all persons of Indian blood, not members of any tribe, a portion of the Indian Territory.*

I cannot help but remember hearing that dad's grandparents were at one time thinking about signing up for the Dawes Allotments, but "something happened" and they never did. I remember my mother mentioning this, and she had no Indian blood, but her family lived next to my great-grandparents on my Dad's side – the Richey's, as well. I wish I knew the right questions to ask back when I was younger, but at the time, I had little interest in these things. Part of my quest in doing research was to find out exactly what happened. Why did they back out, and never even apply for Dawes? This would have been the 1890s. They did live near Fort Smith at one time and we do seem to have some ancestors that "could have been" Catawba. They also lived in the Chickasaw Nation and the Catawba had asked the Chickasaw to accept them, an offer the Chickasaw refused. Did we belong to this organization, the Western Catawba Indian Association — at one time 4,000 strong? That would explain a lot. The Melungeons too, were Eastern Siouan — if not Catawba then they descended from their closest, both genetically and linguistically – allies, the Cheraw or Saponi, both of whom were known to have moved in with the Catawba during recorded history. They were the same people.

I also keep thinking of Catawba Chief Haigler's letter to Gov. Glen of SC when he asked him to give wampum to the Pedee Indians and asked the governor to ask the Pedee to live with them (the Catawba) to make them stronger. And in the 1890s some Catawba in Arkansas and Oklahoma descendants were still doing that — trying to get other Indians to join them in a new land in the west, to maintain a resemblance of a nation, even at that late date. They did not want to go into extinction as a nation, quietly. They did not want their heritage forgotten, utterly. (See Appendices 1 and 2). Up to the present day, no organization has thought to revive these "Western Catawba". They have been forgotten, utterly.

# CHAPTER 4 THE GIST'S

## A. Guess/Gist, Finally!

It literally took us years to find Harriet Guess/Gist's parents. I literally looked to every Gist/Guess/Guest and other variations of spelling – and was able to prove they were NOT my Harriet's line. This took years and I must have spent well over 100 hours proving these were the wrong ancestors. I spent oh, so much time getting nowhere. We knew we came from Lawrence County, Alabama. For years we thought we descended from Thomas Gist and Nancy Roney. We eventually proved that was not the case. I had thought we had checked every Gist in the area and we descended from none of them. Then there was a website — http://www.luftex.com/lawrence_co_al_notes.htm . The author of this website was looking for a Rachel McNutt who married Edmond Nichols. This person says:

*I need help finding the parents of Rachel McNUTT, who married Edmund NICHOLS about 1826 in Lawrence Co, Al. These are my ggg-grandparents. To begin, I will try to clear up some confusion over two different Rachel McNUTT's in the mix. My Rachel was a McNUTT by birth, [1809].* ***The other was Rachel HAVINS, b. 1797 to James HAVINS & wife Sarah MILLER. Rachel HAVENS married 1st to a GUEST [spelling may be incorrect]. Little is known about the 1st marriage or how it ended. Next she married Thomas TOLBERT on 12-07-1820. [TOLBERT had 1st mar. Cynthia HAVINS, Rachel's older sister. That marriage apparently ended with the early death of Cynthia.] Thomas TOLBERT died in 1821, leaving Rachel a widow. She married for the 3rd time to Emanuel McNUTT on Dec 31, 1822.*** *I'm only speculating, but I believe my Rachel McNutt NICHOLS was either a sister or a close cousin to Emanuel McNUTT. Please contact me if you have any information, remarks, or questions.*

*James HAVINS was born about 1770 in Virginia. He was Primitive Baptist between 1770 and 1822. He was listed on the tax rolls in 1800 in Jefferson CO, TN. He appeared on the census in 1820 in Lawrence CO, AL. He died in Jan 1822 in Lawrence CO, AL. He was buried in Jan 1822 in Pinhook, Lawrence CO, AL. He was married to Sarah MILLER (daughter of Thomas MILLER and Sarah GAMBOL) on May 4, 1790 in Greene CO, TN. Sarah MILLER was born between 1770 and 1772 in Pittsburgh, PA. She died after 1850 in Newton CO, MO. She was buried after 1850 in Newton CO, MO. James HAVINS and Sarah MILLER had the following children:*

*Mary Henderson HAVINS.*

*Thomas HAVINS*

*Cynthia HAVINS b. abt 1795, Jefferson CO, TN. Mar. Thomas TOLBERT after 1815.*

*Rachel HAVINS b. about 1797.*

*Charlotte HAVINS*

*John HAVINS b. abt 1803 in Jefferson CO, TN.*

*Louvina HAVINS*

*Ann HAVINS*

**Lawrence County, Alabama Marriages, 1818-1822**

*Thomas TALBOT (Tolbert), m. Rachel GUISS (Guest) on DEC 07, 1820*

*Emanuel McNUTT m. Rachel TALBOT (Tolbert) on DEC 31, 1822*

*Henry McNUTT m. Anna McNAMEE on 22 SEP 1818*

*John McNUTT m. Silphy McNAMEE no date*

*William McNUTT m. Betsy IRWIN on 25 NOV 1818*

*Richard GEST m. Jane McKINNEY on 13 SEP 1821*

*Thomas GEST m. Nancy RANEY on 06 NOV 1818*

*James HAVINS m. Sarah MILLER 04 May 1790 Greene Co., TN USA*

The 1830 census Lawrence Co., Al has Emanuel McNutt 00201, 110201 ⇔ Emanuel is between 20-30 and Rachel his wife is between 30-40. There are 2 girls between 15-20 years old, and 2 boys between 10-15. **The point is these children are too old to have been the children of Emanuel, they were Rachel's by a previous marriage. They are Gist's, not McNutt's.** On the 1840 census of Shelby County, Tn we have Emanuel McNutt, 010001, 0020101. Emanuel is between 30-40, and his wife Rachel 40-50. Of the four Gist children, only one is at home, a female 20-30. Since in 1830 she was between 15-20, she would be between 25-30. The other female between 25-30 is not at home and the 2 males between 20-25 are also not at home. They either died or had moved away from home, perhaps to start their own families.

Harriet's mother and step father had moved to Shelby County, Tennessee by 1840 – THAT'S WHY my great-great-grandparents married in Shelby County, Tennessee in 1841! After 20 years of wondering – finally . . .

**How Do We Know That Rachel Was a Daughter of James Havens? [25]**

Rachel Havens' first husband was a Gist. He died or disappeared by 1820. They had 4 children per 1830 census. Marriage record says the following –

81

*State of Alabama, Lawrence County*

*Know to all men by these present, that we* **Thomas Talbot and James Havins** *are held and firmly bound unto the Governor of said state for the time being, and his successors in office, in the penal sum of 200 dollars, for the due payment whereof we bind ourselves, our heirs, executors and administrators, jointly, severally, and firmly by these presents, sealed with our seals this seventh day of December 1820.*

*The condition of the above obligations is such that whereas the above bound* **Thomas Talbot has this day prayed a license from the clerk of the County Court of said county, to be married to Rachel Guess of said county.** *Now if there is no lawful cause to obstruct this marriage, then the above obligation to be void, otherwise to remain in full force and virtue.*

## Thomas Tolbert, James Havins

Thomas Tolbert/Talbot died within a year. When he died, the following document was created:

*To authorize the Administrator and Administratrix of Thomas Tolbert, to sell and convey certain real estate.*

*Section 1. Be it enacted by the Senate and House of Representatives of the State of Alabama, in General Assembly convened,* **That James Havens and Rachel Tolbert, administrator and administratrix of the estate of Thomas Tolbert,** *deceased, be, and they are hereby authorized to sell the certificate of the south east quarter of section number twenty three, in township number seven, of range number seven, west, in the district of land sold at Huntsville, belonging to the estate of said Thomas Tolbert, deceased, on such terms as they may deem most advantageous; taking bond with sufficient security, for the true and faithful payment of the consideration.*

*Sec. 2. And be it further enacted, That the said administrator and administratrix, are hereby authorized and empowered on the sale of said land, to make, or cause to be made to the purchaser or purchasers (as the case may be,) of the same, a conveyance of such title as the said deceased had or was entitled to, which conveyance shall be equally valid and binding, as if the same had been made by the said decedent in his lifetime.*

*Sec. 3. And be it further enacted, That said administrator and administratrix shall, before the sale of said land, hereinbefore authorized to be sold, enter into bond with sufficient security, payable to the Judge of the County Court, in which said land is situated, for the disposition of the money arising from the sale of said land, agreeably to the existing laws, regulating the distribution of the personal effects of deceased persons.*

*Sec. 4. And be it further enacted, that the administrator and administratrix of Thomas Tolbert, aforesaid, shall give at least thirty days notice, by publishing the time and place of sale of the above described land, in the Florence Gazette or Alabama Republican, and at the Court House door in the town of Moulton and three other public places in said county. (Approved, Nov. 27, 1821.)*

The above documents tell us Rachel was daughter of James Havins.

## McNutt's, Joiner's, and Gist's and Brown's in Shelby County, Tennessee

David Brown and Harriet Guess/Gist's marriage license says —

*Be it known by these presents, that we, David B. Brown and J. E. Randolph, of the county of Shelby in the state of Tennessee, are held and firmly bound unto the governor of said state, for the time being, in the sum of twelve hundred and fifty dollars, to be paid to his excellency, his successors in office, or assigns, to which payment, well and truly to be made, we bind ourselves, our heirs, executors and administrators, and each and every of us and them jointly and severally, firmly by these presents, Witness our hands and seals, this 25th day of August, 1841.*

*The condition of the above obligation is such that whereas David B. Brown hath this day prayed and obtained license to marry Harriet Guess. Now if the said Harriet Guess be an actual resident of the county aforesaid, and there shall not hereafter appear any lawful cause why the said David B. Brown and Harriet Guess should not be joined together in Holy Matrimony as husband and wife, then this obligation be void and of no effect; otherwise to remain in full force and virtue. David (his "x" mark) B. Brown; J. E. Randolph.*

Now we know why David Brown and Harriet Guess/Gist were married in Shelby County, Tennessee. Harriet's mother and step-father had moved there. They are my great-great-grandparents.

So who was Thomas McNutt in the 1850 and 1860 census records living with/near David and Harriet (Guess/Gist) Brown? He was Harriet's half-brother!

Marriage records in Shelby County, Tn have two marriages for Thomas Joiner. The first says: *Sept. 6, 1837 Tho. S. E. Joiner Mary Fuller executed Sept. 15th, 1837*

And the last:

*Oct. 11, 1842 Thomas S. E. Joiner Cynthia McNutt*

Thomas Joiner married Cynthia McNutt in Shelby County, Tennessee. There were no other McNutt's on the 1840 census of Shelby County, other that Emanuel. This explains who Nancy I. Joiner was on their census record (recorded as Nancy I Brown). She was their daughter, meaning she was Harriet's niece. This explains two of the three orphans who David and Harriet raised. More on the Joiner's later.

### The Family of James Gist

James Gist married Elizabeth Frazier 14 Oct 1848 in Shelby County, TN. There is no record of the marriage in Shelby County. In Elizabeth's application for a Union Civil War widow's pension in 1869, she stated they were married 14 Oct 1848 in Shelby County, TN, and there was no public record of the marriage that she could find. In those same pension papers (I purchased a copy). It said he had dark complexion and was born in Lawrence County, Alabama.

James Gist and Elizabeth Frazier moved west after they married, and can found in Dade County, MO for the 1850 and 1860 censuses.

Following James S. Gist

The first place James Gist can be found in a record is the 1850 census. James apparently moved west shortly after he married in 1848, and can be found in Dade County, MO for the 1850 census.

### *1850 Dade County, MO census, Dist. 25, page 303, household 595*

| James S. GIST | 27 AL |
| wife Elizabeth | 20 TN |
| dau Margret | 03 AR |
| dau Francis | 01 MO |

This is James "S." (or "T." ?) Gist and wife Elizabeth Frazier, who married in Shelby County, TN in 1848. The oldest daughter Margret was born in AR indicating that James may have gone to AR first, before continuing on to MO. Or, perhaps Margret was born in AR while the family was moving west. This family was also in Dade County, MO for the 1860 census. David and Harriet [Gist] Brown are first found in Lawrence County, Arkansas in 1848. Maybe Harriet's brother married and went to Arkansas with them, later moving on to Missouri.

### *1860 Dade County, MO census, Lewis Creek, page 007, household #40*

| James E. GUEST | 41 AL Com Laborer |
| wife Elizabeth | 25 AL Seamstress |
| dau Margret | 12 AR |
| son William A. | 08 MO |
| son Edward D. | 06 MO |
| dau Elizabeth | 04 MO |
| dau Mary | 02 MO |

This is James "S." (or "T." ?) Gist and wife Elizabeth Frazier, who married in Shelby County, TN in 1848. James Gist joined the Union Army in 1862 and was discharged as an invalid in 1863. James Gist died in 1865 of complications from a condition he contracted while serving in the Union Army. The vast majority of the information for James Gist comes from his Civil War Pension File, which contains detailed information about James Gist, his wife and children.

**The Civil War Pension file of James S. Gist**

James Gist died in 1865 of complications of Coxalgia - a condition he contracted while serving in the Union Army, the Missouri 29th, in 1862. Elizabeth Gist applied for, and was granted, a Widow's Pension in 1869. The Civil War Pension file for James S. Gist contains 26 pages, primarily affidavits and certificates to verify the following: The service of James Gist; that he was healthy before entering the service; that his illness was service related; his marriage; his death; the names and dates of birth of each of his five children. Quoting from James pension application:

*James S. Gist, born about 1819 in Lawrence County, AL. Married Elizabeth Frazier 14 Oct 1848 in Memphis, Shelby County, TN. No record of the marriage in Shelby County.*

*Five children:*

1. *William H. Gist*   *b. 25 Oct 1851*
2. *Elizabeth B. Gist*   *b. 10 Apr 1856*
3. *Mary H. Gist*   *b. 26 Apr 1858*
4. *James Gist*   *b. 14 Sep 1862*
5. *Sidney Luellen*   *b. 02 Oct 1865*

His pension application also says: ***Entered the service 15 Aug 1862 from Sims Creek, MO, (Co. D. MO 29th Inf. Regt.), age 43, 5'11" tall, dark complexion, dark eyes and dark hair.*** *Discharged July 1863 as an invalid. Reason for discharge: "Coxalgia - producing permanent lameness. Caused by exposure in the field - Has been in hospital six months. He is unfit for military duty or invalid corps."* James Gist died from Coxalgia two years later, 10 Sep 1865. The widow Elizabeth Gist applied for a pension in 1869.

Note: Coxalgia is the medical term for an injured or painful hip joint. Also note he was born in Lawrence County, Alabama. He married in Shelby County, Tennessee. Note it says he was of dark complexion, with dark eyes and hair.

After James' death in 1865, Elizabeth and her children can be found in Camden County, MO for the 1870 and 1880 censuses. Elizabeth died 19 Jan 1911. I have been unable to find Elizabeth in either the 1900 or 1910 census.

***1870 Camden County, MO census, Osage Twp, page 512, household #13***

| | | | |
|---|---|---|---|
| *Elizabeth GIST* | | *36 AL* | |
| *son* | *William A.* | *18 MO* | |
| *dau* | *Elizabeth B.* | *12 MO* | |
| *dau* | *Mary H.* | *09 MO* | |
| *son* | *James* | *07 MO* | |
| *dau* | *Lydia L.* | *04 MO* | *(Sidney Louellen)* |

Elizabeth Gist, the widow of James S. Gist, who died in 1865.

**1880 Camden County, MO census, Osage Twp, page 149D**

Elizabeth GIST          46 AL    (widow)

son   James            17 MO

dau   Louella          11 MO    (Sidney Louellen)

Elizabeth Gist is the widow of James S. Gist, who died in 1865.

The link with Lawrence County, Alabama and Shelby County, Tennessee makes me think he is Harriet's brother. He was born according to the 1850 census about 1823, and Rachel had married Emanuel McNutt by then. However in the 1860 census he states he is 41 years of age, meaning he was born about 1819, which is in the short period of time Rachel would have been married to a Gist (abt 1812-1820). Since there are NO Gist/Guess/Guest's on the 1840 or 1850 census for Shelby County, Tennessee — I think we have enough evidence to infer that this James Gist was Harriet's brother. Interesting, for he served in the Union Army, in the 29th Missouri. Harriet's husband, my great-great-grandpa, David Brown, was in the 8th Arkansas, Confederate. This means Harriet's brother died September 10, 1865, and her husband died May 1, 1865, one for the Union, the other in the service of the Confederacy. One in Missouri, the other in Arkansas. It must have been a hard time for the family. They probably attended each other's weddings.

Recent evidence has come up that one of the four children of Rachel's that I thought was a Gist may have been a Talbot. That might mean we only have one missing Gist sibling, but we still have missing McNutt half brothers and sisters to Harriet..

## B. James Havens and David Smith [25]

I sent off for old papers about David Smith who had moved to Missouri, and these papers were at a small university there. They Xeroxed me copies and I am trying to transcribe them. I will later explain about the Smith's, Gist's, Havens, and others on the "Guess/Gist side of the family. David Smith married Charlotte Havens, sister to my Rachel Havens. Rachel was Harriet's mother). Charlotte and Rachel's father had died leaving Sarah [Miller] Havens a widow. While both were living in Lawrence County, Alabama, the following was part of the package I was sent.

*Two quarter sections of land subject to the dower of Sarah Havens, widow of said deceased, upon the following /audit? [can't make it out] to wit one half at a ? [audit maybe?]*

*of 3 months, and the other half at a ?audit?* **Until the 25th December 1826 they having entered into bond in the sum of fourteen hundred dollars with William McNutt and John Brown as their security.** *A copy. Test John Gallagher. clk.*

The above was recorded shortly after the death of James Havens, Harriet's maternal grandfather. He died in 1822.

We have shown that Sarah's daughter Rachel, married Emanuel McNutt in 1822. Was William his father? And Rachel's daughter by an earlier marriage, Harriet, married David Brown in 1841. David was the son of John Brown. Long before finding this connection between these Brown's and Haven's and Smith's and McNutt's — THIS was the "John Brown" that I have always believed was the father of our David. With these family connections now known, I am certain of it.

**Words on a plaque in Bankhead National Forest in Southern Lawrence County, Alabama**

*This area was the home to Indians, settlers, people of mixed ancestry and their descendants. Local bluff shelters contain evidence of occupation from Paleo Indian (10,000 BC) through the Mississippian Period (1540 AD). Chief Tuscaloosa (Black Warrior), mentioned by Desoto (1540), was a noted Creek Indian leader. A 1733 map identified the southern drainage from these mountains as the Tuscaloosa River.* **The first known written occurrence of "Warrior Mountains" was made by rifle maker John Bull (1777-1840), who engraved one of his rifles "David Smith, Warrior Mountains - 1829" According to family tradition. James Havens (Smith's father-in-law) said, "bury me by my Indian friends on the side of the Warrior Mountain where the magnolia blooms in the spring" (possibly Indian Tomb Hollow).** *James E. Saunders' 1899 book refers to the southern highlands of Lawrence County as the Warrior Mountains. On 15 Jun 1936, Pres. Roosevelt changed the name to the Black Warrior Forest, and on 17 Jun 1942, Congress changed the name to William B. Bankhead National Forest. The Black Warrior Wildlife Management Area, Sipsey Wilderness (1975) and Sipsey Wild and Scenic Rivers are found here.*

David Smith (mentioned above) married Charlotte Havens, sister to our Rachel. Both Charlotte and Rachel were daughters of James Havens, mentioned above. The following was found about them, written by David's son, who was also James grandson. And it mentions MY line of Gist's, as well.

**PAST AND PRESENT OF GREENE COUNTY, MISSOURI; Early and Recent History and Genealogical Records of Many of the Representative Citizens [27]**

BY JONATHAN FAIRBANKS AND CLYDE EDWIN TUCK; VOLUME II, ILLUSTRATED, 1915 , A. W. BOWEN & COMPANY INDIANAPOLIS, GREENE COUNTY, MISSOURI., p 1280-1283

## JOHN RANDOLPH SMITH. M. D.

*Doctor Smith was never named by his parents, being known only by a "nickname" until he was eight years of age when he selected his own name. He comes from an excellent old American family. Robert Smith, his grandfather, was born in England, and he served in the Revolutionary war becoming captain of a company in the Fourth North Carolina regiment. He was a gallant officer and took part in many engagements, including the battle of King's .Mountain. After the war he was a merchant and ship builder of note, owning several vessels which operated between North Carolina ports and the West Indies. Nathaniel Geist, the doctor's great-grandfather, first married Mary Howard, of Baltimore, Maryland, and later Dinah Volker, of Holland. His daughter, Mary Geist, by his first wife, married Robert Smith, our subject's grandfather. Nathaniel Geist served with George Washington in the war with England against France, and he was captured in 1773 at Braddock's famous defeat by the Cherokee Indians, who held him four years. During his captivity he married an Indian maiden and they reared a family. One of their sons* [Vance's note: notice it says one of their sons? Did they have several?], ***George Geist, was a man of exceptional prowess and ability and the Indians called him Chief Sequoyah, and he was for some time chief of the Cherokee tribe. He has been held in great reverence by the succeeding generation of Cherokees in view of the fact that he originated the Cherokee alphabet.***

***David Smith, father of our subject, was born in North Carolina. He lived in Tennessee, Alabama and Kentucky before coming to Missouri in 1836.*** *He was a great cattleman, raising large numbers in the above mentioned states, and in the early days before there were any railroads in the South, he practiced driving immense herds of cattle to Baltimore, Maryland, where he marketed them. Many claim that he originated the familiar term "cowboy." He was left an orphan in infancy, his father and mother both dying at that period of his life.* ***All his life he was a dealer in livestock and was one of the most widely known cattle and horse dealers in his day and generation in the localities where he resided. He was one of the first to import blooded horses, and he raised thoroughbreds for a number of years.*** [Vance's note: Notice David's mother was a Gist also. Remember these relationships later when the discuss Aaron Gist who was hung as a horse thief in 1801. David Smith was a horse dealer whose first cousin was Aaron Gist, earlier hung as a horse thief —

makes me wonder . . . there but for the grace of God . . . Notice the author too, has confused stories of one Nathaniel Gist for another. Remember there were three contemporary Nathaniel Gist's. Two were father and son, the father marrying the Howard girl, the son the Volker. The third was with Washington at Braddock's defeat. The Cherokee were their allies in this battle, not their foes, so parts of the above narrative are in error.]

*He lived to a ripe old age, spending his last years on his large stock farm in Newton County, this state. His family consisted of the following children: Benjamin F. died in infancy: Sarah A. married Thomas Walker; Mary, who is now eighty-two years of age and has never married, is living at the old homestead. "Kent Park," Newton county, Missouri: Dr. John R. of this sketch; Charlotte E. married James W. Roseberry, now deceased; their son Charles II. Roseberry owns and conducts a large deer farm at "Kent Park," Newton County, and is a member of the Society for the Preservation of Wild Animals of the United States Government. Thomas H. Benton Smith died in 186- while in the service of the Confederacy, having been with General Rains' brigade at Ft. Smith, Arkansas, at the time of his death.* [Vance's note: another relative at Fort Smith, Ark.]

***Dr. John R. Smith owns a gun which was made to order for his father in 1829, by John Bull, a gunsmith of Warrior Mountain, Alabama. It is a fine specimen of guncraft of those days, is mounted with silver and has a gold powder pan and bushings. The stock is of curly maple and the barrel of a very soft iron. It is a remarkably accurate shouting piece and it was designed as a "target" gun for the pioneers.*** *The mounting has several inscriptions on the silver plating. The doctor values this heirloom very highly.*

I have left out much of the story about David's son, the one about whom this article was written.

As with many similar accounts, there is some truth and some that is not. For Instance, the Nathaniel Gist who married "Dinah" is NOT the same Nathaniel Gist who was with George Washington at Braddock's Defeat in the French and Indian War of the 1750s and early 60s. They were first cousin's. The Nathaniel Gist who married Mary Howard was the father of the Nathaniel Gist whom he says married Dinah Volker. The Nathaniel Gist who married "Dinah" was killed at Kings Mountain. This article also claims Robert Smith, David's father, also served at Kings Mountain.

From "Warrior Mountains Indian Heritage" by Ricky "Butch" Walker, p 276, we have a confirmation of the previous article mentioning a rifle in the possession of David Smith. Mr. Walker says —

*"John Bull, In 1829, a frontiersman and famous rifle maker by the name of John Bull engraved 2 of his masterpieces from the Warrior Mountains. According to information provided by Mr. Dan Wallace, the exceptional rifle is inscribed on a silver platelet in the stock, "John Bull for David Smith, Warrior Mountain . . .*

*"According to Old land records of Lawrence County, Alabama by Margaret Cowart, David Smith entered 79.92 acres of land . . . near Indian Tomb Hollow on September 18, 1818 and 79.92 acres on September 28, 1818 . . . He married Charlotte Ann Havens, who was the daughter of James Havens. According to Havens family legend . . . James Havens was buried next to his Indian friends on the side of Warrior Mountains. . ."*

One last thing about David Smith. There was an 1828 land transaction in Lawrence County, Alabama whereby David Smith was assignee of Ruth Gist, with Ruth being assignee of Saml. G. Acklin. David Smith purchased 79.92 acres of land, nearly half a quarter section of land, with a section being a square mile, or 640 acres. I do not know who Ruth Gist as this is the only place I have ever seen her name. But it does confirm there was a Gist in Lawrence County, Alabama who knew David Smith. Remember the document above that said his mother was Mary Gist, daughter of Nathaniel Gist by what it calls his first wife, but that first wife was actually the wife of Nathaniel's father, also named Nathaniel. But some of what it says is just wrong. What parts can we trust?

From my research, I know I descend from the same James Havens, and that David Smith's mother was Mary [Gist] Smith, a sister or Aunt to my John Gist found in "Land of the Lake" (more about him later) of whom it said he also was some relation to Sequoyah. The article above said "one of the sons" of this Nathaniel was Sequoyah. Was John another, and was Mary a daughter? The above James Havens is the same man, who once he died, that John Brown and William McNutt were used as security in 1826 (more about this later, as well) to help his widow get by.

David Smith's relatives say his mother was descended from Nathaniel Gist. Which Nathaniel? Let us consider the evidence. Where can we find this Nathaniel Gist? This is another of our breakthroughs, finally! It's about time! I researched LITERALLY every Gist/Guess/Guest family in Alabama/Arkansas/Georgia/Tennessee/Virginia/North and South Carolina/Maryland/Oklahoma and Texas, ruling them out, one by one, a process that took many years, and was more frustrating than you can imagine. The article about the Smith's said Robert Smith, David's father, served in the 4th North Carolina during the Revolutionary War. That article said David Smith's father was Robert Smith, lived in North Carolina. It also said Nathaniel Gist was the father of Sequoyah. However the Nathaniel that was killed at

Kings Mountain was NOT the Nathaniel Gist whose father and grandfather knew George Washington. The Nathaniel Gist who knew Robert Smith, David's father, was the Nathaniel who moved to Southwestern Virginia before being killed at Kings Mountain, during the Revolutionary War, in 1780.

Now that we have a particular Nathaniel Gist to research, let us see what we can find about him.

**The Dorsey's**

These Gist's are recorded [28] by the Dorsey's. Every Gist genealogy researcher starts with the Dorsey's book. They say the following about this family on pages 60-61:

*Nathaniel Gist 4 (Nathaniel 3, Richard 2, Christopher 1). B. c, 1736, Baltimore County, Maryland; d, probably Oct 7, 1780 at the Battle of Kings Mountain, North Carolina. M. Dinah _____. Thought to be a daughter of Aaron Van Hook, who died intestate in Orange County, NC in 1760. His sons, Aaron and Lawrence Vanhook, lived in Washington County, Virginia in the 1780s with the Gist's and Fulkerson's. James Fulkerson married Mary Vanhook, sister of Dinah Vanhook. Benjamin Sharp, son-in-law of James and Mary Fulkerson, said that Nathaniel Gist, was uncle by marriage to his wife, Nathaniel Gist was a young boy when his family moved from Maryland to Virginia. He lived with his father beyond the Dan River in Rowan County, North Carolina, until it was necessary for the frontier families to move to a place of safety. Nathaniel and several of his brothers moved to Cumberland County, North Carolina (see maps pages 10 and 58).*

*The records show that he served on the jury in Cumberland County in January 1759, and again in October of this year, and also in 1761. On August 16m1763, when the court ordered that a road be laid out from John Martinlier's Ford on Cape Fear River to Archibald McNeill's on the Lower Little River in Cumberland County, Nathaniel Gist, Christopher Gist, and Joshua Gist all served on the jury to lay out the road. This same year Nathaniel Gist asked that his mark and brand be granted and recorded (Cumberland Co., NC Ct of Common Pleas, book A, p 21; Bk B, pp. 27, 35, State Dept. of Archives and History, Raleigh.*

***In 1769 Nathaniel Gist bought 100 acres of land from Robert Smith in Cumberland County.*** *[Vance's note: There it is! Robert Smith, father of David Smith, knew THIS PARTICULAR Nathaniel!] On April 18th 1770 he was granted 155 acres situated between Two Little Rivers, adjoining his own and John Smith's and George Robert's lines (Cumberland County, NC Deeds 3m p 442, NC land grant bk 20, p 647, Department of State,*

*Raleigh). On February 13m 1778, Nathaniel Gist and Dinah, his wife, sold their grants of 155 acres and their tract of 100 acres between Two Little Rivers to Isaac Williams (Cumberland County, NC Deeds 4, pp 461, 462).*

*From here Nathaniel Gist and his family and others went to the new lands that were being made available in Washington County, Virginia. Soon after they arrived the Revolutionary War started, and he and his brothers Richard Gist and Thomas Gist enlisted in Col. William Campbell's Regiment of Washington County, Virginia. It is thought that Nathaniel was killed. The name of Nathaniel Gist appears on the monument of those killed during the encounter with the British forces at the Battle of Kings Mountain (L. P. Summers, History of Southwestern Virginia, pp. 859, 164) (record of the monument on the battlefield).*

*Children of Nathaniel and Dinah Gist (thought to have been their children)*

*i.] Nathaniel Gist 5. On October 14th, 1791, Nathaniel Gist by warrant entered 800 acres of land lying on the waters of Holstein River and on the top of White Mountain to have the naked place or old field in the center and running according to law by quantity . . . (Washington Co., Va. Record Entry and Surveys, No. 1, p 99). No records have been found of the sale of this land.*

*ii.] John Gist 5, may have gone to Tennessee.*

*iii.] Aaron Gist 5, may have gone to Tennessee.*

*iv.] George Gist 5, On March 28th, 1796, George Gist bought 50 acres in the Raccoon Valley on a branch of the North Fork of Holston River, from James Walsh. On August 9th, 1797, when living in Russell County, Virginia, he sold this land to William Gilson* [Vance's note: Gibson?] *(Washington County, Va Deeds 2, pp21, 88).*

*Probably others.* [Vance's note: according to the Smith's, they also had a daughter named Mary.]

## Cumberland County, North Carolina

According to the Dorsey Book on the Maryland Gist families our Nathaniel was in Cumberland County, North Carolina. Is there a Robert Smith there? Well let's see what we can find out [29].

First, how do we negotiate the Smith account of Dinah being a "Volker" while the Dorsey's said she was a Vanhook? Well, the Dorsey's said:

*"Nathaniel Gist 4 (Nathaniel 3, Richard 2, Christopher 1). B. c, 1736, Baltimore County, Maryland; d, probably Oct 7, 1780 at the Battle of Kings Mountain, North Carolina. M. Dinah _____. Thought to be a daughter of Aaron Van Hook, who died intestate in Orange*

*County, NC in 1760. His sons, Aaron and Lawrence Vanhook, lived in Washington County, Virginia in the 1780s with the Gist's and Fulkerson's. James Fulkerson married Mary Vanhook, sister of Dinah Vanhook. Benjamin Sharp, son-in-law of James and Mary Fulkerson, said that Nathaniel Gist, was uncle by marriage to his wife . . ."*

BUT, his wife was a Fulkerson on one side and a Vanhook on the other. So Nathaniel's wife might have been a Fulkerson or a Vanhook, either one, according to Sharp's statement. Both these families were Dutch from New York, whose families had been in New York since the days it was known as New Amsterdam. Also I had a conversation by email with a Fulkerson descendant/researcher and they weren't surprised at all, that we found the name Volker. I found out that the original family name WAS Volker and they knew it! Somewhere down the line "son" was added and it was also Anglicized to become Fulkerson. They said this was a very common practice for that culture in those times.

http://www.rootsweb.ancestry.com/~jecain/smit033.html

**Cumberland NC Deed Book 3-442 28 Nov 1767 ROBERT SMITH of Cumberland to Nathaniel Gist of Cumberland,** *50 pds, parcel of land lying in Cumberland Co. between the two Little Rivers. s/ ROBERT SMITH. w/ HUGH SMITH, Adam Killan, John Williamson.*

Shows Robert Smith, father of David Smith, sold land to Nathaniel Gist. Remember David's son said David's mother was Mary Gist, a daughter of Nathaniel. The one that bought land from Robert Smith was Nathaniel Gist (Jr.) b 1736, the one that was killed at Kings Mountain in 1780. His father was also named Nathaniel Gist (Sr.) b 1707.

*Cumberland NC Deed Book 4-155 28 Sep 1769 ROBERT SMITH of Cumberland to Adam Killen to Cumberland for 10 pds, 100a in Cumberland Co. between the two Little Rivers and known by the name of "Rattlesnake Hill". said tract of land was granted to DAVID SMITH by patent dated 03 Oct 1755. The said ROBERT SMITH is lawfully and rightfully the owner of said 100a being entitled to the same by the Last Will and Testament of DAVID SMITH, decd. s/ ROBERT SMITH w/ Thomas Killen, Gerard Craig.*

Apparently Robert Smith's father was also named David Smith, the same name as his son.

**Cumberland NC Deed Book 6-428 19 Jan 1778 ROBERT SMITH, Power of Attorney, to wife MARY SMITH.** *s/ ROBERT SMITH. w/ William Sproul.*

Confirms the Smith (from Missouri) report that Robert's wife was named Mary. The Smith's of Missouri say Mary was a Gist, a daughter of Nathaniel. Even the Dorsey's never found this record, but when they listed his children, after listing four, they said "probably more".

*Cumberland NC Deed Book 18-277 22 Mar 1799 ROBERT SMITH for "love and affection to son DAVID SMITH" s/ ROBERT SMITH. w/ ?????? MacNeele, ?????? MacNeele.*

This confirms that Robert Smith had a son named David, confirming the Smith family story about the origins of their family in America.

So — there WAS a Robert Smith with a wife named Mary and a son named David – this fits exactly what the Smiths of Missouri later say. Nathaniel Gist knew these Smiths well, as he bought land from them. His daughter could very well have married one of them.

## Washington County, Virginia

The Dorsey's say these Gist's went to Washington County, Virginia in the early 1770s. What can we discover about this?

http://www.rootsweb.ancestry.com/~varussel/indian/28.html

*We the Commissioners, etc...do certify that John Dickerson, heir-at-law to Humphrey Dickerson, who was assignee of Joseph Blackmore, who was assignee of Nathaniel Gist is entitled to 310 acres of land lying in Washington county on the north side of Clynch River in Cassell's Woods, to include his improvement. Surveyed the 28th day of May, 1774.* [Vance's note: when discussing the Melungeons, recall Jarvis words, where he said the whites "with the friendly Indians" built Fort Blackmore. OUR Nathaniel Gist – not the famous Nathaniel Gist, but his first cousin — KNEW Joseph Blackmore. Again, interesting.]

http://www.rootsweb.ancestry.com/~varussel/indian/79.html

At the above link we have *"The above writer is referring to the children of Joseph Blackmore, for Captain John Blackmore, builder of Blackmore's Fort, had in the year 1779, left for the area for settlement on the Cumberland in Tennessee. Joseph Blackmore was a brother of Captain John, and owned the adjoining farm to the old Fort tract to the south and down Clinch River."* Joseph and John Blackmore were brothers, and John Built Fort Blackmore, famous in the history of the Melungeons as having been built by the "friendly Indians" who seem to have been relatives of the Catawba, NOT the Cherokee. Those Catawba keep popping up, even here with respect to Nathaniel Gist. It makes me wonder when the Cherokee themselves say his paternal grandpa was White implying his father was half Indian. What if his father was half Catawba, not Cherokee? Well that changes things a bit . . . We will probably never know.

http://www.rootsweb.ancestry.com/~varussel/landgrants/washcosurvbk.html
*Page 149 - Richard Moor...390ac...Commissioners Certificate...on the waters of Beaver Creek, north branch of Holston River...Beginning on the north side of the big ridge...corner to Cornelius Carmacks land he now lives on...corner to Carmack & Nathaniel Gist...June 6, 1782 - Richard Moore...390 ac on a branch of Beaver Creek, surveyed on January 12, 1775, includes improvements, actual settlement made in 1774...August 17, 1781*
*Page 151 - Nathaniel Gist...200 ac...Preemption Warrant #1972...on the waters of Beaver Creek, north branch of Holstein River...Beginning corner to Cornelius Carmacks land he now lives on...corner to Richard Moors land he now lives on...June 5, 1782*

http://www.rootsweb.ancestry.com/~varussel/census/1802tx.html
*1802 Russell County Virginia Personal Property Tax List*
Note: All households have one tithable unless otherwise noted.

*Gess, Nathaniel*
http://www.rootsweb.ancestry.com/~varussel/court/ruscolobk2.html
*P374 - Abrell Meed vs Jesse, Caleb & William Friley, NB, Jury: Richard Long, George McCoy, Austin Bush, Robert Willson, George Gess, Thomas Stapleton, John Deskins, Joseph Tate, Richard Davis, Richard Collier, Bartin Smoot & William Gibson, Jesse Friley found guilty, Caleb & William found not guilty*


http://www.rootsweb.ancestry.com/~varussel/landgrants/ruscosurvbk2.html
*Talks of Guest's River, Guest's Fork, and Guest Mountain*


http://www.rootsweb.ancestry.com/~varussel/families/burk.html
*Mentions a George Gest/Guest Sr. (1707) and Jr. (1747) in a will or wills*
*1801 Russell County Virginia Personal Property Tax List*
*Guest, Nathaniel – 1*


http://www.rootsweb.ancestry.com/~varussel/landgrants/ruscosurvbk.html
*361 - March 20, 1799 - Samuel Ewing - 150 ac - part Treasury Warrant 2083 dated December 23, 1796 - on the waters of Clinch River in Castles Woods - by a path corner to*

*David Calhoun and Richard Long - corner to William Robinson - by a path – on the bank of Clinch River corner to Robinson's corner to Stephen Gest's.*

There were still Gist's in the region after the death of Nathaniel in 1780. Brother Richard had also settled there and he too, was killed at Kings Mountain. Kings Mountain is found right next to the Catawba lands on the North/South Carolina border. Both Richard and Nathaniel had sons named Nathaniel. Also of note only amongst these Gist's do we see the given name "George".

## King's Mountain

We have heard that Nathaniel was killed at Kings Mountain. So I need to discuss this battle, just a little. Recall the Dorsey's quoted Summers, saying:

*From here Nathaniel Gist and his family and others went to the new lands that were being made available in Washington County, Virginia. Soon after they arrived the Revolutionary War started, and he and his brothers Richard Gist and Thomas Gist enlisted in Col. William Campbell's Regiment of Washington County, Virginia. It is thought that Nathaniel was killed. The name of Nathaniel Gist appears on the monument of those killed during the encounter with the British forces at the Battle of Kings Mountain (L. P. Summers, History of Southwestern Virginia, pp. 859, 164) (record of the monument on the battlefield).*

So what happened at this battle? I have read many articles about all the Nathaniel Gist's that there were. Especially confusing are the discussions about the Nathaniel who descended from Christopher, and his first cousin who descended from Nathaniel Sr. The son of Christopher knew George Washington, personally. The Nathaniel, son of Nathaniel, was killed at Kings Mountain, in 1780, and had moved to Southwestern Virginia shortly before the start of the Revolutionary War started, earlier in the 1770s. So many start talking about one of these Nathaniel's,, and up writing about the other one. Benjamin Sharp also lived near our Gist's in Old Washington County, in Southwestern Virginia.

However he was around the other Nathaniel when he switched sides, as he started the war as a Tory and switched to the side of the Revolutionaries in 1777. Sharp, like many writers, confuses the two Nathaniel Gist's who were first cousins of one another. From a Letter of Benjamin Sharp, in "American Pioneer", 237, dated Warren County, Missouri, March 3, 1843, we take the following, which gives some light upon the history of the Gist's:

*"In the year 1776, he (Col Nathaniel Gist) was the British Superintendent of the Southern Indians, and he was then in the Cherokee Nation. And when Col. Christian carried his expedition into the Indian country, he surrendered himself to him, and although the*

*inhabitants were so exasperated at him that almost everyone that mentioned his name would threaten his life, yet Christian conveyed him through the frontier settlements unmolested; and he went on to head-quarters of General Washington, where, I suppose, their former friendship was revived. He became a zealous Whig and obtained through the General's influence as was supposed, a colonel's commission in the Continental Army, and served with reputation during the war. He afterwards settled in Kentucky, where he died not many years ago.*

     *I well recollect of the friends of General Jackson boasting that a luxuriant young hickory had sprung out of his grave, in honor of old hickory face, the hero of New Orleans.*

     **One of his uncles, also a Col. Nathaniel Gist was uncle to my wife by marriage; and his younger brother Richard Gist, lived a close neighbor to my father in 1780, and went on the expedition to Kings Mountain, and fell there, within 25 or 30 steps of the British lines, of which I am yet a living witness."**

One thing I have learned is that in old age, we sometimes recall the past incorrectly, not intentionally trying to deceive, but as a result of life's experiences. The Dorsey's also

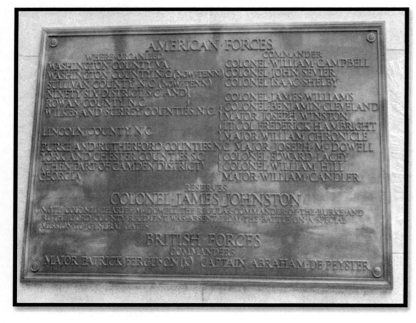

read this, saw Nathaniel (the one killed at Kings Mountain) and then assumed the wife of Nathaniel was a Fulkerson, aka Volker, or a Vanhook, as Benjamin's wife was a Vanhook on one side, and a Fulkerson on the other. The Nathaniel at King's Mountain was an Ensign by rank, not a Colonel. Sharp says that he saw Nathaniel's brother, Richard, killed at Kings Mountain with his own eyes. Well, since he knew the other Nathaniel had survived the war, did he confuse Richard with Nathaniel? Nathaniel's name was on the list of the dead, and his name is inscribed on a plaque at the battle site. We might never know the exact truth. The Nathaniel Gist at Kings Mountain was

NOT the Nathaniel Gist Sharp was speaking about, whom he called "the Colonel". They were first cousins and had the same name.

The bottom plaque at the battlesite, lists the dead at Kings Mountain. The third name from the top in the middle collumn is "Nathaniel Gist". You can just make it out. His commander was the first name on the upper plaque – Colonel William Campbell, of Washington County, Virginia.

## C. DNA Testing Results

DNA testing is a powerful tool and can be used to confirm or reject long held family stories and census records. Here are excerpts of a copy of an email I was sent about the Gist's my family are related to:

An analysis of the test results for those of Group 1 of the FTDNA Gist/Gest/Gues(s)(t)

 Y-DNA Project.
 Y-DNA test lab
 http:www.familytreedna.com

As of Mar 2011, the Gist/Gest/Gues(s)(t) Y-DNA Project has 60 members, 6 of whom are in Group 1. A complete list of all the Project Y-DNA test results can be found online at:

www.familytreedna.com/public/gistgestguessguest

**The oldest known ancestors of those represented in Group 1:**

*1. Major Thomas GIST, born estimated 1765 in Union District, SC. Lived in Knox County, TN in 1797. Helped establish the town of Smithland in Livingston County, KY in 1798. Sheriff of Livingston County, KY when he died in early 1807.*

*2. Christopher GIST, born about 1804 in TN, married to Mary McNutt [in Lawrence County, Alabama]*

*3. Aaron and Nancy GIST, born about 1807 and 1815 respectively in KY. Aaron Gist and Nancy were probably the parents of the following three men:*

*4. Thomas O. GIST, born about 1830 in KY. Married Sarah Gist, daughter of Christopher Gist, about 1858.*

*5. James Harvey GIST, born Feb 1836 in Wayne County, KY per Civil War records. [Vance's note: his son wrote one of those dust bowl era papers for IPP]*

*6. , born about 1837 in KY. Elijah, 23 and unmarried in 1860, with 45 year old Nancy GIST (his mother?) living in the household with him for the 1860 census.*

*7. Nathaniel Gist, born 1707, son of Richard Gist and Zipporah Murray of the Maryland Gist families.*

There are other Guest's in Lawrence County, Alabama – Moses, Martin and others associated with them – we apparently are not related to that bunch. Number 7 is Nathaniel Gist, b. 1707. This is the father of OUR Nathaniel. These families are VERY closely related to my family, per genealogical records. Notice number 2, Christopher's wife was a McNutt and he too can be found in Lawrence/Winston/Walker County area of Northern Alabama very close to some Brown's. I too have Brown's and a McNutt married my g-g-g-grandma, the same generation as Christopher. Some think Emanuel McNutt and Mary McNutt (Christopher's wife) were brother and sister. Notice also one of these people, through a paper trail, goes back to Nathaniel Gist b. 1707. This Nathaniel had a son named Nathaniel who was killed at Kings Mountain, the same person the descendants of David Smith wrote about. I have talked to descendants of many of these people, and have yet to find any who didn't also have a family story of having an Indian ancestor somewhere down the road. And many of these people had never heard of each other, their families having lost contact for generations.

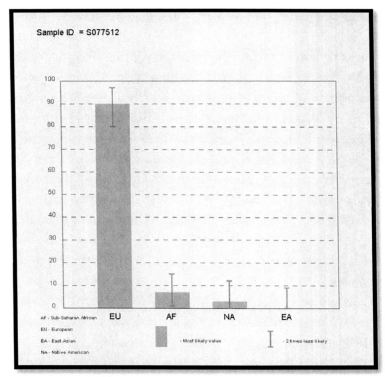

Here is a bar graph of an autosomal DNA test I took in 2005. It came back almost completely Caucasian (EU), but we did have a little American Indian (NA) and a little sub-Sahara African (AF) autosomal DNA as well. These tests are still being perfected. This test suggested about 1/32nd American Indian and about 1/16th sub-Sahara African, and the rest (29/32) Caucasian. There is a margin of error of about 1/16th either way, but you can't get zero or less percent of DNA that was present.

## D. Gist Station and Gist Station's Camp

http://www.rootsweb.ancestry.com/~varussel/other/forts.html

There was a place called "Gist's Station" in what is now Wise County, in southwestern Virginia. But in the past it was part of Washington County. The author of the article below didn't know any Gist's ever lived in the area – but ours did!

## GUEST STATION

*Of all the frontier stations along the Clinch this one presents the greatest enigma. The location is between Big and Little Tom's Creek, on Guest River at the present site of Coeburn, Wise Co., VA.*

*Outside of deed references which mention this station frequently no other direct reference has been found pertaining to it, and no militia correspondence or pensions applications make mention of it.* **Charles B. Coale, in "Wilburn Waters" tells of the Indians going to this station in 1777, after their capture of Jane Whittaker and Polly Alley, and finding it well defended make no attack upon it.** *Coale gives no authority for this statement and search for it has proven fruitless. Who built the station and for what purpose is unknown. There are several opinions, but opinions unless backed by factual data should never become a part of written history. This writer does categorically deny that it has any relation with Christopher Gist as has been written, since Gist did not travel through the present bounds of Wise County.*

*Elder Morgan T. Lipps, who settled on Tom's Creek in the spring of 1838, states in his diary: That the old settlers showed him some of the logs of the old fort and chimney rocks still lying upon the ground when he arrived there in 1838. Even if Christopher Gist did visit this spot in 1750, he could never, with the help of a small Negro boy, have built a structure whose remains would have lasted 88 years after his departure.*

**That some sort of fortification existed at Coeburn is unquestioned, since from the earliest times the place was called Guesses Station, and retained that name until the coming of the railroads when the name was changed.**

When I read this I said to myself – Christopher's nephew – MY Nathaniel WAS THERE! I think it was OUR family that founded this fort. Wise County was a part of old Washington County. I really need to look at the description of the location of the Gist's lands, and compare it to the location of Guest's Station. But our Gist's were the only Gist's to ever live there!

## Gist's Station's Camp

Don Sticher, Gist researcher but not directly related to my branch of the Gist's who claims Indian blood, found the following and forwarded it to me —

Early Times in Clinton County (Kentucky), Jack Ferguson, 1986, *Page 8*

*Sometime in early 1775 Benjamin Price and a small company retraced the Maniker party's path and established a camp in the "Great Meadows," an open grassland near the present Mill Springs. Because in a few years after the opening of the nineteenth century*

102

*there was considerable litigation involving land grants in that area, requiring the depositions of witnesses, quite a large amount of information involving land grants in this area has been preserved concerning Price's settlement(15). One of those who gave their testimony was an erst-while companion of Price - Nathaniel Buchanan (16). He testified that sometime in 1775, he, Price and some others launched a canoe into the Cumberland above the mouth of "Meadow Creek" - later known as "Lick Branch" - and crossed the river to the south side. Because Price was in charge of the company of hunters the place was ever afterwards known as Price's Landing. An old Indian trace led from the Landing to what later became known as the "Great Meadows" or "Price's Meadows," an open grassy glade or valley free of trees which extended in a northeasterly direction from where Price later established his camp. Initially the hunters camped in a large salt petre cave near the meadows. Buchanan testified that he marked out a new trace from the salt petre cave to Price's Landing, which was a more direct route, intersecting the old trace some distance above the river cliff. He asserted that his party used the new trace from February until the following July. Apparently they then erected a log house near the meadows - Buchanan testified that he assisted in building "this cabin" - apparently, as far as the records indicate, the first settler's dwelling erected in this part of the Cumberland valley. According to Buchanan, no one else was hunting in "these woods" at that time, but later Michael Stoner, a man name Green, and some others came to them at the "Great meadow."*

**Several miles upriver from Price's camp a hunter named Gist, possibly Nathaniel, had a hunting camp called Gist's Station Camp, in Pulaski County, on the southern side of the river nearly opposite the mouth of Pitman Creek. A trace led from Price's camp to Gist's Station Camp, which was generally used by Buchanan's companions - "It was our crossing place when we came to or returned from Price's Meadows."**

*John McClure testified that he and some others wanted to trap along the Cumberland in the fall of 1783. They were told that they could find Price's landing by the noise made by the fall of the creek near its mouth. They followed Buchanan's trace from the landing to the salt petre cave where they camped about seven or more months.*

*After a cabin was erected at Price's Station, the camp was enlarged and a blockhouse built, in 1777 - "the year of the bloody sevens"- when all of Kentucky was aflame with Indian hostilities, only Price's Station, Harrodsburg, and Fort Boonesboro survived.*

So there was a hunting camp called "Guest's Station's Camp" dating back to 1775 at least. This would be a hunting camp associated with Guest's Station, which was run by our Gist's! If our Gist's were hunters, they were traders as well I suspect. On the Cherokee Nation's own website it says Sequoyah's mother was a trader. If our Nathaniel Gist was a hunter and trader, and spent time in the Cherokee hunting grounds in North Tennessee and Southern Kentucky in the 1770s, he very well might have come across Cherokee hunting parties. Please refer to Appendix 5 for Buchannan's reference to "Gist's Station's Camp".

## E. John and Aaron Gist, Jason Cloud and John Brown

The Dorsey's said John and Aaron Gist might have gone to Tennessee. We found John and Aaron in "Land of the Lake" by Dr. Ridenour, in Tennessee, on pages 7 and 8.

By Dr. G. L. Ridenour, LaFollette, TN, 1941, excerpt taken from Pages 7 and 8.

### ELK, DEER, BUFFALO PERISH IN COLD

*The winter of 1779-1780 was very cold. So many elk, deer and buffalo gathered in the shelter around the meadows and cane-brakes along the creek between Pine mountain and Walnut mountain that the food for these large animals was soon exhausted, and scores of the them perished in severe continued cold. Hunters and Indians alike avoided the beautiful valley in the spring and early summer of 1780 on account of the stench from the dead game. The name Stinking Creek has persisted for the scenic stream until the present.*

*In the summer of 1785 several parties of surveyors were running the metes and bounds of North Carolina land grants of the south side of Clinch River. At the same time the surveyors could not resist crossing the stream to select the choice locations for land grants with reference to Henderson and Company's Great Survey. Thomas Hutchins, a brother-in-law and a Deputy Surveyor under Stockley Donelson during the fall and winter of 1785-86, surveyed tracts on both sides the river.*

*Brooks and a number of woodsmen in company that year surveyed land "Including a Large Buffalo lick." This party gave the name of Reed's Creek to one of the streams. George Brooks, a brother of Castleton Brooks, a Long Hunter who settled in Hickory Cove and had been killed by the Indians in 1776 or 1777 at his cabin, and Andrew Reed were skilled woodsmen and famous hunters and were often directing parties of woodsmen for the protection of the surveyors.*

**One 340 acre tract of land calls for a location on both sides Beaver dam Creek "including William Sharp's improvement at Reed's corner along a conditional line between William Sharp and John Brady on a cross fence down a small branch, thence along the fence twenty-nine poles striking the creek at a bent so up said creek to Miller's line where John Guest (Gist) now lives."**

**This John Gist was the son of an Indian trader and a Cherokee woman. He was kinsman of Sikwayi, or Sequoya, whose English name was George Gist, the inventor of the**

*Cherokee alphabet of syllables.  Years later Aaron Guest of Kentucky acknowledge the receipt of his part of "the estate of my father Aaron Guest, Deceased, where Jason Cloud and John Guest (Gist) were executors."*

Notice the time frame above was about 1785 when the land was first being surveyed. I can't but help but recall Aunt Lorena's letter – she told me that she was told by her mother (Lona [Richey] Hawkins 1883-1963, my grandma) that her, Aunt Lorena's great-grandma (Harriet) was either Sequoyah's niece or great niece. If the John Gist mentioned above WERE to have been Sequoyah's brother or half-brother – AND if John was Harriet's grandpa – then it would make Harriet out to be Sequoyah's great niece, and that is what grandma told Aunt Lorena, according to her letter.

The following is from "Land of the Lake" by Dr. G. L. Ridenhour, which was printed by Campbell County Historical Society. In the Preface his daughter, Crea Ridenhour says *"Much detailed research and time went into the writing, and the information included in the book was painstaking historically correct. . . . much that he knew died with him." Crea Ridenhour, Nov. 11, 1991.*

**The Trial and Hanging of Aaron Gist**

Both the Dorsey's and Ridenhour mention John and Aaron Gist. They appear to be father and son, although the Dorsey's portray them as brothers. John is hardly mentioned in any historical document, but Aaron, the unfortunate one, was hung as a horse thief. What? Well, yes that's true. This Aaron Gist was either a son of Nathaniel or a son of John, who was a son of Nathaniel, the man killed at Kings Mountain in 1780. DNA records and genealogical records say our ancestor descended from this Nathaniel as well. Dr. Ridenhour said Aaron's probable father (John) was part Indian and was related to Sequoyah, perhaps an unknown brother, and my aunt wrote me saying our great-great-grandma was a niece or great niece of Sequoyah. There is a record of Sequoyah apparently visited a descendant of the well-known Nathaniel Gist saying that he was looking for his White relatives. But what if he descended from "the other" Nathaniel Gist, the Nathaniel who died at the battle of Kings Mountain? Maybe the reason Nathaniel never visited his Cherokee family was because he was dead.

But back to the hanging of Aaron Gist. As for being one of the few men hung it seems, in that era, you'd think more would have been written about him. Below is an account of what we have found.

*Grainger County, Tennessee Court Minutes, Vol. 1, 1796-1802*

*Abstracted from LDS Film #968587, Grainger County Court Minutes 1796-1823*

*Page 167 — 18 Feb 1801 - "Ordered that John Ward Deputy Sheriff of the County of Grainger be allowed the sum of seven Dollars for the conveyance of Aron Guest (sic) to the goal (jail) of the District of Hamilton & that Jeremiah Vardamon and Seamon Cockrill be allowed the sum of Two Dollars and Twenty five cents each for their services each."*

*Superior Court Minutes, 1793-1809, Knox County, Tennessee Historical Records Survey*

*LDS Film # 24725, (Film of 1939 WPA transcribed records)*

*Page 255 — Tuesday, 6th of October 1801 - State vs Aaron Gist*

*Horse Stealing, pleads not guilty. A jury sworn (to wit) — Andrew McCampbell, Ebenezer Byran, Oliver Alexander, David Stuart, Robert Patterson, James Cozby, <u>George McNutt, Joshua Gist</u>, William Coleman, Arthur Crozier, John Sterling, Moses Looney.*

*Do say they find the Defendant Aaron Guest guilty of the Felony and Horse Stealing in manner and form as charged in the bill of Indictment.*

*Court adjourned till tomorrow morning 9 O Clock*

*Page 257 — Friday Morning, 9th of October 1801 - State vs Aaron Guiss Court met according to adjournment, present all judges*

*Horse Stealing, Verdict Guilty. Aaron Guiss being led to the bar and asked if anything he had to say why the sentence of the Law should not be passed against him. Saith nothing - Sentence therefore was passed that he should be Hanged by the neck until Dead, and that the Sheriff of Knox County shall put this sentence in Execution at the public gallows in Knox County on Wednesday the 14th October instant between the Hours of 12 and 4 o'clock in the afternoon. Anderson County, Tennessee Court Minutes 1801-1809, WPA transcript 1936*

*Page 7 — 8 Mar 1802 - The last will and testament of Aaron Guest was proved in open court by Hugh Montgomery Esquire, one of the subscribing witnesses thereto & ordered to be recorded.*

*Page 22 — 14 Jun 1802 - Ordered that Jason Cloud & John Guest be qualified as executors of the Last Will & Testament of Aaron Guest deceased they having given bond and security accordingly to law.*

*Page 36 — 14 Sep 1802 - Jason Clouds exhibits an Inventory of the Estate of Aaron Guess deceased which is ordered to be recorded.*

*Page 55 — 14 Mar 1803: William Hancock Deputy Sheriff made oath in open court that the taxes returned on due by the following persons could not be collected they having removed out of the county (viz) John Guess, Owen Willis, Jonathan Rains, for the year 1802. Page 56 — 14 Mar 1803 - Ordered by the court that Jason Cloud of the Executors of the last will and testament of Aaron Guess deceased have leave to sell the property belonging to said Estate agreeable to the tenor of the will.*

Aaron Gist's trial started on the 6th of October, 1801 and he was sentenced to be hung on the 9th of October, 1801. Aaron's father, John Gist, of whom it was said was "some relation to Sequoyah", left the county in 1802. There is no further mention of him in any documentation whatsoever. Where did he go? What became of his family? Before John Gist left the county, both he and Jason Cloud were executors of the estate of poor Aaron. But his father, John — leaves the county, and only Jason is made executor and has leave to sell the deceased Aaron's belongings.

Below is an account of the actual record of what proceeded and the reason for the trial and hanging of Aaron Gist.

## Petitions to the General Assembly of Tennessee

Abstracted from Tennessee State Library and Archives Microfilm Legislative Petitions 1799-1801, Roll 1 (partial list, as relevant to Aron Gess and John Gess only)

*Petition #26, Series 1, 1801: Petition of William Grisham (no county given) for compensation for a bay mare stolen from him in 1800 by Aaron GEST. Grisham is a poor man with a large family of small children and cannot afford to sue GEST. No settlement is indicated on the document.*

*Petition #4, Series 2, 1801: Petition of William Grissem, by his next friend William Hord, for compensation as the state's witness against Aaron GAST, "who was condem'd and Executed in the month of October last for horse stealing..."*

*Petition #6, Series 2, 1801: Petition of Jeremiah Vardeman for compensation for his services in the case of Aron GESS. "... in the month of November 1800 I had the unhappy misfortune to swap horses with a certain Aron GESS, and I received from him a certain mare which has since proven to be stolen, the property of William Grasam of Grainger County; whereupon I pursued the said GESS from Kentucky into this Commonweth and arrested him according to Law and committed him to the publick jail in this town..." Vardeman's petition is endorsed by Wm McGeehee, Esq., Elisha Wallen, Matthew Sims and Jas. Lea.*

A friend, Don Sticher wrote a summary about the hanging of Aron Gess. He was the researcher who found these documents and credit should go to him for his hard work. Here are a few excerpts from that summary.

*From the Court Minutes of Anderson Co., Tennessee, Book I, 1801-1909 we have this record of Aron Gess, John Gess and Jason Cloud.*

*8 Mar 1802: The last will and testament of Aaron Guest was proved in open court by Hugh Montgomery Esquire, one of the subscribing witnesses thereto & ordered to be recorded.*

*14 Jun 1802: Ordered that Jason Cloud & John Guest be qualified as executors of the Last Will & Testament of Aaron Guest deceased they having given bond and security accordingly to law.*

*14 Sep 1802: Jason Clouds exhibits an Inventory of the Estate of Aaron Guess deceased which is ordered to be recorded.*

*14 Mar 1803: William Hancock Deputy Sheriff made oath in open court that the taxes returned on due by the following persons could not be collected they having removed out of the county (viz) John Guess, Owen Willis, Jonathan Rains, for the year 1802 - -*

*14 Mar 1803: Ordered by the court that Jason Cloud of the Executors of the last will and testament of Aaron Guess deceased have leave to sell the property belonging to said Estate agreeable to the tenor of the will –*

Apparently Aaron Gist was accused of stealing a horse from William Grissem. He went to Kentucky and swapped horses with Jeremiah Vardeman. Vardeman for some unknown reason suspects the horse is stolen, and pursues Aaron back to Tennessee and arrests him.

John Gess was on the 1802 tax list for Anderson Co., TN - Jason Cloud's Company. I have a copy of that tax list. There are 65 names on that list. One is James McNutt, another John Gess, and Jason Cloud is also there. But we have John Ridenour Jr. and Joseph Ridenour, as well, as being 2 of those 65 names! So members of the Ridenour family, a descendant of whom wrote that book, "Land of the Lake", were neighbors of and PERSONALLY KNEW John Gess, Aaron Gess, and Jason Cloud. So when they speak of John Gess as being a son of Nathaniel Gess and a Cherokee woman, they are speaking of knowledge held in their family.

Finally, remember in the Ridenour book that he mentioned Aaron Guest later acknowledged receiving the possessions of his deceased father, also named Aaron? Well here is a record of those documents:

*Campbell County, Tennessee Deed Book D, Pages 150 and 151*

*Know all men by these presents that I Aaron Guest Jun'r of the County of Livingston and State of Kentucky for divers good causes and considerations do nominate and appoint*

108

*Silas Williams Junior of the town of Jacksborough County of Campbell and State of*
*Tennessee my true and lawful agent and attorney for me and in my name to ask for demand*
*and receive or sue for and collect all my Right, Title, Clame, Interest and Demand that I have*
*of in and to the estate of my father Aaron Guest Dec'd where Jason Cloud and John Guest*
*were the Executors of said Estate and had the care of said money and the aforesaid Silas*
*Williams hereby as fully authorised to collect said money and receipt for it in my name as I*
*could do was I personally present at the doing of the same and I do hereby ratify and confirm*
*whatsoever my said attorney may lawfully do touching the premises in my name. In witness*
*whereof I have hereunto set my hand and seal this 22nd day of November 1822.*

> *In the presents of, Jos Hart, Aaron Guest (seal), Charles Maysey*
> *State Of Tennessee )        Court of Pleas and Quarter Session*
> *Campbell County   )          5th December 1822*

*The execution of the within Power of Attorney from Aaron Guest to Silas Williams*
*was this day proven in open Court by the Oaths of Joseph Hart and Charles Maysey*
*subscribing witnesses thereto and ordered to be Registered.*

> *State of Tennessee )          Test  Jos Hart     Clk*
> *Campbell County   )          13th December 1822*
> *A True Copy , Test. Silas Williams     Regis'd*

So I suspect the younger Aaron Gist was the infant son of the unfortunate Aaron Gist
who was hung some 21 years earlier. He wanted his part of the estate of his father, perhaps
this was when he turned 21. So what Ridenhour said about his son later returning for his
rightful inheritance is proven true. This is evidence that what he said about John's relation to
Sequoyah is also true.

On pages 70-74 of "Colonel Return Jonathan Meigs, Day Book Number 2" [30] there
is a story of James Vann pleading for a Cherokee Indian accused of horse stealing. Mr. Vann
claims he was innocent, and blames the Creek Indians instead. Meigs says he is going to try
to get the case transferred to a court other than the local courts, fearing he will receive the
death penalty. From the record in this book, What is interesting is that Vann seems to have
started his pleas for the life of his Cherokee friend in December of 1801. Aron Gess was
hung on the 14th of October, 1801. Vann had obviously heard about the hanging of Gess, and
Meigs saw to it that he wouldn't be in the same type of local court as Gess, knowing the
probable result.

And what became of Aaron Gist, Jr.? There are Cloud's living near him in Western
Kentucky. Perhaps Aaron Sr. had married Jason Cloud's daughter. There is another John Gist

living in the area, but there are clearly two John's, as the one other is well known. Just what became of this John, the half Indian John, we may never know. However I strongly suspect he is my Harriet's grandpa, so I want to find him, real, real bad . . .

There is one possible reference. Davy Crockett [31] wrote an autobiography. In it he mentions Richard and John Brown, having gone by both their houses (p 42, 46, 50, 58). On page 73 he mentions travelling for a short while with a "John Guess" during the Creek Red Stick War, which was part of the War of 1812. I suspect this is speaking of another John Guess, not mine. But still, it is there.

### Jason Cloud, Cherokee John Brown, and John Gist

Jason Cloud, as we know from the documents above, was an executor of the estate of Aaron Gist, hung in 1801 as a horse thief. In the "Land of the Lake", by Dr. G. L. Ridenour are a couple of other interesting items about Jason Cloud.

*p. 34 —Captain Jason Cloud and several river men transported the heavy hammers and the irons for the forge. **Captain Cloud was active in the flatboat trade down the river** and was associated with the small groups of men who played an important part in the settlement of the Mississippi River Valley.*

*p 97 — [speaking of the war of 1812] — several Campbell County men under the direction of **Captain Jason Cloud** and the Haley's built the retaining wall at **Suck Creek on the Tennessee River** to enable the flatboats to transport provisions to General Andrew Jackson's Army.*

The following excerpts are from "Footsteps of the Cherokee: A Guide to the Eastern Homelands of the Cherokee Nation", by Vicki Rozema, John F. Blair Publisher, Winston-Salem, North Carolina, 2nd edition, © copyright 2007 by Vicki Rozema.

On page 66 is the following:

*Around 1800, **John Brown, a mixed-blood Cherokee** who became prominent in the area, ran a ferry across the Tennessee River at Williams Island. He was known as the best guide for navigating the treacherous waters at The Narrows and **the Suck along the Tennessee River.***

John Brown was a top class navigator around "The Suck" and Jason Cloud, flatboat captain, helped build a retaining wall at "The Suck" to make it easier to navigate. Jason Cloud knew my Gist's, and from this — he knew some of the Cherokee Brown's, also.

## F. Our Gist's per Genealogical Records

Much of the credit for this section should go to Don Sticher. Don doesn't descend from this family, but has studied both DNA and genealogical records about us and other branches of the Gist surname. There were three Gist/Guess/Guest family groups that were early pioneers in the area of Alabama west of Huntsville. Two seem to be related to us, per DNA test results, so our genealogical study is of these two branches.

## The First Migration of Our Gist's to Northern Alabama

Ricky Butch Walker in "Warrior Mountain Folklore" [32] mentions a little about our families, but not much. He does say many mixed-Indian families lived in/near Lawrence/Winston/Walker Counties in Northern Alabama. Both our Brown's and Gist's were living there as well, but we had all left and were not present to tell out stories. We are speaking, now.

The first of these two families appears about 1818 in Lawrence County, Alabama. Thomas Gist, Richard Gist, Rachel Gist (wife of unknown Gist, possibly "?James?") and Christopher Gist - apparent brothers, all born in Tennessee around 1800. These families first show up in Alabama in Lawrence County around 1818 where Thomas and Richard can be found in the marriage records (Thomas married in 1818 and Richard married in 1824). They first show up in Walker County, AL for the 1830 census. This family probably has origins in Tennessee in the area around Anderson County.

### 1830 Walker County, AL, pages 258, 270, 271, 272

| | | | |
|---|---|---|---|
| GUEST, Richard | 20-29 | page 258 | 2 1 0 0 1 0 0 - 2 0 0 0 0 1 0 |
| RONEY, Lewis | 30-39 | page 270-14 | 4 2 1 0 0 1 0 - 0 2 0 0 2 0 0 0 1 |
| GUEST, Nancy | 30-39 | page 270-15 | 0 1 0 0 0 0 0 - 0 0 1 0 0 1 0 |
| GUEST, Christopher | 20-29 | page 272-4 | 1 0 0 0 1 0 0 - 1 1 0 0 1 0 0 |

This group of Guest families appears to have origins in Lawrence County, AL, which is just north of Walker County. The correct spelling of the name appears to be GIST. There was a series of marriages in Lawrence County from 1818 to 1825 that matches this family. The Guests who married in Lawrence County were possibly all brothers and sisters from one family. These Lawrence County, AL marriages were:

| | | | |
|---|---|---|---|
| Gest, Thomas | Roney, Nancy | 06 Nov 1818 | Lawrence, AL |
| Guess, Rachel | Talbert, Thomas | 07 Dec 1820 | Lawrence, AL |
| Talbot, Rachel | McNutt, Emanuel | 31 Dec 1822 | Lawrence, AL |
| Gest, Richard | McKinney, Jane | 13 Sep 1821 | Lawrence, AL |
| Guest, Susan | Bowlen, Lewis | 07 Oct 1824 | Lawrence, AL |

| | | | |
|---|---|---|---|
| Guest, Jane | Miller, Isaac | 11 Aug 1825 | Lawrence, AL |
| Guest, Susanna | McDaniel, Wiley | 10 Dec 1825 | Lawrence, AL |

The last three names seem to spell their names "Guest" and we are not related to them. Lewis Roney who lived next door to Nancy Guest in 1830 is thought to be Nancy's brother. Richard Guest moved across the border into Mississippi around 1836 and can be found in Itawamba County, MS for the 1840 census and Pontotoc County, MS for the 1850 census (wife's name "Jane"). Both of these Mississippi counties are just west of Walker County, AL. Rachel (my ancestor) had a third marriage to Emanuel McNutt and they moved to southwestern Tennessee, Shelby County. Thomas Gist disappears and his wife Nancy divorced him. She remarried a Rackley, and they move to northwestern Tennessee nearer the Mississippi River.

**1840 Marion County, AL, page 059**

GUESS, Christopher 30-39          1 1 1 0 0 1 0 - 0 0 0 0 1 0 0

This is Christopher Guest who had been living in Walker County, AL for the 1830 census. Marion County, AL is the next county NW of Walker County. Richard Guest, who was in 1830 Walker County, AL with Christopher, moved west into Mississippi about 1836. Christopher Guest cannot be found anywhere for the 1850 census but can be found in 1860 and later, living in Winston County, the county just east of Marion County and between Lawrence County and Walker County. In 1880 Winston County Christopher Guest was living in the household of James H. Haw, listed as grandfather, 76 years old and born in TN.

**1840 Itawamba County, MS, page 147 (On MS border NW of Walker County, AL**

GESS, Richard          30-39          0 1 1 1 0 1 1 - 1 3 2 0 0 0 1

This appears to be the Richard Guest who had been living in Walker County, AL for the 1830 census. The number of children and approximate ages of everyone matches the 1830 Alabama family. There were two adult men in the household for this census, one 30-39 years old and one 40-49 years old. Which one was Richard, who was about 40 years old? And who was the second man?

Richard Guest married Jane McKinney 13 Sep 1821 in Lawrence County, AL. Richard kept moving west and can be found in Pontotoc County, MS in 1850 with a wife named "Jane" (next county west of Itawamba).

Christopher Gist not found anywhere in Alabama in 1850, by any spelling variation. He was in Winston County, AL for the 1860, 1870 and 1880 censuses. Richard Gist was living in Pontotoc County, MS in 1850. A search of Fayette, Marion and Hancock (renamed Winston in 1858) counties turned up nothing.

## 1850 Pontotoc County, MS census, page 69b, household #219, and #220

| | | | |
|---|---|---|---|
| GUEST, R. | 50 | birthplace "Unknown" | Farmer |
| Jane | | 50 birthplace "Unknown" (Jane McKinney) | |
| Catherine | 16 AL | | |
| Docia | 15 AL | | |
| Elizabeth | 13 MS | | |
| GUEST, J. | 26 AL | Farmer | |
| Jinsy | 26 SC | | |
| John | 6 MS | | |
| Harriet | 5 MS | | |
| Johnson | 2 MS | | |

This is the family of Richard Guest and Jane McKinney who married 13 Sep 1821 in Lawrence County, AL. Richard was in Walker County, AL in 1830 and Itawamba County, MS in 1840. The daughter Docia was born in AL in 1835 and the daughter Elizabeth was born in MS in 1837, indicating the family moved from AL to MS around 1836.

This family disappears after this census. One bunch of this family appears in Lawrence County, Arkansas, later.

## 1860 Winston County, AL census, Littlesville, page 1203, household #92

| | | | |
|---|---|---|---|
| Christopher GIST | 56 TN | Farmer | abt 1804 |
| Mary Gist | 53 TN | | abt 1807 |
| Angeline Gist | 24 AL | | abt 1836 |
| Frances C. Gist | 19 AL | | abt 1841 |
| Martha J. Gist | 17 AL | | abt 1843 |
| William H. Gist | 16 AL | | abt 1844 |
| Romay E. Gist | 12 AL | | abt 1848 |
| Christopher C. Gist | 10 AL | | abt 1850 |

This is the family of Christopher Gist and wife Mary McNutt. There were two daughters not shown here; Sarah, who married Thomas O. Gist, and a daughter recalled as

113

"Rowena Eveline" Gist. Sarah's death certificate gives her parents' names as Christopher Gist and Mary McNutt. Per family recollections "Rowena Eveline" was born about 1845 and married William Richard Pace. "Rowena Eveline" may be the daughter Angeline shown above.

Angeline Gist married a "Pace" and was widowed for the 1870 census (Civil War widow?). See the 1870 and 1880 censuses for more information.

I was told the photo to the left was a son of Christopher Gist and Mary McNutt, born in 1849. That would make him Christopher C. Gist (b. about 1848) or Romay Gist (b. about 1850).

**The Next Migration of Our Gist's to Northern Alabama [32]**

The other of these two families that is related to us came from the Southern Kentucky family of Aaron (b.1807) and Nancy Gist of KY. With apparent sons Elijah Gist, Thomas O. Gist, James Harvey Gist and perhaps Bowlen Guest. They first show up in Alabama in Marion County for the 1860 census. DNA testing in 2006-2007 shows this family is related to the Christopher Gist families above. While this family was from Kentucky, there were several of the Gist families from the Anderson County, TN area who lived just across the KY border in Whitely and Wayne County on the Tennessee border.

**1860 Marion County, AL census, Allens Factory, page 688, household #518**

| | | |
|---|---|---|
| Harvy GUESS | 25 KY Farmer | (James Harvey Gist) |
| Nancy J. Guess | 20 AL | (Nancy Jane Pace) |
| Nancy E. Guess | 4 AL | |
| Talitha Guess | 1 AL | |

This is James Harvey Gist. Harvey lived next door to a Pace family (Moses, 31 NC and Martha J. , 32 AL). Harvey was apparently a son of nearby Nancy Gist, who was the wife of Aaron Gist. Per Harvey's Civil War records he was born Feb 1836 in Wayne County, KY. Wayne County, KY is just across the Tennessee border from Campbell County, TN, where many early Gist families are found. Harvey married 2nd Mary Ann Meek 1864 in Barry County, MO. Barry County, MO is in the southwest corner of the state near both AR and OK.

**1860 Marion County, AL census, Allens Factory, page 690, household #527**

| | |
|---|---|
| Thomas O. GIST | 28 KY Farmer |
| Sarah Gist | 21 AL (Sarah Gist, daughter of Christopher Gist) |

Lucy A.                        1 AL

Thomas O. Gist is apparently another son of nearby Nancy Gist (wife of Aaron Gist).
Thomas O. Gist married Sarah Guest, a daughter of Christopher Guest who lived in
neighboring Winston County.  Descendants claim both Thomas O. Gist and his wife Sarah
Gist were Indian or part Indian.  They also claim the second wife of Harvey Gist (Mary Ann
Meek) was half Choctaw.

**1860 Marion County, AL census, Allens Factory, page 690,  household #???**
Elijah GIST              23 KY Farmer
Nancy GIST              45 KY (mother?)

Elijah Gist was a son of Aaron Gist (b.1807 KY) and Nancy.  Aaron Gist was born
about 1807 in KY and died after the 1870 census in Colbert County, AL (NW corner near
Lauderdale County where many Gist families lived from 1830 on).  Elijah Gist can be found
in 1870 Colbert County, AL with his father Aaron 63 and mother Nancy 53 in the household.
Where was Aaron for this 1860 census?  Perhaps Aaron was looking for the next place for
the family to live.

**1870 Colbert County, AL census, Newburg, page 43a and 43b, household #66**
Elijah GIST              34 KY Farmer
Catherine Gist          27 AL
James Gist               8 AL
Nancy Gist               6 AL
Louiza Gist              3 AL
Lou Ellen Gist           1 AL
Aaron GIST              64 KY  Retired Farmer
Nancy Gist              53 KY  At Home

This is the same Elijah and Nancy Gist found in Walker County, AL for the 1860
census.  Colbert County is in the very NW corner of Alabama.  Evidently Aaron and Nancy
Gist are the parents of Elijah.  Only Nancy and her son Elijah were listed in the 1860 Walker
County household.  Nancy's husband Aaron was not at home in 1860.  Where was Aaron for
the 1860 census?  No trace of Thomas O. Gist who lived near Elijah and Nancy Gist in 1860
Walker County.  James Harvey Gist moved to Barry County, MO before 1864 and can be
found there in 1870.

Per land records in Marion County, Alabama, 1857-1859, Christopher Gist and Aaron Gist had consecutive land certificate numbers (27048 and 27049) indicating they probably visited the land office together. Were they brothers?

Some descendants of James Harvey Gist moved to Indian Territory, per Indian Pioneer Papers. Jim Sanders, a friend and fellow researcher, found a transcription of that document here: http://www.okgenweb.org/~okmurray/Murray/indianpioneerpapers.htm and I have already included it in this report.

Where did these Gist families in Northwestern Alabama come from? Aaron can be found in Wayne County, Kentucky. James Harvey Gist aid in his Civil War pension application that he was born 15 Feb 1836 in Wayne County, KY.

**1860 Winston County, AL census, Littlesville, page 1203, household #92**

| | | | |
|---|---|---|---|
| Christopher GIST | 56 TN | Farmer | abt 1804 |
| Mary Gist | 53 TN | | abt 1807 |
| Angeline Gist | 24 AL | | abt 1836 |
| Frances C. Gist | 19 AL | (female) | abt 1841 |
| Martha J. Gist | 17 AL | | abt 1843 |
| William H. Gist | 16 AL | | abt 1844 |
| Romay E. Gist | 12 AL | | abt 1848 |
| Christopher C. Gist | 10 AL | | abt 1850 |
| Harvy GUESS | 25 KY | Farmer | (James Harvey Gist) |
| Nancy J. Guess | 20 AL | | (Nancy Jane Pace) |
| Nancy E. Guess | 4 AL | | |
| Talitha Guess | 1 AL | | |

**1860 Marion County, AL census, Allens Factory, page 690, household #527**

| | | |
|---|---|---|
| Thomas O. GIST | 28 KY | Farmer |
| Sarah Gist | 21 AL | (Sarah Gist, b.1838, daughter of Christopher Gist) |
| Lucy A. | 1 AL | |

Thomas O. Gist lived next door to Elijah Gist (and Nancy) and is apparently another son of Nancy Gist (Nancy the presumed wife of Aaron Gist). Thomas O. Gist married Sarah Gist, a daughter of Christopher Gist who lived in neighboring Winston County. Descendants claim both Thomas O. Gist and his wife Sarah Gist were Indian or part Indian.

## 1860 Marion County, AL census, Allens Factory, page 690, household #528

| | | |
|---|---|---|
| Elijah GIST | 23 KY Farmer | |
| Nancy GIST | 45 KY (mother?) | |

Elijah Gist was apparently a son of Nancy (and Aaron Gist b.1807 KY?). Aaron Gist was born about 1807 in KY and died after the 1870 census in Colbert County, AL (NW corner near Lauderdale County where many Gist families lived from 1830 on). Elijah Gist can be found in 1870 Colbert County, AL with his presumed parents Aaron 63 and Nancy 53 in the household. Where was Aaron for this 1860 census? Some researchers believe he may be the 52 year old (in 1860) Aaron GUESS found living in a Joseph Smith household in Whitley County, KY in 1860.

DNA tests show all these Gist families are very closely related. Moreover they are not related to most of the Guest families found in this same region.

## 1870 Colbert County, AL census, Newburg, page 43a and 43b, household #66

| | | |
|---|---|---|
| Elijah GIST | 34 KY Farmer | |
| Catherine Gist | 27 AL | |
| James Gist | 8 AL | |
| Nancy Gist | 6 AL | |
| Louiza Gist | 3 AL | |
| Lou Ellen Gist | 1 AL | |
| Aaron GIST | 64 KY | Retired Farmer |
| Nancy Gist | 53 KY | At Home |

## 1870 Franklin County, AL census, Nelsonville Twp, page 535, Household #12

| | | |
|---|---|---|
| Thomas GIST | 40 KY Farmer | abt 1830 |
| Sarah Gist | 32 AL | abt 1838 |
| Lucy Gist | 11 AL | abt 1859 |
| Eliza Gist | 9 AL | abt 1861 |
| Rona Gist | 7 AL | abt 1863 |
| Fannie Gist | 2 AL | abt 1868 |

This is Thomas O. Gist who in 1860 was in Marion County, Alabama.

## 1870 Franklin County, AL census, Nelsonville Twp, page 535, Household #11

| William GIST | 26 AL | works on farm | abt 1844 |
|---|---|---|---|
| Melissa Gist | 24 GA | | abt 1846 |
| Andrew Gist | 5 AL | | abt 1865 |
| William Gist | 3 AL | | abt 1867 |

William Gist was a son of Christopher Gist of Marion County, AL, making him a brother-in-law of next door neighbor Thomas O. Gist. Franklin County, AL is the next County north of Marion County.

There was a third bunch of Gist's, often spelled Guest, who migrated to the same region. DNA testing shows that we are not related to them at all.

## Southern Kentucky Gist's

This second bunch of Gist's we are related to came from Southern Kentucky. It is time to discover more about them while living in Southern Kentucky.

Our origins in Southern Kentucky go back to that report given in Early Times in Clinton County (Kentucky), Jack Ferguson, 1986, Page 8: *Several miles upriver from Price's camp a hunter named Gist, possibly Nathaniel, had a hunting camp called Gist's Station Camp, in Pulaski County, on the southern side of the river nearly opposite the mouth of Pitman Creek. A trace led from Price's camp to Gist's Station Camp, which was generally used by Buchanan's companions - "It was our crossing place when we came to or returned from Price's Meadows."* Also remember Aaron was accused of going to Kentucky to trade a horse they said he'd stolen.

### Wayne County, Kentucky Deed Book B, 1811-1822, (name index only)

| | | |
|---|---|---|
| 190 | Haven, Joseph | Indenture (Deed) |
| 213 | Havens, Joseph | Indenture (Deed) |
| 216 | Havens, Joseph | Indenture (Deed) |
| 217 | Havens, Joseph | Indenture (Deed) |
| 325 | Havens, Joseph | Indenture (Deed) |
| 332 | Havens, Joseph & Mary | Indenture (Deed) |
| 334 | Havens, Joseph & Mary | Indenture (Deed) |
| 336 | Havens, Joseph & Mary | Indenture (Deed) |
| 338 | Havens, Joseph & Mary | Indenture (Deed) |
| 261 | Havens, Joseph & Samuel | Indenture (Deed) |

| 617 | Havin, John | Indenture (Deed) |
|---|---|---|
| 39 | Havin, Joseph & Polly | Indenture (Deed) |
| 162 | Heavin, John J. | Indenture (Deed) |
| 392 | Heavin, John | Indenture (Deed) |
| 731 | Heavin, John | Indenture (Deed) |
| 874 | Heavin, John | POA (Power of Attorney) |
| 849 | Heavin, Samuel & John | POA (Power of Attorney) |
| 255 | Smith, David | Indenture (Deed) (Matches Beeson No. 254) |
| 257 | Smith, David | Indenture (Deed) |
| 522 | Smith, David | Deed (Matches Beeson No. 521) |
| 852 | Smith, David | Indenture (Deed) (Matches Haven No. 849??) |

Plenty of Haven's and Smith's. Remember David Smith's mother was a Gist, and he married a Haven's girl, but she was a daughter of James, and James Havens isn't listed.

### 1810 Census Pulaski County, KY, Somerset Twp, page 147

GESS, Nathaniel      4 1 0 1 0 - 0 0 0 1 0

1M    26-45   (born 1765-1785, about 1775-1780 per later information)

1F    26-45

1M    10-15   (born 1795-1800)

4M    0-9   (born 1800-1810)

I can't help but remember "Gist's Station's Camp" mentioned in 1777 was also in Pulaski County, Kentucky. There is a Nathaniel Gess living there some 33 years later, and we are related to him.

### 1820 Census Wayne County, KY, No Twp, page 81

Gest, Nathaniel      1 0 1 1 1 0 - 0 0 0 1 0

1M, 1F  26-45   (b.1775-1795, probably born about 1775-1780)

1M    18-25   (b. 1795-1802)

1M    16-17   (b.1803-1804)

1M    0-9   (b. 1810-1820)

### 1830 Census, Wayne County, KY, page 258

Gist, Nathan   0 0 1 0 0 0 0 1 - no females

1M    50-59   (b.1770-1780)

1M    10-14  (b.1815-1820)
In neighboring Pulaski County, KY in 1830 was:

**1830 Census, Pulaski County, KY, page 026**

Gist, Thomas        2 0 0 0 1  -  0 0 0 0 1
       1M, 1F  20-29  (born 1800-1810)
       2M        0-5

Thomas Gist is probably a son of the Nathaniel Gist who was in Wayne County, KY (an adjacent county) for the 1820 and 1830 census.

**1840 Census Whitley County, KY, page 205**

GESS, Aaron        1 2 0 0 1  -  0 0 0 0 1
       1M, 1F  20-29    (born 1810-1820.  Son of Nathaniel GIST?)
       2M        5-9
       1M        0-4

This is the Aaron Gist who later shows up in AL - born about 1807 and married to Nancy.  The ages of the sons match those of Thomas O, James Harvey and Elijah who would have been about 8, 5 and 3 respectively in 1840.

**1850 Census, Whitley County, KY, page 380**

| | | |
|---|---|---|
| Gist, Aaron | | 50 TN |
| wife | Mary | 45 KY |
| son | Allen | 18 KY (b.1832) |
| son | William | 16 KY  (b.1834) |
| dau | Polly | 14 KY |
| son | James | 13 KY   (b.1837.  James Harvey Gist?) |
| dau | Lennida | 11 KY |
| son | John | 9 KY (b.1841 |
| son | Lewis | 7 KY (b.1843) |
| dau | Jemima | 5 KY |

This Aaron Gist was born about 1800 and is not the same person as the Aaron Gess who was in Whitley County in 1840. Is this the Aaron whose father was hung in 1801, whose father was John, of whom it was said, his mater was Cherokee and some relation to Sequoyah? This then, takes us full circle, back to Northern Tennessee, and then back to Southwestern Virginia and was mentioned in the Dorsey book on the Gist's, back to Nathaniel Gist, the one killed at Kings Mountain, and back to Maryland. However there is Aaron Gist of Livingston County, Kentucky who was born in Tennessee in 1801 per the 1850 census. This Aaron received eight land grants in Livingston County between 1831 and 1853 totaling 1,487 acres. Aaron Gist lived between two "Cloud" families for the 1840 Livingston County census and there were two "Cloud" children in Aaron's household for the 1850 Livingston County census. We know Jason Cloud knew the Gist's, and we know he also knew the Cherokee John Brown who was at Brown's Ferry in Hamilton County, Tennessee. So we have two possible sons of the Aaron who was hung. In either case, we have come full circle.

### 1860 Census, Whitley County, KY, page 758

| SMITH, Joseph | 50 VA |
| wife | Mary | 40 VA |
| dau | Hanah | 11 KY |
| son | William R. | 5 KY |
| ?? | GUESS, Aaron | 52 KY |

This Aaron seems to be the one mentioned in 1840, not 1850. It is confusing. This is the Aaron who later appears in Northwestern Alabama. There appear to be two Aarons from the same region, one born about 1800 in Tennessee, and the other born about 1807 in Kentucky. And we have the third Aaron born about 1801 living in Lexington County, in Western Kentucky.

### Wayne County, KY Tax Books, 1801-1825, LDS Film 008269

Note by Don Sticher Feb 2009: These tax lists are in a very mixed state of legibility. Some pages are very clear while others are completely faded out. Some years are completely faded. Searched for Gist (all variations) and Havens.

| 1801 | David Smith |
| 1802 | ?? |
| 1803 | Joseph Havens |
| 1804 | ?? Poor condition, hard to read |
| 1805 | Completely faded out |
| 1806 | David Gass or Gess (hard to read) |

1806   John Haven
1807   Nath Gess                Poor condition, hard to read
1807   James Haven              Poor condition, hard to read
1808   James Guess              Clean page, clearly "James Guess" he appears only here
1809   Faded out
1810   Very faded and hard to read
1810   census James Heavin
1811   ??
1812   Nancy Guess?
1812   Joseph Havens  150 acres cleared
1813   Joseph Havens
1814   Joseph Havens
1815   ??
1816   Richard Havens
1817   ??
1818   ??
1819   Nathaniel Gess
1820   Nathaniel Gest
1821-1824 Nothing found

So our David Smith, our James Havens, and several other Smith's and Gess/Gist's and Havens are also mentioned. Was James Guess/Gist Rachel's first husband? Rachel's father James Havens lived here near James Gist. However our family story doesn't mention Kentucky – only Tennessee and Northern Alabama. However other of our Gist's do mention Kentucky. So . . .

# G. True Stories and Tall Tales

Much has been written online about a band of Cherokee found in Southern Kentucky in the same region our Gist's lived. Did my Gist's belong to it? I hate to burst anyone's bubbles, but in historic times, there is no physical evidence for such a band.  There were people of mixed race who moved into in Pulaski/Wayne/Whitley County region, but the stories of "Cornblossom" and "Tuckahoe" are fiction. Comet Press Books, in 1958, published "Legion of the Lost Mine, Stories of the Cumberland" by Thomas H. Troxell.

Most of the stories you see online about this Cherokee community of Southern Kentucky originate from here. In the forward of the book we see the following:

**Foreword**

    *The location of this story is along the Cumberland River and the Great Cumberland Plateau in Eastern Kentucky and Tennessee. The time is before Kentucky became a commonwealth or Tennessee became a state. **The names of some of the characters are fictitious, and any resemblance these may have to those of persons now living is purely coincidental.***

    If you have ever read a novel about World War Two, the names of the generals and politicians and a few of the characters may be correct, and the geographical locations may be accurate. BUT – the story line is fictitious, something that makes good reading. On page 8 Troxell mentions Christian Priber in the footnote section. He says Priber lived at Great Tellico during his stay with the Cherokee. He also mentions Collins book "History of Kentucky" as a source. He even mentions "great bars of silver" being carried off. Of course we all know there are no silver mines in Eastern Kentucky.

    There was an excellent book published in 1983. On the back cover it says *"The Kentucky Historical Society said that it provided 'an exceptional reading experience'"*. The book is "South Fork Country" by Samuel D. Perry [33].

    On page 106 Perry says:

    After 1805, no Cherokee had any legal claim to South Fork Country [Vance's note: meaning Wayne, McCleary, and neighboring counties in Southern Kentucky] . . . though they did not own the land, Cherokees continued to be a visible part of the regional scene. Many individual Cherokees had allied themselves with White families through marriage . . . The mixed blood offspring of these marriages blended easily into the frontier scene and experienced few difficulties as a result of their racial heritage.

    I emailed Mr. Perry for a few months, and purchased this book from him. Mr. Perry sent me two attachments. One he said was property of a local newspaper in South Kentucky and said I didn't have permission to copy it to anyone, but he said he'd be more than welcome to let me foreword this to others.

    Many people have all seen and heard about the Cherokee still in Southern Kentucky as it is all over the internet. So now please listen to the "rest of the story", as Paul Harvey would have said. Please know the man who wrote this is a descendant of the "Slaven" family and their family history is mentioned in these stories. Here is what his research showed —

Mr. Perry also sent me the following –

## YAHOO FALLS AN HISTORICAL OVERVIEW

*Located in McCreary County, Kentucky, Yahoo Falls is considered to be Kentucky's highest waterfall, although it is believed that a similar waterfall in the Red River Gorge exceeds Yahoo Falls in height by a few inches. It is a very scenic waterfall and is surrounded by magnificent vistas and natural arches. In the gorge into which Yahoo Falls plunges there exists a rarity in Kentucky, a sizeable tract of virgin timber, protected from harvest over the years by the inaccessibility of the gorge.*

*When the Cumberland National Forest was created in 1937, ownership of the Falls and surrounding second-growth timberland passed to the Federal government and management of it was entrusted to the U.S. Forest Service, an agency of the Department of Agriculture. Always off the beaten track, so to speak, the Yahoo Falls area languished for more than twenty years as the Forest Service gave the land an opportunity to heal itself after decades of high-grade logging abuse, uncontrolled burning, and erosion.*

*In 1953, supervision of the Cumberland National Forest was assigned to Robert F. Collins, a professional forester, sportsman, and far-sighted manager of natural resources. Collins was also a history buff and admirer of the Kentucky explorer and pioneer, Daniel Boone. So much so, that in 1966, he was almost solely responsible for having the name of the Cumberland National Forest changed to that of Daniel Boone National Forest. In his seventeen-year tenure as Forest Supervisor, Collins made a name for himself as a progressive land manger and undertook many innovative projects that transformed the Forest from a virtual wasteland into a haven for lovers of outdoor recreation and a sustainable source of wood products.*

*Collins had a sincere interest in the history of the region that became the Daniel Boone National Forest and sought to establish sites on the Forest where that history could be used to attract visitors and educate the general public. As a Boone enthusiast, he was, naturally, attracted to the northern reaches of the Forest where Boone had spent most of his time while in Kentucky. However, the southern districts could not be ignored and Collins began to look around for something he could use as a basis for interpreting the history of that region. He found it in an obscure booklet entitled LEGION OF THE LOST MINE, published in 1958 by a Scott County, Tennessee resident, Thomas Harlan Troxel.*

*LEGION OF THE LOST MINE is a short collection of stories based upon the traditions of the Troxel family and centers around an intriguing person in the history of the*

Cherokee, Chief Doublehead. In the book, Troxel creates additional characters to supplement the Doublehead story. Big Jake, Princess Cornblossom, Hans Blackberne, and the romantic Brave Tuckahoe all romp through the pages of LEGION OF THE LOST MINE like characters in a Walt Disney drama. Although Thomas H. Troxel was careful to note in the foreword to his book that the names of some of the characters are fictitious, many well-meaning persons have used his work as a framework upon which to build a fraudulent history of the region drained by the Big South Fork of the Cumberland River. Robert Collins used it to create the Yahoo Falls Recreation Area on the Stearns Ranger District.

Knowing that it would be cost-prohibitive to attempt to extract the mature timber from within the Yahoo Creek gorge, the decision was made to turn Yahoo Falls into a scenic attraction and lure visitors to the Stearns Ranger District. An all-weather road was built from the Alum Ford road to the top of the gorge and a picnic area was established with sources of potable water, fire pits, and toilets. Trails were constructed and a long flight of steel stairs led visitors down into the gorge past towering cliffs and nearly vertical slopes lush with mountain laurel, rhododendron, and not a few threatened and endangered species of plants.

For the history buffs, Collins ordered the construction of a cemetery at the entrance to the Yahoo Falls Recreation Area. This cemetery would contain only one grave, that of a Jacob Troxel, one of the major players in LEGION OF THE LOST MINE. With the help of a local congressman, a government-issued marker was acquired and installed at the head of the "grave". The marker would identify Jacob Troxel as a veteran of the Philadelphia County Militia in the Revolutionary War.

Today, management of the Yahoo Falls area is the responsibility of the National Park Service and hundreds of visitors come to stand under the immense overhang beneath the Falls and to navigate the trails that penetrate the pristine creek gorge. Presumably, some of these visitors also pause at the entrance and look at the lone gravestone enclosed by a rustic fence, not knowing that the stone stands over an empty grave, and that it honors a man who, in all probability, never existed. To his credit, in LEGION OF THE LOST MINE, Thomas H. Troxel never mentions Jacob Troxel, referring, instead, only to a Big Jake, going so far, even, as to suggest that he might be "Jacob the conjuror, as spoken of in connection with Indians in Virginia colonial history." However, because of the intercession of Robert Collins and others, it has been assumed that Big Jake was, indeed, Jacob Troxel.

Shortly after his retirement, in 1970, Robert Collins was commissioned by the Forest Service to write a history of the Daniel Boone National Forest. Since its publication in 1975,

125

*A HISTORY OF THE DANIEL BOONE NATIONAL FOREST has become the definitive work (and the only work) on the subject, even though it has been the object of negative criticism within the agency, itself. In his book, Collins perpetuates the Big Jake-Princess Cornblossom-Chief Doublehead legend and enhances it, going so far as to lend credence to what is, perhaps, the most notorious of the myths, the alleged massacre of innocent Cherokee at Yahoo Falls by Indian-hating whites. This grievous indictment of the non-Indian citizens of Wayne County, Kentucky, particularly the Gregory family, is an unforgivable breach of professional ethics by Collins or any reputable historian. By making such charges without proof, Collins ensures that he can never be taken seriously as a historian and leaves all of his work open to question and debate. In his wisdom, even Thomas H. Troxel makes no mention of a massacre at Yahoo Falls in his published writings.*

*For many years, I was a believer in the Big Jake-Princess Cornblossom-Yahoo Falls Massacre legend. When I undertook the research which culminated in the publication of my own book, SOUTH FORK COUNTRY, I quickly learned that much of what I had believed in my younger days about the legend was based upon pure speculation, wishful thinking, and, as time went on, deliberate attempts to deceive. After much study, I concluded that, although there was, indeed, a Chief Doublehead (though bearing no resemblance to the Doublehead of the legend), both Big Jake (Troxel) and Princess Cornblossom were, both, simply, figments of Thomas H. Troxel's imagination and that the Yahoo Falls Massacre was simply an add-on to the legend designed to serve personal agendas.*

*The oft-repeated (even on the Internet) story of a mass murder at Yahoo Falls is based, not upon empirical data, but upon hearsay and revisionist history. It is an unconscionable smear of the descendants of Hiram Gregory, who is charged with leading the assault upon the Cherokees, and serves, not to unite the people of the Big South Fork region, but to divide them.*

*In the past, good, but misinformed persons have sought to create a heritage for the people living within the drainage basin of the Big South Fork whom they regarded as having none. They used their influence to put up historical markers and headstones, wrote about the region in national forest histories, and, patronizingly, tried to give what they thought was the region's due. They cannot be faulted for this because they did what they believed was right. But, we are at the dawn of a new era in historical research and the citizens of Wayne, Pulaski, and McCreary counties now know that their true heritage can be based upon real people and real events. We must not be afraid to subject our sacred cows of tradition to the historical method and evaluate the data objectively and responsibly. I have done that to the*

126

*Chief Doublehead-Big Jake-Cornblossom-Yahoo Falls Massacre, and have found it to be what it always will be-a series of fanciful stories not based upon factual evidence.*
        *Samuel D. Perry, Copyright: 2002*
        *So although there were admittedly many mixed race families living in the area where some of our Gist's lived, the stories you see online mentioning Cornblossom, Tuckahoe, and the Yahoo Falls Massacre – these people and events are fictitious.*

## Priber

There is one other often quoted Cherokee story I feel I need to mention before ending this writing. Christian Gotlieb Priber is mentioned with respect to Doublehead's wife. They say Priber's daughter married Doublehead. With all due respect, there is no proof Doublehead ever married her, or if she even existed. Doublehead was said to be Sequoyah's great uncle, so mentioning Priber is a legitimate subject of this short family history.

A well-known Cherokee Historian, Robert J. Conley, was asked by the Cherokee Nation to write a history of the Cherokee Nation. The end result is "The Cherokee Nation, a History" published by the University of New Mexico Press, copyrighted by Robert J. Conley and the Cherokee Nation in 2005. So many people say Christian Gottlieb Priber was a major personality in the 1700s in Cherokee history. Was he? Here is what Robert Conley says of him:

*Once again, the English chroniclers and their followers who have blindly followed them have given us a tale full of contradictions. Priber was German, but was a French agent. He was a Jesuit priest, but railed against religion. He was a dangerous French agent who urged the Cherokee to trade with both the French and English . . . Among a matrilineal society, he spoke of wives as property without being killed, thrown out of town, or even laughed at. Among a people with a strong clan system, he advocated that children be raised as 'public property'.* **The man himself has been painted as a bundle of contradictions, and the idea he is supposed to have proposed to the Cherokees and supposed to have influenced them would never have been listened to by Cherokees. The entire tale is ludicrous.**

So much of earlier history is simply unknown and much is also unknowable. Priber did exist, but all we know of him was written by the English who were his enemies. It is possible most of the things were written of him never happened. Did mixed race families exist in Southern Kentucky. Evidence says overwhelmingly, yes. Are the stories of Tuckahoe, Cornblossom, and the Yahoo Falls Massacre true? We see them all over the internet! They are fiction. There were mixed race families who lived like the neighboring whites, and like their neighbors, just tried to do the best they could raising their families. Many of these people are well-meaning and sincere. But I can't with a good conscience say Tuckahoe or Cornblossom ever existed. They are good and interesting stories well written by Thomas Troxell. But he himself said some of the characters in his book were fictitious. If you ask the Cherokee themselves about this "Cornblossom" (and I have) all you usually hear is "Corn has no blossoms!" with a light hearted chuckle as they walk past.

## H. More About Sequoyah [34]

So we have established that we *might be* related to Sequoyah. The next section is more information about him. Much has been written about Sequoyah. George Everett Foster says in "Se-Quo-Yah, the American Cadmus and Modern Moses: A Complete Biography of the Greatest of Redmen (1885)" his father was a German Salzberger trader named George GiBt (my keyboard can't make the exact German letter that looks sort of like an uppercase "B". This letter has a long "sssss" sound. Salzberg is in Austria now, but once was part of southern Bavaria. His family came to America about the same time as the Moravians who came with Oglethorpe when Georgia was just being settled. But there is no proof that he even existed. In Grant Foreman's "Sequoyah" he says Sequyah's father was Nathaniel Gist, the son of Christopher. Mr. Foreman wrote on p. 77, *In the Bureau of American Ethnology in Washington is a letter written by John Mason Brown of the Louisville bar, a descendant of Nathaniel Gist* [Vance's note: He is not talking about MY Nathaniel. Brown descended from the famous one], *who stated that Sequoyah had visited the Gist descendants in Kentucky, probably on his way to or from Washington in 1828. On this occasion he was looking for his White kin.* Apparently Sequoyah thought his father was named Nathaniel Gist. But what if he was seeking the *WRONG* Nathaniel?

### The Cherokee Phoenix and Other Writings

There are many who claim Sequoyah was just 1/4th Cherokee Indian. However those who knew him personally say he looked full blood Cherokee. Some suggest he had NO White blood. The truth is probably in between. He had some White blood, probably ranging between ½ and 3/4ths Cherokee. Dad once bought a small book "The Mysteries of Sequoyah, Centennial Edition" written by C. W. "Dub" West. The author signed it for him. This was a hard cover, "special edition" of 1776. His copy says "387 of 1000 copies". So I know at one time Dad was interested in the family stories. West explores all the contradictions. Some put his birth about 1760 and others at 1775-7. As for Sequoyah's mother, every researcher except one, Mooney, say his mother was a full-blood – Capt. John Stuart, Jack Kilpatrick and others, they all agree. Mooney is the only researcher that says Sequoyah's mother was a Watts. But when reading other researchers, they all say his mother was full-blood Cherokee. Alice Marriott says his mother was Wut-tee and her brothers were Tahn-yan-tah-hee and Tahlonleeska. Mr. Payne who lived near Sequoyah said his grandfather on his mother's side was Shawnee. So just who were his parents? If people only read Mooney they will get one opinion saying she was a "Watts", but EVERY OTHER Sequoyah researcher – and there are about a dozen of them — rejects this notion!

From "Chronicles of Oklahoma, Volume 11, No. 1, March, 1933, CAPTAIN JOHN STUART'S SKETCH OF THE INDIANS", By GRANT FOREMAN we have the following:

*The Arkansas Gazette for June, 1837* carried the following advertisement:

*"Just published and for sale at office of Arkansas Gazette **'Sketch of the Cherokee and Choctaw Indians,'** by John Stuart, Captain U. S. Army, price 37 ½c."*

Grant Foreman then quotes from this 1837 article by Stuart, as recorded by the Arkansas Gazette:

*"George Guess, the inventor of the Cherokee alphabet, is a man of about sixty years of age. He is of a middle stature, and of rather a slender form, and is slightly lame in one leg, from disease when young. His features are remarkably regular, and his face well formed, and rather handsome. His eyes are animated and piercing, showing indications of a brilliancy of intellect far superior to the ordinary portion of his fellow men. His manner is agreeable, and his deportment gentlemanly. He possesses a mild disposition, and is patient, but is energetic and extremely persevering and determined in the pursuit or accomplishment of any object on which he may fix his mind. He is inquisitive, and appears to be exceedingly desirous of acquiring information on all subjects. His mind seems to soar high and wide; and if he could have had the advantages of an enlightened education, he would no doubt have brought himself to rank high among the acknowledged great men of the age in which he lives. He has been in the habit, ever since he could apply his language in that way, of keeping a journal of all the passing events which he considered worthy of record: and has, at this time, (it is said), quite a volume of such matter.*

*"**His connection in blood with the whites, is on the side of the father. His mother was a fullblood Cherokee; and he was raised entirely among the uncultivated portion of the Cherokees, and never received much, if any, advantage from an intercourse with the whites. He does not speak one word of the English language**.* [Vance's note: when this was written, Sequoyah was still alive and lived only a few miles from the Arkansas border. The

129

author, Capt. John Stuart, had personally met him.] *From a very early age, he has possessed a natural talent for drawing, and very far surpasses any man in his nation in that art; but he never received any kind of instruction from any practical artist. He can draw a horse, hog, deer, &c. remarkably well; and no man in the United States can surpass him in drawing a buffalo. He can also draw rough portraits, a circumstance which, connected with his fondness for drawing, contributed very much toward inducing him to attempt the formation of a type for his language.*

*"Mr. Guess, when engaged in the very laudable purpose of inventing his alphabet, had to encounter many very serious obstacles, and which but few men would have surmounted. No one had the least confidence in the success of his project, and thought him to be laboring under a species of mental derangement on that subject. He was laughed at by all who knew him, and was earnestly besought by every member of his own family to abandon a project which was occupying and diverting so much of his time from the important and essential duties which he owed to his family—they being, in some measure, dependent on his daily labor for their subsistence. But no argument or solicitation could induce him to change his determination. And although he was under the necessity of working much at night, by lights made from burning pine, he persisted until he accomplished fully the object of his desire. Even after he had completed the alphabet, and the art of applying it to writing, and when he was fully able to write anything that he might wish, and when he made records in books, and kept a running book account of his monied transactions, &c.— even then, it was with great difficulty that he could induce the members of his own family to believe that it was anything more than a wild delusion. At length, however, he prevailed upon one of his young daughters to learn of him his newly invented alphabet, and its arrangement, she being the only one of his family, and in fact the only person, he could prevail on to undertake the supposed useless task. She made rapid progress in learning, and soon became able to write and read with ease and fluency anything the father would write. This began to open the eyes of the family and of some of the neighbors, but did not prove to be entirely satisfactory. A meeting, therefore, was held, of the people, on the subject, and by separating the father and daughter, and requiring them to write, as dictated to, by the company, and to read, while separated, the writing of each as dictated to them by others, and that being accordingly done in every instance, led the persons present into a full conviction of the truth, as well as the utility, of the invention. And several of the most influential men in the nation immediately learned it, and discovering all its practical advantages, recommended it in high terms to the*

*people. From that time it spread into a general use; and the people of the nation are at this day in the full enjoyment of its great benefits.*

*"George Guess, in forming an alphabet for the Cherokee language, found that eighty-six distinct characters would be necessary. To make so many distinct figures differing so much in their shape, as to be easily distinguished from each other, and, at the same time, to be easily and quickly made with a pen on paper, was a matter of much difficulty. But, being one day on a public road, he found a piece of newspaper, which had been thrown aside by a traveler, which he took up, and, on examining it, found characters on it that would be more easily made than his own, and consequently picked out for that purpose the largest of them, which happened to be the Roman letters, and adopted them in lieu of so many of his own characters—and that, too, without knowing the English name or meaning of a single one of them. This is to show the cause and manner of the Roman letters being adopted."*

The only other record of his parents made while he was alive was in by the Cherokee themselves was in the Cherokee Phoenix, part of which is quoted below. I have the entire article in Appendix 1, and the end of this report.

## Cherokee Phoenix; Invention of the Cherokee Alphabet

This was written in 1828 by an acquaintance of Sequoyah's, a Cherokee. It was published in the Cherokee Phoenix in both English and in Sequoyah's own syllabry. He was still alive at the time and he was a reader of every issue of the Cherokee Phoenix. Had he disagreed what was said about his family, don't you think he would have responded to it? It says that although he appeared to be full blood Cherokee, his paternal grandpa was a White man.

## Sequoyah - according to an acquaintance

*CHEROKEE PHOENIX Wednesday August 13, 1828 Volume 1 No. 24 Page 2 Col. 1a-2a*

### INVENTION OF THE CHEROKEE ALPHABET

*Mr. Editor- The following statement respecting the invention of the Cherokee Alphabet, may not be altogether uninteresting to some of your readers. I have it from a particular friend of Mr. Guess, who lived near him at the time he made his invention.*

**Mr. Guess is in appearance and habits, a full Cherokee, though his grandfather on his father's side was a white man. He has no knowledge of any language but the Cherokee,** *consequently, in his invention of the alphabet, he had to depend entirely on his own native*

131

*resources. He was led to think on the subject of writing the Cherokee language by a conversation which took place one evening at Sauta. Some young men were making remarks on the superior talents of the white people. One said, that white men could put a talk on paper, and send it to any distance, and it would be understood by those who received it. They all agreed, that this was very strange, and they could not see how it could be done. Mr. Guess, after silently listening to their conversation for a while, raised himself, and putting on an air of importance, said, "you are all fools; why the thing is very easy; I can do it myself:" and, picking up a flat stone, he commenced scratching on it with a pin; and after a few minutes read to them a sentence, which he had written by making a mark for each word. This produced a laugh and the conversation on that subject ended. But the inventive powers of Guess's mind were now roused to action; and nothing short of being able to write the Cherokee language, would satisfy him- He went home, purchased materials, and sat down to paint the Cherokee language on paper. He at first thought of no way, but to make a character for each word. He pursued this plan for about a year; in which time he had made several thousand characters. He was then convinced that the object was not attainable in that way: but he was not discouraged. He firmly believed, that there was some way in which the Cherokee language would be expressed on paper, as well as the English: and, after trying several other methods, he at length conceived the idea of dividing the words into parts. He had not proceeded far on this plan, before he found, to his great satisfaction, that the same characters would apply, in different words, and the number of characters would be comparatively few. After putting down, and learning all the syllables that he could think of, he would listen to speeches, and whenever a word occurred which had a part, or syllable, in it, which he had not before thought of, he would bear it on his mind, until he had made a character for it. In this way he soon discovered all the syllables in the language. In forming his characters, he made some use of the English letters, as he found them in a spelling book, which he had in his possession. After commencing upon the last mentioned plan, I believe he completed his system in about a month.*

*During the time he was occupied in inventing the alphabet, he was strenuously opposed by all his friends and neighbors (sic). He was frequently told that he was throwing away his time and labor (sic), and that none but a delirious person, or an idiot, would do as he did. But this did not discourage him. He would listen to the expostulations of his friends, and then deliberately light his pipe, pull his spectacles over his eyes, and sit down to his work, without attempting to vindicate his conduct. After completing his system, he found much difficulty in persuading the people to learn it.- Nor could he succeed, until he went to*

132

*the Arkansas and taught a few persons there, one of whom wrote a letter to some of his friends in the Nation, and sent it by Mr. Guess, who read it to the people. This letter excited much curiosity. Here was a talk in the Cherokee language, which had come all the way from the Arkansas sealed up in paper, and yet it was very plain. This convinced many that Mr. Guess' mode of writing would be of some use. Several persons immediately determined to try to learn. They succeeded in a few days, and from this it quickly spread all over the nation, and the Cherokees ( who as a people had always been illiterate,) were in the course of a few months, without school, or expense of time, or money, able to read and write in their own language.*

*This astonishing discovery certainly entitles Mr. Guess to the warmest gratitude of his country; and, should the Cherokee language continue to be spoken, his fame will be handed down to the latest posterity.-*
*G. C.*

## From the Cherokee Nation's Official Website

The following was taken straight off of the web page of the Cherokee Nation of Oklahoma where they speak of Sequoyah and the Syllabry.

*Family tradition tells us that Sequoyah (S-si-qua-ya) was born west of Chillhowee Mountain, which is approximately one and a half miles east of Tasgigi, Monroe County, Tennessee. This location is only about 8 miles from Echota, the capital of the old Cherokee Nation. As far as his birth year, the best estimation is from 1760 to 1765. Sequoyah stated that when an Iroquoian Peace Delegation visited at New Echota in 1770, he was living with his mother as a small boy and remembered the events. While in Washington in 1828, he told Samuel Knapp he was about 65.*

*As the traditional Cherokee society is matrilineal, and one's clan is obtained through the mother, this information is of most relevance when researching the man's history and background. **Her name was Wu-te-he, and she belonged to the Red Paint Clan. She had two brothers, Tahlonteeska and Tahnoyanteehee. The only certain information regarding his father is a statement made during Sequoyah's lifetime about his father, which appeared in the Cherokee Phoenix (August 13, 1828). This stated his paternal grandfather was a white man. Sequoyah's father was half Cherokee and his mother a full blood.** His father's name has been identified as either George Gist, a German peddler, or Nathaniel Gist, a friend of George Washington's and ancestor of the Blair family of Washington, D.C. Sequoyah also had at least two brothers; one was named Tobacco Will who was a blacksmith* *in Arkansas and also a signer of the Cherokee Constitution. The Old Settler Chief, Dutch (U-ge-we-le-dv), was another brother.*

*Copyright ©1998-2002. Cherokee Nation. All rights reserved.*

So according to the Cherokee themselves, Sequoyah had a little White blood, but not much. His mother was a full blood. His mother was Wut-tee or Wu-te-he, and his father was either Nathaniel Gist or a German peddler named George Gist. The truth about his parentage is we really don't know much about them. Some said he was a Baptist Minister but the people who personally knew him said he wasn't even a Christian. There are so many contradictions.

And about Captain Dutch being his brother – we have
http://digital.library.okstate.edu/chronicles/v009/v009p233.html
Chronicles of Oklahoma, Volume 9, No. 3, September, 1931, THE CHEROKEE WAR PATH, With Annotations, By Carolyn Thomas Foreman

The Cherokee War Path, Written by John Ridge in Washington City as Narrated by the Cherokee Warrior of Arkansas, John Smith who was present and principal actor in the Warlike Expeditions in the Pararies of the Far West. March 25th, 1836. It says:

*The Cherokees are divided into 7 clans; each clan having a peculiar name, & are considered one family & are not permitted to intermarry in their own clan under the penalty of death. It is an ancient, civil institution of our forefathers.* **The names of these clans are the Wolf, the Deer, the Paint, the Blind Savana, the Green Holley, with the sharp thorney leaf, The Long Flowing Down Hair, and the Deaf. The last of these is mine & that of Dutch—we are brothers.**

Sequoyah's mother (and thus Sequoyah) was said to be Paint Clan. Dutch and Sequoyah have different clans! This means they have different mothers. The only way we can have them being brothers is if they had the same father. As I have said before and will continue to say, there are many contradictions.

# CHAPTER 5 THE BROWN'S

## A. Lawrence County, Alabama

We know less about our Brown's than any other surname. Part of the reason for this is that there are so many John Brown's. Which John Brown belongs with which family? We still have much work to do. A mixed-race Joiner married into our family and they seem to be related to the Joiner's mentioned below. As I said, we still have much work to do on our Brown's.

Here is what we have on our Brown's in Alabama. John Brown married Polly Black Dec 23, 1820 in Lawrence County, Alabama.

This marriage is found in early Lawrence County, Alabama marriage records. John Brown's family is still in Lawrence County in 1830.

1830 census Lawrence County, Alabama

John Brown 100001, 010001 ⇔ John Brown, 30-40, Mary 30-40, 1 daughter 5-10, 1 son 0-5. They live near the Emanuel McNutt household where John's son, David's future wife lives. There is also a William McNutt nearby. Is he Emanue's father? There is also the head of a household named "David Black" living nearby as well, perhaps his wife's relations.

By 1840 they are on Walker County, Alabama's census. On 1847 tax records John Brown is still alive. A second John Brown is already deceased and his wife Hannah is mentioned. David Brown was on the same 1847 tax records. So after marrying Harriet in Shelby County, Tn (the Memphis area), he has returned to the place of his birth. Marriage problems? Did she go with him? They had no children during those years. Perhaps we will never know. By 1850 census, my John's widow Mary is head of household in Walker County, Alabama, so he seems to have died between 1847 and 1850. Nothing is known of him before his marriage to "Polly" [Mary] Black. There was a "Brown's Ferry" on the Lawrence/Limestone county lines across the Tennessee River. Melton's Bluff is nearby. We have Gist relations who knew Jason Cloud, who knew the John Brown of *the other* Brown's Ferry near what is today Chattanooga, Tennessee. But we have hit dead ends at this point. Maybe one day we will find more. Once we thought it was impossible to discover our branch of the Gist's, but we have with the help of others. Maybe what is needed is for all the Brown's to get together and compare notes. Perhaps something else. Maybe we'll never know.

There are two other Brown's on the 1840 census of Walker County within three houses of our John. They are Coleman Brown 10001, 10001 and William Brown 00010001, 0000001. There was also an elderly John Brown in 1830 census, between 60-70 years old, of Walker County, Alabama. Perhaps he was John's father, and when he passed on, John took over his property. Unfortunately I understand old records have been lost for that county. I already have provided the census records for 1850 in an earlier section, for Mary and the family.

David Brown married Harriet Guess in 1841 in Shelby County, Tennessee per Shelby County records. Why Shelby County? David Brown's Tax Records show him in 1847 Walker County, Alabama where his family lived, and where Harriet's family had lived previously. In 1848 he is on tax records of Lawrence County, Arkansas. David and Harriet [Guess/Gist] Brown have NO children until after they appear in Arkansas. They were married in 1841 in Shelby County, Tennessee, but he apparently went back to Alabama. We may never know what happened. After he goes to Arkansas she is with him and they have 4 children after that.

In "Warrior Mountain Folklore" by Ricky Butch Walker, on page 10, we have:

*. . . the Cherokee people began a massive movement into North Alabama . . . the Cherokee . . . moved into present day Lawrence County during the 1770s. . . .*

*The Cherokees established towns in Lawrence County at Brown's Ferry, (Moneetown), Melton's Bluff, Courtland,, and the mouth of Town Creek. Doublehead established a village near the mouth of Blue Water Creek in Lauderdale County.*

His whole book is about the Indian families of Lawrence, Winston, and Walker Counties in Alabama. Some of the surnames however, are Eastern Siouan (Riddle, Minor), so I wonder. There is a state recognized Cherokee Tribe called "Echota Cherokee" found in these three counties. Apparently some mixed-race families were not removed from the region in the 1830s. And my family lived right there, as well – my Gist's, Brown's, McNutt's, Havens', Smith's – all were right there.

## A Little More about the Brown's of Walker County, Alabama

1830 Walker County, Alabama

Richard Guest 21001, 200001 ⇔ 2 males and 2 females under 5, 1 male 20-30, 1 female 30-40.

Nancy Guest 01,001001 ⇔ 1 male 5-10, 1 female 10-15, 1 female 30-40. (divorced wife of Thomas Gist. He disappears while she goes on to northwestern Tennessee, after marrying a Rickley male).

1830 census, Walker Co, Alabama

(2nd name on the page)
William Brown 002100001,000000001 ⇔ 2 males 10-15, 1 male 15-20, 1 male 60-70; 1 female 60-70

(4th name on the page)
Christopher Guest 10001, 11001 ⇔ 1 male and 1 female under 5, 1 female 5-10. 1 male and 1 female 20-30.

(7th name on the page)
John Brown 111000001, 2112001 ⇔1 male under 5, 5-10, and 1 male 60-70; and 10-15, 2 females under 5, 1 female 5-10, 10-15, 2 females 15-20, 1 female 40-50
   1840 Walker County, Alabama
   Christopher Gist  111001, 00001 ⇔ 1 son under 5, 5-10, 10-15, 1 male 30-40; 1 female 20-30
   1840 Walker County, Alabama
   William Brown 00010001, 0000001 ⇔ 1 male 15-20, 1 male 50-60; 1 female 40-50
   Coleman Brown 10001,10001 ⇔ 1 male and female under 5, 1 male and 1 female 20-30.

(2 names later)
**John Brown 10120001, 0110101 ⇔ 1 male under 5, 1 female 5-10, 1 male and female, 10-15, 2 males 15-20. ⇔ mine**
   The elder John and William Brown's on the 1830 census are gone by 1840, and there is a younger William and John Brown in their place, and they are still living near Christopher Gist, making it appear that a younger generation has moved into their parent's old place.
**1840's Walker County Tax Record, Cerca 1847**
   http://www.rootsweb.ancestry.com/~alwalker/1840TaxRecord.htm
   William Robins, Collector.  circa 1847.
   (Contributed by Peter J. Gossett, Winston County ALGENWEB and Barbara Dunn)
   Beat 3; Thomas Brown, William Brown, <u>David Brown</u> ⇔ [my g-g-grandpa]
   Beat 4; Isaac Brown, Isaac Brown, Agt. for William Looney
   Beat 5; Jarret Brown, James Brown, William Brown - 1 slave
   Beat 7; Russel Brown, Hannah Brown [her husband was said to be Cherokee, and was also named John Brown], Hugh Brown, Agt. for David Wolf & Gibson Wolf [There is a grave saying Hugh Brown was the father of  John Brown]
   Beat 9; N.M. Brown
   Beat 11; Allen Brown, Est. of J.M. Brown [Is this John Brown, husband of Hannah?]

Beat 12; William Brown
Beat 13; **John Brown** ⇔ **[MINE, David's father]**, William Brown

## Other Brown's

I can't stop without mentioning another bunch of Brown's living in the same general area. There was another John Brown living in the area. Mine arrived about 1820 at least, but other Brown's showed up a little later. My family left Alabama for Arkansas and Oklahoma, but it is my understanding that these other Brown's remain in North Central Alabama to this day.

In my research, at first when I came upon them I heard they were claiming Cherokee heritage. At first I was elated. The more I read about them, the more I realized they were *not* talking about my Brown's. Their John Brown had married Hannah Rice, mine had married Polly/Mary Black. Then for a time I started to thinking this other family was claiming the heritage of my family! Who were these usurpers! They are descendants of John Brown and his wife, Hannah Rice. Hannah is mentioned in that 1847 tax list as though her husband had just passed on. My John is still alive and is listed in those 1847 tax records, but his wife, Mary is head of household in the 1850 census, making me think he died between 1847 and 1850. The fact that the 2 John Brown's died only a few years apart also makes researching them a difficult task.

These other Brown's also seem to have Indian blood. They have a lineage that goes back to the Guion Miller rejected rolls. Mine don't go back to the rolls as I know my great-grandparents never applied. Family story says they thought about it, but "something" happened, they got discouraged or angry, I don't know. But they changed their mind and never applied. We don't know why.

There is an old grave in Winston County, Alabama and it says that John Brown was the son of Hugh Brown. Their Brown's do have a lot of "Hugh Brown's" in their line, so I don't think that John who was son of Hugh, is mine. I was so hoping it was mine! But he is their's, and a clue for them.

I have also thought of the Catawba. There were Catawba Brown's, also. There is a record the Catawba have that several hundred of them were adopted into the Cherokee Nation. I have never seen a Cherokee record of these adoptions. Maybe that is the real reason why so many are on the rejected rolls – not because they are not Indian, but rather because they are not Cherokee. Are the descendants of the other Brown's actually Catawba? Are mine? See Appendix 2 at the end of this report. It speaks of a Catawba saying many Catawba moved in with the Cherokee just before or after removal of the late 1830s. Maybe these Catawba "thought" they were being adapted into the tribe when in reality they just moved near them as neighbors.

I don't hold any animosity towards those other Brown's. I'm over it. ☺ Those families are just trying to do the same thing I am – discover their roots. Maybe the two John Browns are related. I think we go back to one or perhaps both Brown's Ferry's. We have evidence but not proof. I want to be a good researcher and not just make claims I can't back up emperically. That's my burden. I wish the other Brown's my best and hope one day maybe we can untangle this mess. Maybe if my Brown's had signed up for Dawes we would know the connection (if there was one) to those other Brown's. There are just too many John Brown's, too many unanswered questions.

## B. Hartwell H. Houston and the Joi(y)ners

Please denote in the following, the surname "Joiner/Joyner" and the relationship to Cherokee John Brown of Hamilton County, Tennessee. I copied and pasted this from the internet. Someone calling themselves "Bright Star" had placed it online – yeah, I know . . . but the material seemed of interest to my family. I have explained it near the end of this report.

*Freedmen Project—Miller app # 17703— Hartwell Houston, Joynar, Brown, Allison, Thompson, Turtina, Davies, Russian, Joiner*

*PLEASE NOTE ALL RESPONSES TO QUESTION ARE IN CAPS.*

*Below are the questions asked on the Miller Applications I have sent you info on in the Freedmen Project work. I hope to get at least one a week submitted. For those of you who cannot afford these NARA applications, I would advise that after you confirm it is your line, that you send for the packet, for source proof. Remember genealogy is nothing without documentation.*

*Application #—17703*
*Action Taken—REJECT*
*Name of applicant— HARTWELL H. HOUSTON*
*No. of children—*
*Residence—ROLAND, OKLA.*
*Reason—-APPLICANT BORN IN 1834 BUT DOES NOT APPEAR ON EITHER 35 OR 57 ROLL. NOT AN ANCESTOR THROUGH WHOM APPLICANT CLAIMS APPEARS*

*ON ANY ROLL. THE ANCESTERS IT APPEARS WERE NOT PARTIES TO THE MONIES ON 35-36. APPLICANT WAS A SLAVE. MISC.LIST,P,2883*

    *Second Note: OKLA.-FIELD*
*#17703*
*HARWELL HOUSTON*
*with #-SALLISAW*
*Remarks— 28725-6,31299*
*FIELDS, OKLA.*
    *UNABLE TO LOCATE ANCESTERS OF APPLICANT ON ROLL WITH ANY DEGREE OF CERTAINTY.*
    *ROLAND SPECIAL COMMISSIONER of the COURT of CLAIMS,601 Ouray Building, Washington D.C.*

    *Sir, I hereby make application for such share as may be due me of the fund appropriated by the ACT of CONGRESS, approved June 30, 1906, in accordance with the decrees of the COURT of CLAIMS of May 18,1905, and May28, 1906, in favor of the Eastern Cherokees. The evidence of identity is herewith subjoined. Note: Answers to all questions should be short, but complete. If you cannot answer, so state.*


*Question # 1) State full name:*
*English name-HARTWELL H. HOUSTON*
*Indian name-*
*#2) Residence —ROLAND, INDIAN TERRITORY*
*#3) Town and Post Office—ROLAND, INDIAN TERRITORY*
*#4) County — DISTRICT NUMBER ELEVEN*
*#5) State—INDIAN TERRITORY*
*#6) Date and place of birth?—ASHVILLA, NC-JUNE 23 ,1834*
*#7) **By what right do you claim to share? If you claim through more than one relative living in 1851, set forth each separately: JOHN BROWN OF HAMILTON COUNTY, TENNESSEE***
*#8) Are you married?—YES*
*#9) **Name and age of wife or husband——NARCISSUS HOUSTON, AGE 63***
*#10) Give names of your father and mother, and your mother's maiden name before marriage.*
*Father- English name—-*
***Indian name—ALMON JOYNAR***
***Mother- English name—ANNA BROWN MARRIED ALMON JOYNAR***

*Indian name—-*
*Maiden name—ANNA BROWN*
*#11) Where were they born?*
*Father- NORTH CAROLINA*
*Mother—NORTH CAROLINA*
*#12) Where did they reside in 1851, if living at this time?*
*Father—TENNESSEE*
*Mother—TENNESSEE*
*#13) Date of death of your father and mother:*
*Father—JULY 11,1880*
*Mother—NOV.21,1880*
*Page 3-*
*#14) Were they ever enrolled for money, annuities, land, or other benefits? If so, state when and where.*
*I DO NOT KNOW, CANT ASCARTAIN*
*#15) Name all your brothers and sisters, giving ages, and residence if possible.*
*Name: ELLAN ALLISON*
*dob: DON'T KNOW*
*dod; DEC.24,1894*
*Name: PHILLIP JOYNAR*
*dob: DON'T KNOW*
*dod; DON'T KNOW*
*Name: ISAAC THOMPSON*
*dob: DON'T KNOW*
*dod; DON'T KNOW*
*Name: ELIZABETH TURNTINA*
*dob: DON'T KNOW*
*dod; DON'T KNOW*
*Name: WINNIE DAVIS*
*dob: DON'T KNOW*
*dod; DON'T KNOW*
*Name: RUTHIE RUSSIAN*
*dob: DON'T KNOW*
*dod; DON'T KNOW*
*#16) State English name and Indian names of your grandparents on both father's and mother's side, if possible.*
**Father's side:—BILLY JOYNAR,  BATTIA JOYNAR**
**Mother's side:—JOHN BROWN, WINNIE BROWN**
*#17) Where were they born?*

*Father's side:— DON'T KNOW*

*Mother's side;— DON'T KNOW*

**#18) Where did they reside in 1851, if living at that time?—GRANDPARENTS ON MOTHER'S SIDE RESIDED AT LOOKOUT VALLEY,HAMILTON COUNTY, TENN.**

**#19) Give names of all their children, and residence, if possible:**

**English Name:— ANNA BROWN, MY MOTHER & JAMIMA BROWN**

*Indian Name:—*

*Residence:—DIED NOV. 21,1880*

**English Name :— JAMIMA BROWN**

*Indian Name:—*

**Residence:—DIED IN TENNESSEE, ABOUT 1846**

**English Name :— ALFRED BROWN**

*Indian Name:—*

**Residence: — DIED IN TENNESSEE ABOUT 1842—TO1846**

**English Name:—ABRAHAM JOYNAR**

*Indian Name:—*

**Residence: — DONT KNOW ANYTING ABOUT HIS DEATH**

**English Name:—ALMOND JOYNAR**

*Indian Name:—*

**Residence: — DIED IN BEDFORD COUNTY, TENNESSEE**

*#20) Have you ever been enrolled for money, annuities, land, or other benefits? If so, state when and where ,and with what tribe of Indians.—-NO*

*#21) To expedite identification, claimant should give the full English and Indian names, if possible, of their paternal and maternal ancestors back to 1835.——-DON'T KNOW*

*Remarks- Section)*

Under this head the applicant may give any additional facts which will assist in providing his claim.—-I SAW JOHN BROWN TWICE. BOTH TIMES HE OWNED ME AS BEING HIS GRANDCHILD. MY FATHER OFTEN WENT TO SEE HIM. THE LAST TIME I SAW HIM .HE WAS ON HIS WAY BACK FROM GETTING A PAYMENT IN THE INDIAN TERRITORY AT FT.GIBSON AND HE GAVE MY MOTHER MONEY.

**Legal Section**

Note: Answers should be brief but explicit; the words "yes", "no", "unknown" etc., may be used in cases where applicable. Read the questions carefully.  I solemnly swear that the forgoing statements made by me are true to the best of my knowledge and belief. Signature—-HARTWELL H. HOUSTON

Subscribed and sworn to before me this 28TH day of FEBRUARY, 1917.

Notary Public- signature— W.H. DUUBLAJIES

*My commission expires: JULY 6, 1908*

*Affidavit) (The following affidavit must be sworn to by two or more witnesses, who are well acquainted with the applicant.) Personally appeared before me W.H.JACOBS and J.M.WOOD, who being duly sworn, on oath depose and say they are well acquainted with HARTWELL H. HOUSTON who makes the foregoing application and statements, and have known HIM for 15 years and 24 years, respectively, and know HIM to be the identical person WHO represents HIMSELF to be, and that the statements made by HIM are true, to the best of their knowledge and belief, and they have no interest whatever in HIS claim. Witnesses to mark-BLANK Signatures of witnesses—W.H.JACOBS, J. M. WOOD*

*Subscribed and sworn to me, before me this 28TH day of FEBUARY, 1917.*

*Notary signature—-W.H. DUUBLAJIES*

*Notary commission expires—-JULY 6TH, 1908*

*NOTE: Affidavits should be made, whenever practicable, before a notary public, or clerk of the court, if sworn to before an Indian agent or disbursing agent of the Indian service, it need not be before a notary, etc.*

*BRIGHTSTAR'S PERSONAL NOTE: Pages after that include letters written to the BIA about their claim. Some have additional papers, others do not. ADDITIONAL PAPERS WITH THIS APPLICATION ARE;*

*Add; Letter—#1*

*No.17703*

*Hartwell Houston, being duly sworn, deposes and says; MY NAME IS HARTWELL H. HOUSTON: MY POST-OFFICE IS ROLAND,OKLA.,BOX 32; I WAS BORN IN ASHEVILLE, N.C. IN 1834; I CLAIM RELATIONSHIP TO THE CHEROKEE INDIANS THROUGH MY MOTHER, WHOSE MAIDEN NAME WAS ANNA BROWN; HER NAME AFTER MARRIAGE ANNA JOINER; MY MOTHER WAS UNDER THE GUARDIANSHIP OF BETSY MOSS AND WHEN SHE DIED BETSY MOSS DIED AND WE WENT TO THE GUARDIANSHIP OF HER CHILDREN,*

*AND I WENT TO M.F.NEIL; I WENT TO THE WAR FROM N.F.NEIL; WHEN I CAN FIRST REMEMBER WAS LIVING IN BEDFORD CO.,TENN. I WAS THEN ABOUT FOUR YEARS OLD. I WAS HELD TO SERVICE UNTIL THE WAR BROKE OUT; MY MOTHER WAS A HALF-BLOOD INDIAN; SHE NEVER CAME TO THIS COUNTRY; I AM NOT ON THE FINAL ROLLS OF THE DAWES COMMISSION; JOHN BROWN WAS THE NAME OF THE INDIAN WHO WAS MY GRAND-FATHER AND MY GRAND-MOTHER WAS A NEGRO WOMAN.*

Signed; HARTWELL H. HOUSTON

Subscribed and sworn to before me this 17th day of Sept., 1908 at Sallisaw, Okla.
Signed— Guion Miller Special Commissioner of Court of Claims 2883
Add: Letter #2
MARCH 16TH, 1908
ANSWER- I HAVE MADE THE SAME PROOF TO THE COMMISSION AS I HAVE
MADE TO YOU  BUT THEY FAILED I HAD EX CHIEF JOHN ROSS WHO KNEW ME ALL
MY LIFE AND WHO MADE IN HIS AFFIDAVIT THAT BROWN OWNED X WINNIE
CHILDREN AS HIS BY BLOOD I CLAIM MY CHEROKEE BY MOTHER MY FATHER
BLOOD WAS CROSSED BY CREEK AND CHEROKEE I WAS SO INFORMED THE
GUARDIAN OF MOTHER MRS BETSY MOSE HER OLDEST SON WAS A SOLDIER IN
WAR OF 1812 & HAVING AN OFFICER BY THE WELL KNOWN SAMUEL HOUSTON HE
WANTED MY NAME CALL THAT AND I GIVE THAT NAME WITH MY OTHER NAMES
BY SOME MISTAKE BY THE —-i—- THAT ENROLL ME IN THE ARMY WHEN I NOTICE
HIM CALLING ME CORPL HOUSTON HE TOLD ME THE PAPERS HAD BEEN SENT TO
WASHINGTON D.C. **MY MOTHER SAID MR HENDERSON ENROLLED THEM BY
NUMBER AND SHE WAS ONE OF THE HALF BREEDS I AFFILIATED WITH MY
FATHER AS SON  I FOUND A COUSIN OF THE CREEK NATION BY THE NAME
OF BILLY JOYNER WHICH HE IS NOW DEAD HE TOLD ME ... PARENT,S CAME
FROM NORTH CAROLINA AND HIS GRANDPARENTS NAMES THAT I KNOW
THAT FATHER GIVE ME & HE CLAIMS ALMON AS HIS UNCE I KNOW NOT
ANYTHING ABOUT BROWN'S PARENT'S. BUT THE JOHN BROWN GRAND
FATHER WAS ENROLLED ON THE 25TH DAY OF SEPT. 1835 IN LOOKOUT
VALLEY, HAMILTON COUNTY TENN. I THINK HE DIED THERE, OR AT LEAST I
HEARD THAT IN 1858. I SAW GRANDFATHER TWICE ABOUT MY 4 YEARS OLD.
WHEN I WAS 17 OR 18 YEARS OF AGE HE HAD WITH HIM 2 SISTERS. SALLIE
BROWN, I DONT REMEMBER THE OTHER NAME, I THINK NANCY WAS THE
NAME SHE WAS CALLED IS MY REMEMBERANCE AS I WAS HELD UNDER
GUARDIAN. I WAS NOT TREATED AS A SLAVE.** I WAS TREATED WELL & NO
OVERSEER, NO ONE EXCEPT SOLDIER SON WHO TAKEN MOTHER PLACE. MOTHER
AND FATHER HAD NO GUARDIAN.  MOTHER GUARDIAN WAS A WHITE LADY & SHE
TAUGHT HER T..... AND WRITE & SHE TAUGHT ME WHAT SHE COULD UP TO MY 12
YEARS. YOU ASK ME TO STATE WHY I HAD NEVER BEEN ON ANY CHEROKEE ROLL
BEFORE THE WAR. WAS WITH THE INDIANS NOT VERY OFTEN AND THEN THEY

*WOULD COME TO SEE ME IS THEY HAD TO KEEP CLOST.  THE FIRST DAWES COMMISSION THAT CAME DOWN HERE & GIVE THEM SOME THING NEAR THE SAME EVIDENCE I AM GIVING YOU, ADING EX CHIEF JOHN ROSS, THE WHITE INTER MARRIAGE, IF WE T... HAVE THE NEGRO BLOOD IN US, WOULD AND WILL DO ALL THAT THEY CAN AGAINST ME AND ALL OF THIS LINAGE.  THERE IS A WHITE CITIZEN OF THE INDIAN LIVING IN THIS TOWN, TOLD ME IF I TOLDS THE COMMISSION I WAS A DEMOCRAT THEY WOULD HAVE PUT YOU ON THE ROLLS. I TOLD HIM I WOULD BE LEFT OFF.*

*RESPECTFULLY YOURS, H.H. HOUSTON*

*Add. Letter # 3, 1770,  F.S.T., ROLAND OKLA.  MARCH 18TH,1908*

*MY DEAR ELBA C. KELLER,*

*I THINK I HAVE SAID ALL THAT I CAN THINK AT PRESENT, IT HAS BEEN ALONG TIME SINCE THOSE THINGS HAPPEN. I GIVE THIS EVIDENCE TO THE COMMISSION AS NEAR AS I COULD WITHOUT ANY RECORD BUT THE HEART AND HEAD AND THEN THEY WOULD NOT LET MY NAME ON THE ROLLS AS MEMBER OF THIS NATION. BUT W. R. W. C. KEYS WAS ENROLLED ON THE SAME EVIDENCE OF HIS GRANDFATHER. HE'S SO WHITE I DON'T SEE HOW THE COMMISSIONERS CAN SEE ANY INDIAN ON HIM & CAN'T SEE IT ON ME ,BUT THE INDIANS OFTEN STRANGERS MEET ME AND ASK ME, IS YOU CHEROKEE OR CHOCTAW.*

*HARTWELL H. HOUSTON*

*ROLAND, OKLA.*


*ROLAND OKLA.*

*JUNE 19TH 1909*

*HON COMMISSIONER MILLER, YOUR LETTER RECIEVED AND CAREFULLY READ.  I CANNOT SEE THAT I CAN MAKE THE CASE ANY BETTER BY MAKING A NEW APPLICATION. THE COMMISSIONER OF INDIAN AFFAIRS SENT ME A CARD NO. 17703, ACCEPTING THE APPLICATION. THEN I RECIEVED A LETTER TO HAVE MY CHILDREN AND GRANDCHILDREN PUT ON THE ROLL. I SENT THIS TO LET THEM. THEN THEY COME TO MY HOME, WE WENT TO FORT SMITH ARK, MADE THEIR APPLICATIONS. MY SON P.H. HOUSTON WAS LIVING AT FOSTERVILLE, BEDFORD CO. TENN. AT THE. I HAD HIS APPLICATION MADE & SENT TO HIM WITH INSTRUCTIONS TO PUT HIS CHILDREN & SEND IT IN BY AUG 31TH 1907.*

*HARTWELL H. HOUSTON*

*ROLAND OKLA.*

*IF I UNDERSTAND THIS LETTER IF NOT EXCUSE ME PLEASE & LET ME*
*HEAR FROM YOU AGAIN.*

*PRINCE A. HOUSTON*

*MARY F. HOUSTON*

*LOUISA E. HOUSTON*

*THIS IS THE NAMES ALL MY LEGITIMATE CHILDREN LIVING. I THINK THAT*
*LAWSUIT, SO I SEE THAT I COULD EXCEPT OF THE OMITTED OR IMPROPERLY ........*
*ON THE ROLLS. I DID NOT HAVE ANYTHING TO DO WITH LOUISA, LET A LAWYER*
*HAVE HER CARD, AND SHE SAID THE LAWYER TOLD HER HE HAD LOST IT. SO I*
*KNEW IF ANY ONE GOT ON THE ROLLS IMPROPERLY BY. I AM NOT IT FAULT &*
*HOPE YOU WON'T PUT ON ME, I DID ALL RIGHT TO HAVE THE PAPERS SEN IN*
*AUG 31, 1907. THEY WOULD THOSE THAT DONE GONE & SHOULD BE DEBARED*

So there was a man applying for Cherokee Freedman status named Hartwell. H.
Houston. He says his father was Almon Joyner and his mother was Ann, a daughter of a
slave woman named Winnie and John Brown. What else do we know about the John Brown
who was Cherokee, and lived at Brown's Ferry in what is today Chattanooga, Tennessee?
Well. more about this particular John Brown is found at
http://www.chattanooga.net/fmbnp/timeline2.htm, where it says –

**The Cherokee Tenure**

*Around the time of the American Revolution, the Cherokee moved into the region.*
*Under duress from the emerging Colonial economy, they shifted from a village-based*
*lifestyle to farm-steading, which allowed for individual ownership of 1 square mile (640*
*acres) per head of household. One such property on the Bend was owned by a 1/8 Cherokee*
*named John Brown, who operated the ferry at what is still known as Brown's Ferry.*

So the John Brown who had a daughter named Anna, who was mother to Hartwell,
was mostly White, having little Indian blood. Hartwell's father though, according to
Hartwell, had both Cherokee and Creek blood. So Hartwell was tri-racial. The census record
for Bedford County, Tennessee does include an Almon Joiner in 1850 and 1860, his race in
1860 is listed "M" – meaning mulatto.

## 1850 Marshall County, Mississippi

| | | | | |
|---|---|---|---|---|
| Thomas Joiner | 48 | M | Tn | farmer and minister |
| Elizabeth Joiner | 45 | F | Tn | |
| John T. Joiner | 17 | M | Tn | |
| Martin M. Joiner | 14 | F | Tn | |
| Sarah F. Joiner | 12 | F | Tn | |
| Analisa Joiner | 10 | F | Tn | |
| Helan M. Joiner | 7 | F | Tn | |
| Caroline D. Joiner | 4 | F | Tn | |

Do you remember the marriage on Oct. 11, 1842 of Thomas S. E. Joiner to Cynthia McNutt? Do you remember Cynthia is half-sister to my Harriet [Gist] Brown? If you will look on a map, Marshall County, Mississippi is just south of Shelby County, Tennessee. We have a man named Thomas Joiner in Marshall County, Mississippi who is listed on his census records as being a Minister, and my relative, Cynthia McNutt married a man by that same name a few miles to the north in Shelby County, Tennessee 8 years earlier. Are the 2 Thomas Joiners related? And are they related to the tri-racial families of Joiner's in Bedford County, Tennessee?

Well I saw online where some were asking if anyone knew it there were any Joiners who were Indian. I contacted them including a descendant of this minister. Yes, there was a story/rumor that they had Indian blood. Okay, well they could they be connected to the Joiners in Bedford County, Tennessee. On this score, all I found was one short document. I wouldn't have found it if I hadn't had a lot of Guess/Gist/Guest research material on hand. There is a PDF file online. Here are a few excerpts from it.

*MORDECAI6 YELL (JANE5 GIST, JOSHUA4, NATHANIEL3, RICHARD2, CHRISTOPHER1) was born 01 Aug 1809 in Jefferson County, Tennessee, and died 30 Jan 1897 in Hayes County, Texas. He married LOUISA M SMITH 27 Oct 1845 in Rutersville, Fayette, Texas, and daughter of WILLIAM B SMITH. She was born Abt. 1822, and died Abt. 1865.*

*Notes for MORDECAI YELL:*

*Circuit riding Methodist preacher. Called the "Father of North Texas Methodist Church." Died in Hays County, Texas on 30 January 1897 at age 87. Died at his son's home of pneumonia, contracted from cold while visting son at Chrismas. Buried in Lytton Springs Cemetery, Lytton Springs, Caldwell County, Texas. He was the Father of the original NW for a detailed description of him and how he died.) He was visiting his son and caught pneumonia.*

## Mordecai Yell

*He was the father of this conference, having organized the Springfield District in 1849, when item braced all of our conference territory that had been reclaimed from the Savage. His face has been so long absent from us that many of this body did not know him and few are familiar with his history.* **He was born in Jefferson County, Tennessee, August 1, 1809 and grew to manhood in Bedford County of the same State.** *He was converted at Holts campground under the ministry of Joshua Buther on the 12th day of September, 1830, being twenty-one years and one month old. He was at once appointed class leader under Wiley Ledbetter, preacher in charge.* **He was licensed to preach by Thomas Joiner,** *and admitted on trial into the Tennessee Conference, at Nashville, in 1832, Bishop James O. Andrew, presiding. He was ordained deacon in 1834 by Bishops Soule and McKendree, and elder, in 1836 by Bishop Andrew. When the Tennessee Conference was divided he fell into the Memphis conference, where he served two years on the Pontotoc, and two on the Salem Districts.*

The man above listed as Nathaniel 3 Gist was the father of Joshua, but he was also the father of MY Nathaniel Gist, the one killed at the Battle of Kings Mountain during the Revolutionary War.

It goes on to say Mordecai Yell (a Gist on his mother's side closely related to mine) grew to manhood in Bedford County, Tennessee, he goes on to say Mordecai was licensed to preach in September 1830 by our Thomas Joiner and was transferred to the Memphis Conference. Since he grew to manhood in Bedford County, Tennessee. It says he was transferred to the Memphis Conference — Well apparently so was Thomas Joiner as he was preaching one county to the South of Memphis, in Northern Mississippi's Marshall County by 1850! So all the evidence so far does not contradict that these Joiners are the same that ones that knew the Cherokee Brown's. And my Gist's by family story married the Cherokee Brown's.

## Other Joiners and Carla Davenport's E-mail

As I mentioned earlier, Carla Davenport is the wife of J. L. Davenport, a descendant of my great Aunt Ettie. She wrote this year's before I ever heard of Hartwell H. Houston's freedman application.

148

*Vance,*

*I found this interesting tidbit. Now, I am sure they are Indians and not black as the census states. 1. When asked if they were Indian they probably said no. and they were processed as "colored or black" which I am sure you are already aware of.*

*Anyway, since Harriett has Looney and Joiner I am submitting these for your perusal*
*Knox Co. Tn Subdivision 15*
*William Looney 40 B b. TN*
*Polly 40 B b. TN*
*Abner J. Joiner 16 B b. TN*
*Rebecca J. Joiner 10 B b. TN*
*Sarah E. Joiner 7 B b. TN*
*Next door at the "white" household of Anderson M. Sands is*
*Nelson Joiner 16 B. B. TN*

*I also thought it was interesting that one of the little girls is named Rebecca. I am trying to find the husband of Rebecca Joiner b. 1790 in NC. She has a daughter Pernetta who married Jordan Payne in Shelby Co. TN in 1838 and then removed to Mississippi before 1840. Rebecca and 2 sons are living next door to Jordan and Pernetta. I also did a run down on Rufus Joiner who married Eliza Santina Baird, and find in the Mississippi census a "black" family with a son named Rufus Joiner. Anyway the only other marriage is for Thomas S. E. Joiner who married 1. Mary Fuller in 1838. Mary must have died, but I cannot find where he is in the 1840 census. The same Thomas S. E. Joiner married Cynthia McNutt in 1842. As you know, on 30 September 1843 our Nancy Joiner was born and admitted to the family Bible just as a child of Harriet and David B. Brown. Now, I cannot find Thomas S. E. Joiner and Cynthia ANYWHERE. So, I am wondering are these the parents of our little Nancy Joiner?*

*Carla*

At the time we were emailing, we thought maybe McNutt's or Joiner's had married into the family, but had no idea how. Now that we know Harriet's mother's 3rd husband was a McNutt, well it all falls into place. One branch of these "Black" Joiners, per Hartwell Houston, were really bi or tri-racial – They were Indian, White, and Black! And some of them DID remove to the region near Shelby County, Tennessee.

## C. Two Powell Brown's and The Swetland Rolls

From the Swetland Rolls, 1869

Brown, Cinda 934

Brown, Eliza 1398

Brown, Gabriel, 1402

Brown, John 1401

Brown, Josephine, 1404

Brown, Martha A. 1403

Brown, Narcissa 1400

Brown, Obsiah 932

Brown, Polly 1399

***Brown, Powell 1405***

Brown, Sally 933

Brown, Wash 935

Brown, William Sherman 1406

**This family was also recorded online:**

James Daniel Brown 17 Feb 1816, in Cherokee, NC, d. 25 Dec 1903 Niescoop Prairie, Adair Co, Ok., b. New Hope, Chance, Adair Co., Ok.

Father: Alfred Brown, b. 16 Sep 1790 in NC

Mother: Narcissus Brown, b. 29 Dec 1793 in NC

Marriage 1: Eliza Raper, b. 7 Aug,1827 Cherokee, NC.

Married: 19 May, 1843 in Cherokee, NC.

Children:

Mary A. "Polly" Brown b. 15 Feb 1845, Adair, Cherokee Nation, IT (Ok)

Narcissus Love Brown b. 30 Dec 1849 Cherokee Nation, Tn

John W. Brown. b. 30 Dec 1849. Adair, Cherokee Nation, IT (Ok)

Henry Marshall Brown b. 30 Jan 1854 in Niascoop Prairie, Adair, Cherokee Nation, IT (Ok)

A. Martha Brown b. 16 Apr 1854, Cherokee Nation, IT (Ok)

Josephine Brown, b. 10 Oct 1858, in Cherokee, NC.

Jane S. Brown, b. 1860, Cherokee, NC

James Brown, 20 Oct 1850, Adair, Cherokee Nation, IT (Ok)

Florence Brown, b. May 1, 1871, Niascoop Prairie, Adair, Cherokee Nation, IT (Ok)

***Powell Brown, b. 2 Nov. 1872, Cherokee, NC***

## There was Another Powell Brown

Notice Swetland Rolls, Powell Brown was born in 1872. But there is another Powell Brown, one who lived near my David Brown in Lawrence County, Arkansas.

### 1850 Census Jackson County, Alabama

| | | |
|---|---|---|
| *Powell Brown* | *27* | *Ga* |
| Sarah | 27 | Al |
| John | 9 | Tn |
| Elvira | 8 | Tn |
| Francis | 7 | Tn |
| Mary | 5 | Al |
| Martha | 4 | Al |
| Nancy | 3 | Al |
| George | 1 | Al |

### 1860 Census Lawrence County, Arkansas Brown/Griffith

*Powell Brown*

Sarah Brown

John Brown

David B. Griffith, b. 1811 NC

Catherine Griffith (wife), b. 1811

Amanda Griffith (daughter) b. 1843,

Lucinda Griffith, b. 1847

Oliza Griffith b, 1851,

Mary A. Griffith b. 1854 Ark (actually daughter of Anderson Griffith and Nancy Wayland Griffith)

Josephine Griffith b. 1856 Ark (actually daughter of Anderson Griffith and Nancy Wayland Griffith)

These names are very similar, but not exact. However the odds these names are randomly so similar aren't very high. If it is random, then why are they so similar?

Also this shows these Brown's in Arkansas (who arrived in Arkansas from Northeastern Alabama, and Georgia before that) knew some of my Wayland's in Arkansas – the Nancy Wayland spoken of descended from my William Wayland. Coincidences do occur. I need more info to conclude anything more than that, about these Wayland's and Brown's.

151

But there is a Powell Brown who is a child when there is also an old man in Arkansas by that same name who has Wayland/Griffith children in his household. The child named Powell Brown is on Swetland Rolls. I can't conclude anything more about the Brown's – I wish I could. Add this coincidence with the story of Hartwell H. Houston and his Brown's/Joiner's marrying one of my Gist's, and add that coincidence to the coincidence that Jason Cloud knew my Gist's, and he also knew John Brown of Brown's Ferry, well then we have three coincidences. A series of coincidences with a central theme and pattern eventually ceases to be a coincidence. I don't know if we've reached that threshold or not, though. Probably not, but still.

Oh, before I forget, there was an Alfred Brown mentioned with respect to these Swetland Roll Cherokee. I also have an Alfred.

**The Reservation Roll Brown's**

http://www.accessgenealogy.com/native/rolls/reservation_roll.htm

Several Brown's are on the Reservation Rolls. Each family who signed up for the Reservation Rolls agreed to settle back East in or near the Old Cherokee Nation. Each were to be given 640 acres. There are seven Brown's: *Alexander, James, John, John Sr., John Jr., Polly, and William.* There are a John and a William in Walker County, Alabama living near one another. Old men by those names are alive in 1830, while on the 1840 census younger men, also named John and William, are living in the places of their fathers. We know they are the same because both Coleman Brown and Christopher Gist are close neighbors of them in both the 1830 and 1840 census records. The website above provides a search feature, which is where I obtained the seven names listed. There is a caution, where the website says; *"This is only an index of applicants, the people listed here did not in most instances receive the reservation they requested."* But there are just so many people who claim one or another of these seven, and how can we know which John belongs to which family. More information is supposedly stored at the National Archives in various locations, but I have tried and tried to get information from the National Archives in Fort Worth, and all I have ever gotten is the run around. I have both mailed and emailed them, and called them on the telephone, and they will not make me a copy (for a fee) of the information I ask of them. Why, I don't know. I'll keep trying.

## Two Brown's Ferrys [32 and 33]

That's right, there were two of them. There was the one mentioned above near what is today Chattanooga, Tennessee, run by 1/8th Cherokee John Brown. That is the one everyone knows about. But there was a second Brown's Ferry on the Tennessee River in Northern Alabama, on the border between Limestone and Lawrence Counties. Ricky Butch Walker says in "Warrior Mountain Folklore" (p 11) that *Doublehead's Village was originally located in present day Lawrence County, Alabama at Brown's Ferry and was known locally Moneetown. Moneetown refers to "Big Water Town".* Melton's Bluff is just a few miles down the Tennessee River from Brown's Ferry. Walker says (p 10*) According to Ann Royalle's letter, originating from Melton's Bluff, dated January 14, 1818, the Cherokee Village of Melton's Bluff was established between 1788 and 1793.*Vicki Rozema in "Footspeps of the Cherokee" says virtually the same thing, although I suspect their sources are not independent of one another.

From "Doublehead, Last Chickamauga Cherokee Chief", also by Ricky Butch Walker, p 73, we have the following; *Historical records indicate that Doublehead lived at his Chickamauga Indian town at Brown's Ferry from the 1770s through December 1801. According to "History of Alabama by Albert James Picket (1851), "Dec. 1801: Emigrants flocked to the Mississippi Territory . . . constructing flat boats at Knoxville, they floated down the river to the head of the Muscle Shoals, where they disembarked at the house of Double-Head, a (p 74) Cherokee Chief." . . .From Doublehead's town, the Emigrants followed the Brown's Ferry Road to Gourd's Settlement (Courtland, Alabama) where it intersected with Gaine's Trace.*

And I remember as I read this, what was said of Jason Cloud of Ridenhour's "Land of the Lake," mentioned earlier — p. 34 — *Captain Cloud was active in the flatboat trade down the [Tennessee] river and was associated with the small group of men who played an important part in the settlement of the Mississippi River Valley.* Bingo! Cloud was a flat boat captain, and these settlers constructed flatboats at Knoxville (where our mixed-blood Aron Gist was hung, also late in 1801). Jason Cloud knew John Brown, and here we have flatboats landing at the second of the two Brown's Ferry's, in Lawrence County, Alabama, which is the county where OUR John Brown married in 1820, and where our Gist's are first mentioned in 1818. Per the historic record, these settlers disembarked at the house of Doublehead! Jason Cloud seems to have known Doublehead, as well. John Chisholm, grandfather of Jessee Chisolm for whom the Chisholm Trail was named, probably knew Jason Cloud, as he was a business partner of Doublehead's.

**The Melton's**

     This brings us to an interesting family – the Melton's, about whom Melton's Bluff was named. In *Doublehead,* Walker quotes another book, Lore of the River, by William Lindsay McDonald. McDonald is quoted as saying:

     *John Melton and his Cherokee wife had a number of children; the names of some of them are believed to have been Moses, James, Charles, <u>David</u>, Thomas, and Merida. Walker adds Moses Melton is listed in microfilm archives as the son of <u>Lewis</u>.* Let us consider the two men I have underlined:  <u>David and Lewis</u>.

     http://digital.library.okstate.edu/kappler/vol2/treaties/com0435.htm

     At the above website a treaty signed by only 2 Cherokee – Captain Dutch and David Melton. It was signed in 1835, the treaty following the events that keep popping up, the Dragoon Expedition of 1834 in Indian Territory where the American Army first encounters the Comanche, Kiowa, and Wichita Tribes of Western Oklahoma.

**The Act of Union**

     The following website takes us to "The Cherokee Act of Union"

     http://www.oklahomagenealogy.com/actofunion.htm, and it says:

***Act of Union Between Eastern and Western Cherokee, 1838***

     *Whereas, our fathers have existed as a separate and distinct nation, in the possession and exercise of the essential and appropriate attributes of sovereignty, from a period extending into antiquity, beyond the records and memory of man; and, Whereas, these attributes, with the rights and franchises which they involve, remain still in full force and virtue; as do also the national and social relations of the Cherokee people to each other, and to the body politic, excepting in those particulars which have grown out of the provisions of the treaties of 1817 and 1819, between the United States and the Cherokee Nation, under which a portion of our people removed to this country, and became a separate community; but the force of circumstances have recently compelled the body of the Eastern Cherokee to remove to this country thus bringing together again the two branches of the ancient Cherokee family; it has become essential to the general welfare that a Union should be formed and a system of government matured, adapted to their present condition, and providing equally for the protection of each individual in the enjoyment of all his rights.*

     *Wherefore, we, the people composing the Eastern and Western Cherokee Nation, in national convention assembled, by virtue of our original and unalienable rights, do hereby solemnly and mutually agree to form ourselves into one body politic, under the style and title of the 'Cherokee Nation.'*

*In view of the union now formed, and for the purpose of making satisfactory adjustments of all unsettled business which may have arisen before the consummation of this Union, we agree that such business shall be settled according to the provisions of the respective laws under which it originated, and the courts of the Cherokee Nation shall be governed in their decisions accordingly. Also, that the delegation authorized by the Eastern Cherokee to make arrangements with Major General Scott, for their removal to this country, shall continue in charge of that business, with their present powers until it shall be finally closed.*

*And, also, that all rights and titles to public Cherokee lands on the East or West of the river Mississippi, with all other public interests which may have vested in either branch of the Cherokee family, whether inherited from our fathers or derived from .any other source, shall henceforward vest entire and unimpaired in the Cherokee Nation, as constituted by this Union.*

*"Given under our hands, at Illinois Camp Ground, this 12th day of July, 1838.*
*"By order of the National Convention.*
*GEORGE LOWREY, "President of the Eastern Cherokee.*
*GEORGE GUESS, his (X) mark, "President of the Western Cherokee.*

## Eastern Cherokee

*R. Taylor, V. P., James Brown, V. P., Te-KE-chu-las-kee, V. P., George Hicks, John Benge, Thomas Foreman, Archibald Campbell, Jesse Bushyhead, Lewis Ross, Edward Gunter, TE-nah-la-we-stah, Stephen Foreman, Daniel McCoy*

*By order of the National Convention; John Ross, "Principal Chief, Eastern Cherokee; GOING SNAKE, Speaker of Council.*

## Western Cherokee

*Tobacco Will, V. P.,* **Dave Melton, V. P.,** *John Drew, V. P., James Campbell, Looney Riley,* **Charles Gourd, Lewis Melton,** *Young Wolfe, Charles Coody, Ah-sto-la-ta, Jack Spears, George Brewer, Thomas Candy, Mosses Parris, Looney Price.*

*By order of the National Convention; August 23, 1839; JOHN Looney', his (X) mark; Acting Principal Chief, Western Cherokee*

*The foregoing instrument was read, considered, and approved by us, this 23d day of August, 1839.*

*Aaron Price, Major Pullum, Young Elders, Deer Track, Young Puppy, Turtle Fields, July, The Eagle, The Crying Buffalo*

First, notice Charles Goard. Did he come from Goard's Settlement mentioned a few paragraphs back by Walker, as today known the town of Courtland, Lawrence County, Alabama? David and Lewis Melton BOTH signed this document on behalf of the Old Settlers. These Melton's came from Melton's Bluff, just a few miles downriver from the second Brown's Ferry. These KNOWN mixed-Cherokee Melton's were from Lawrence County, Alabama. They were right next to Brown's Ferry where Jason Cloud most probably landed on many occasions. Jason was executor of the will of Aron Gist. Aron's father John Gist was said to be some relation to Sequoyah, and Doublehead, who was said to be Sequoyah's Uncle, lived right there as well until after the end of 1801, shortly after out Aron Gist was hung in October of 1801.

Another name found in both Lawrence County, Alabama and the Act of Union is from the Looney family. John Looney signed it. He was known as the nephew of Cherokee Chief Black Fox. There was a famous Union sympathizer during the Civil War known as Bill Looney, whose nickname was "The Black Fox". Several Old Settler Cherokee families in Arkansas, Oklahoma and East Texas seem to have come from Northern Alabama families.

Before going off any further onto this tangent, I must say these things are just supporting evidence, just clues. In a court of law I believe this is called circumstantial evidence. Is it enough? That's easily answered — I don't know.

156

# Conclusion – So Where Is Our Indian Blood

We have provided evidence of a possible Catawba link. Brown and Wayland/Gibson are both Catawba surnames. Even Nathaniel Gist lived near the Catawba, not the Cherokee, for much of his life. We have shown Catawba migrations away from their homeland, one of which was to the Oklahoma/Arkansas border where my family eventually lived. But the Brown's and Gist's do seem to have links to the Cherokee as well.

We have two possible connections a generation apart between our Gist's and the Cherokee Brown's – the Jason Cloud connection about 1800-1815, and the Joiner connection in the 1840s. I also took that autosomal DNA test showing me to be mostly Caucasian, but with a little American Indian and a little sub-Sahara African DNA as well. This, together with the Ridenour book, and the family stories – it all adds up. The Swetland Roll Brown's seem to have many names similar to ours, even the man named "Powell Brown" lived near our Brown's in Arkansas, but ours was an old man when theirs was a child. And we both have an Alfred Brown, but theirs was older than mine. And there are other names similar as well. The reservation rolls might be a clue.

It took me a long time (two decades or more), searching in libraries, court houses, books, magazines, journals, the internet, travelling hundreds of miles, and hundreds of hours pursuing dozens of wrong genealogical alleys. Grudgingly I had to realize all those hours were wasted effort. I might yet find some more blind allies, or perhaps rich veins of valuable ore. I have a lot more background material on hand, but I might have shared too much of that already. I did not intend for this report to be as long as it is. I just hate not mentioning a lot more families whose descendants might one day be doing the same research. Maybe I'll write that all down later. I have included evidence for the paternity of Sequoyah, knowing I have proven nothing, knowing I have only provided evidence. I hope others will consider the possibility that the Nathaniel Gist who was killed at Kings Mountain in 1780 might be Sequoyah's father. Appendix 3 explores this possibility a little further.

I should take more time to organize all this stuff, but I am tired and have other things to do. If I included much more material I am afraid it would not only be far longer, but it would also be pretty boring – all those census records don't make for interesting reading.

I've tried to include interesting local or family historical tidbits. I didn't know our family had or knew so many interesting characters. Well, I have to end this sometime and somewhere. So I suppose for now, well — this is it.

I'd hoped to include anything about my family that would show our long tenure in Indian Country. We have for generations had stories of being Indian-mixed, but it wasn't written down. We are not on the Indian rolls except maybe the Mulay, Siler, or Reservation Rolls. Brown's Ferry's (there are two of them) seems to be a connection as well. I found stories which connected our family stories to old tales about one bunch of Gist's, proven to be related to one another, which seem to indicate the family stories might be true, about us being related to Sequoyah. Our Gist's and Brown's did live in a region in Northern Alabama where a Alabama state recognized band of Cherokee resides today. I won't argue about whether states can recognize tribes or not – I'm not recognized as Indian by any state, either. Years back, I used to try to contact them, but they never responded, and I gave up on them.

Also, we do seem to have a Melungeon connection to the Eastern Siouans, the Catawba, Saponi, Cheraw/Saura/Xualla (What the early Spanish chroniclers with De Soto called them).

I have poured my heart and soul into this writing. I've been consumed by it. I'll keep looking into it.

Well, I guess this'll have to do for now – gotta run or I'll be late for work and I'll have my boss yellin' at me. That's not true. Some other poor sucker who thinks it'll help him to get ahead will be ordered to do the yelling. (Just joking, the boss would *never* do that. :)

Neither pre-conceived yet unproven beliefs, nor ambition and greed will comprehend logic that is not skewed like a magnet, drawn towards that nursery rhyme jingle — *mirror, mirror on the wall.* Logic is always just out of view of the skewed perception, diametrically opposed to its equal and opposite. Knowing that, I have tried to make my own research unbiased. That has always been difficult, as every moth knows when encountering a flame. I hope I am not just seeing what I want to see. I don't think I am.

Oh, one more thing. With me, there's always one last thing that I forgot to say.

We get whiter every generation as a result of being left off the rolls, and soon our Indian blood will be forgotten utterly, erased like footprints in melting snow. Like the Western Catawba. Like them and others, we'll likely be forgotten, too.

So where is our Indian blood? It seems to be drying up, like a creek bed in the drought of the heat of the summer sun. But once upon a . . .

I suppose that's one reason I've been compelled to write this — It is evidence for generations to come, that we, their ancestors, were once here.

# Appendix 1 - Catawba King Haiglar's Letter to Gov. Glen of South Carolina

From "History of the Old Cheraws," by Alexander Gregg.

p 13 — That the Pedees [Indians] owned slaves will appear from the following notice, published in the Gazette of the day, Aug 30-Sep 6, 1748 —

*"Taken up by Michael Welch, overseer to the subscriber on an island called Uchee Island, a Negro fellow, who gives the following account of himself, viz., that he belonged formerly to Mr. Fuller, and he was by him sold to Billy, king of the Pedee Indians; that the Catawba Indians took him from King Billy, and carried him into their nation, and that in endeavoring to make his escape from the Catawba's, he was lost in the woods, and had been so a considerable time before he was taken. Any person having any right or property in the said fellow, may apply to the subscriber, now in Charleston."*

*still p 13 —*

*The Pedees and other smaller tribes who now lead a wondering life, were in constant danger of being enticed off by the more powerful and hostile nations of Indians, to join them in their predatory excursions.*

*The following letters indicate the anxiety felt on the subject by the Catawba's, as well as by the provisional government of this period, the first was addressed by the King of the Catawba's to his excellency, James Glen, Esq : —*

*"There are a great many Pedee Indians living in the settlements that we want to come and settle amongst us. We desire for you to send for them, and advise — page 14 — this, and give them this string of wampum in token that we want them to settle here, and will always live like brothers with them. The Northern Indians want them to settle with us; for they are now at peace, they may be hunting in the woods or straggling about, killed by some of them, except they join us, and make but one nation, which will be a great addition of strength to us."*

*his mark, the (x) King"*
*[21 Nov, 1752]*

# Appendix 2 - Some Catawba Moved Away

The following is from Senate Document 144 (54th Cong, 2d sess.). A descendant of the Mr. McDowell, a man who prepared a part of this document for the Guy and Jeffries families, was kind enough to share this document with me.

*On the 21st of November, 1887, James Kegg, of Whittier, North Carolina, in addressing the Secretary of the Interior (# 31383), made the following statement, viz:*

**Many years ago, this people, the Catawba Indians, leased the land they owned in South Carolina and became a wondering tribe without homes for their wives and children. They made applications he states, to the Cherokees of North Carolina for homes upon their land and that about 500 or so were adopted that have been identified as such, that some 300 of them were removed west under the Cherokee treaty of New Echota, made December 29th, 1835, leaving a few living among the Cherokees . . . and a small portion remaining in South Carolina.** . . . *Those Catawba remaining in South Carolina, Mr. Kegg states, had no interest whatever in the lands which were leased out by those who became Cherokee by adoption.* [Vance's note: this clearly implied that most Catawba left the Catawba Nation. Those who left the Catawba Nation before the 1840 treaty, where those lands were given to the state of South Carolina, as no one could have "leased out" lands after that date.] it is interesting in p 53 of Dr. Blumer's book, "Catawba Nation, Treasures in History", he says of James Kegg that he was "not at all impassioned over preserving the Catawba reservation" and that *"He thought that a move to join the Cherokee in North Carolina might be a good idea".* So we have a schism between the Catawba who left, and those Catawba who wanted to stay. According to Kegg, the majority left.

In "The Catawba Indians" by Douglas Summers Brown, he says (p 319): *In 1840 when the Treaty of Nation Ford was signed, many of the Catawba's were already living among and near the Eastern Band of Cherokees.* [Vance's note: ambiguous – before the removals of 1838-1839, before the "Trail of Tears" – ALL of the Cherokee east of the Mississippi were considered "The Eastern Band" — including Rosses followers, the vast majority of Cherokee.]

Some Catawba "moved west" about 1835, others moved to live near the Eastern band of the Cherokee about the same time, about 1840. According to Kegg, only a small number of Catawba remained on their former lands in South Carolina. If he is right — hundreds had left. What became of them?

# Appendix 3 - Evidence that Sequoyah's Father Might Have Been *the Other* Nathaniel Gist

In the past I have heard of two men who have been said to be Sequoyah's father. One was from "Se-Quo-Yah, The American Cadmus and Modern Moses: A Complete Biography of the greatest of Redmen (1885)" by George Everett Foster. He speaks of a Swabian-Franconian emigrant who settled in the new community of Ebenezer. They arrived in Georgia when it was just being settled by Oglethorpe about 1735. They had a baby and named him George. George became an Indian trader. While trading in Cherokee county, he had a son, Sequoyah. But before Foster's book, there was the September 1870 issue of Harper's Ferry by Phillips. This story was this George Gist was a sort of a shady character, and never cared about his Indian son, totally disappearing from history. And that is the problem with this story – this immigrant German Gist family has never been found.

According to Chronicles of Oklahoma, Volume 1, No. 2, October, 1921, THE PATERNITY OF SEQUOYA, THE INVENTOR OF THE CHEROKEE ALPHABET, By Albert V. Goodpasture, we have a discussion of another possible father of Sequoyah, Nathaniel Gist. It says —

Only one other man—Nathaniel Gist—has ever been suggested as the father of Sequoya, and his claim has not received serious consideration on account of the manner in which it was presented. The story as told by John Mason Brown is that Nathaniel Gist was captured by the Cherokees at Braddock's defeat in 1755, and remained a prisoner with them for six years, during which time he became the father of Sequoya. On his return to civilization he married a white woman in Virginia by whom he had other children, and afterwards removed to Kentucky, where Sequoya, then a Baptist preacher, frequently visited him, and was always recognized by the family as his son. In reply to this claim Mooney points out that the Cherokees were allies of the British during the war in which Braddock's defeat occurred; and that Sequoya, so far from being a Baptist preacher, was not even a Christian. For these positive errors, and some other improbabilities in Brown's story, he classes it as one of those genealogical myths built on a chance similarity of name.

So Nathaniel was never captured by the Indians for six years, and he was never a Baptist Minister. With some falsehoods, can't we suspect there might be others in this account? Yet it is the most popular story as to just who was Sequoyah's father.

From Mysteries of Sequoyah, by Dub West, p. 2 & 3:

161

*The house resolution accepting Sequoyah's statue for Statuary Hall gives his father as "a German trader named George Gist who dealt with contraband articles, and who abandoned his wife before Sequoyah was born." Mooney said it is generally conceded that his father was George Gist. McKinney and Hall, Foster, Starr, and Phillips also subscribe to the George Gist theory. Foreman is the proponent of the theory that Sequoyah's father was Nathaniel Gist. He says that Major Gist Blair, who was owner of the Blair House in Washington at the time and a descendant of Nathaniel Gist, stated that Sequoyah was a son of Nathaniel Gist. In the Bureau of American Ethnology in a letter written by John Mason Brown of the Louisville Bar, who was a descendant of Nathaniel Gist, stated Sequoyah visited the Gist descendants on his way to or from Washington in 1828. On this occasion, he was looking for his White kin . . .*

*Jack Kilpatrick rejects the paternity of either George Gist or Nathaniel Gist, indicating that he possibly had some Caucasian blood, but very little — that he appeared to be a full-blood. He further says that it is a mistake to emphasize the father of a Cherokee family, as the Cherokee society is matrilineal. Weaver says that Sequoyah appeared to be a full-blood.*

As for me, I have read several books, as many as I could get my hands on (and will continue to do so), about Sequoyah. My opinion, based on my own reading which I admit has a bias, is that he was neither a son of this German Indian trader named George Gist, nor the Nathaniel Gist who was the son of Christopher Gist, friend of George Washington.

There have always been families who had family stories of a Guess/Gist/Guest ancestor who was related to Sequoyah in Northern Alabama by 1820, with a second bunch arriving years later. Now we have DNA tests that say literally all of these families with this family tradition, many of whom had lost track of each other over the years, are very closely related to one another. They are NOT closely related with other Gist/Guess/Guest families who do not have these family traditions of having some Indian blood, or having been related to Sequoyah. Through the research shown in this report there is a thin thread or ribbon or connecting documents that might show how these families are related, and show as well, how they might be related to Sequoyah.

Evidence points to a different Nathaniel Gist, a settler and founder of Gist's Station in Wise County, Virginia, who had a hunting Camp in Southern Kentucky. Another bunch lived in northern Tennessee. Perhaps he also had a Cherokee child named Sequoyah as well. They were not a band of Indians that hid in the woods 200 years to suddenly pop up out of nowhere. They were mixed blood families just trying to survive as best they knew how.

162

Dr. G. L. Ridenour said in "Land of the Lake" John Gist was "some relation to Sequoyah." Dr. Ridenour had ancestors who were close neighbors of this John Gist. The Dorsey's in their book on the Maryland Gist's say this John Gist was a son of this same Nathaniel Gist. He unfortunately, was killed at the Battle of Kings Mountain in 1780 during the American Revolution. This left his children essentially orphaned. Perhaps Sequoyah's father was killed and that is why he abandoned his Indian sons.

Remember Foreman said:

*Major Gist Blair, who was owner of the Blair House in Washington at the time and a descendant of Nathaniel Gist, stated that Sequoyah was a son of Nathaniel Gist. In the Bureau of American Ethnology in a letter written by John Mason Brown of the Louisville Bar, who was a descendant of Nathaniel Gist, stated Sequoyah visited the Gist descendants on his way to or from Washington in 1828. On this occasion, he was looking for his White kin.*

It appears Sequoyah was looking for his White kin, and that he went to the decendants of the famous Nathaniel Gist in search of them. This appears to be saying he had heard his father was named *Nathaniel Gist!* Now our family (and others) has been proven to descend from the other Nathaniel, who was contemporary with the famous Nathaniel. All of us that I have come across have family traditions of being related to Sequoyah. Dr. Ridenour in "Land of the Lake" also makes this same argument – independently stating these Gist's were Sequoyah's family. Well, it makes me suspect we might just be Sequoyah's unknown family.

Lastly, my autosomal DNA test said I do have a small amount of American Indian autosomal DNA.

But this means nothing other than "maybe". All we have done is provide evidence, and we haven't been able to disprove our hypothesis, that we might be related to Sequoyah. We haven't proven that Nathaniel Gist, the one killed at the Battle of Kings Mountain, was Sequoyah's father.

No good scientist leaves something hanging that might be proven. Yes, now we have a way to prove or disprove it, through the autosomal DNA test. I make no claims – this could be wrong. I only suggest this as a possibility, and would like to see others look into it. Maybe Sequoyah's descendants would like to know who his father was as well. Since our DNA is unique and doesn't match the other Maryland Gist's, it means we can prove or disprove the notion that we are related to Sequoyah's true known descendants. However I would never try to put any burden on them. They have every right to be or not to be tested if that is their desire.

Albert Einstein hypothesized light from a distant star passing towards us would bend slightly if passing near the sun, and would show that space around a massive object would bend or distort light. Mathematically, it worked. But that wasn't enough. A means of testing this distortion was possible, and they had to wait for a solar eclipse to prove it. After a couple of failed attempts, they eventually succeeded in proving his mathematical calculations were correct.

Well, I have researched all of the documents, or a sufficient number of them. We can make some educated guesses based on them, and we too have a means of testing them. And no, it won't have the shattering consequences that Einstein's theories of relativity and special relativity had – but it would be cool . . . ☺ And if we're wrong – well, darn it . . . ☹ . . . won't be the first time. As with the glass being half empty (as it seems is usually the case), those known relations of Sequoyah would have to take the test first, and maybe they won't want to take it. And that's alright, too. So it's unlikely we will ever discover absolute proof that we are related to Sequoyah – but we might. Again, half empty. But we have come a long way from where we were.

# Appendix 4 - IPP Papers Written by Two of Sequoyah's Descendants

TONEY,
INTERVIEW        #6751

> *(Cherokee)*
> *Texanna, Oklahoma*
> *Interview - July 12, 1937*
> *Indian-Pioneer History*
> *Jas. S. Buchanan, Field Worker*

*Note - the following statement of Mrs. Susan Toney, who does not speak English, only the Cherokee language, was interpreted through her son, Calvin Toney.*

*I (Susan Toney) was born in a refugee camp on Red River in the Choctaw Nation January 6, 1862, where my parents, with other Cherokees, had fled to escape the dangerous conditions that existed in the Indian Territory brought on by the Civil War.*

*My father was William Fields, fullblood Cherokee and my mother was Sallie (Gist) Fields, the daughter of Teasy Gist, the son of George Gist, or Sequoyah, Cherokee.*

*After the Civil War my parents moved back to their home place at the mouth of Dutch Creek on the Canadian River where my grandfather, Teasy Gist, died in 1869, when I was seven years of age. I remember his burial in the old Cherokee burial ground on the hill beside the old Dutch Creek trail two and one-half miles southeast of Texanna, or one and one-half miles west of the old home place. I have known of the old burial ground of the Cherokees since my earliest recollection and it was a very old burial ground at that time. It was abandoned about fifty years ago. There are only two white people buried in the place. They were two little white girls, children of a poor family that was living in the vicinity when their children died about 1911.*

*There were many of the early Cherokee buried at that place and it was always known as the Cherokee burial ground and no other name. There never was any grave markers with inscriptions at any of the graves, as the Indians in the early days kept the burial place of their dead sacred in their memory and the location designated by land-marks.*

*My great-grandfather, George Gist, prominent in Cherokee history, was born in Tennessee about 1760, and at an advanced age he came to the Indian Territory alone, leaving his family east of the Mississippi River. His short time in the Indian Territory was among the early Cherokee settlers.*

*Shortly after he came to the Territory he was joined by his son, Teesey Gist, my grandfather. Shortly thereafter George Gist (Sequoyah), Teesey Gist, his son and another Cherokee by the name of Ellen Boles, for reasons unknown, left the Indian Territory for Old Mexico. George Gist died on that journey somewhere in Mexico about 1847. After the death of Sequoyah, Teesey Gist and Ellen Boles left Mexico and went to Texas where they remained for some time and through a transaction of some description acquired a tract of land from Mexico, then attempted to colonize it with Cherokees which involved them in a difficulty with the Texas government that lead to the killing of Boles.*

*The story as it was handed down through my mother, that when they were involved in the trouble with the Texas people over the treaty they had made with Mexico, Boles and Teesey Gist attempted to escape from Texas with the treaty and was being pursued by their enemies when Boles was shot. Boles took the treaty from where he had it hid in the fold of his saddle blanket, handed it to Teesy Gist and said; "They have got me, you take this and ride for your life for this is what they are after." Teesey Gist made good his escape with the treaty, though he never returned to Texas. I remember seeing the paper many times in later years as I grew up, I don't know what became of it.*

*Page 415 - - Three family charts showing various relationships, as follows:*
*Teesey Gist (died 1869 Dutchers Creek)*
*Daughter Sallie Gist married William Fields*
*Daughter of Sallie Gist and William Fields was Susan Fields Toney, born 1862*
*Teesey Gist*
*Daughter Kate Gist married Downing, children of Kate Gist Downing:*

1. *Joseph Edward Downing (youngest 1883)*
2. *Nannie - - married L. McClure*
3. *Lucile - - - married Van Jargill*
4. *Teesey Downing*
5. *George Downing*
6. *Maude Downing*

166

**Lineage of Calvin H. Toney**

*George Guess*

*Teesey Gist (Guess)*

*Sallie Fields*

*Susan Fields Toney*

*Calvin H. Toney, children of Calvin Toney are:*

*Lucy Toney*

*Ellis Toney*

*Susie Toney*

## TONEY, CALVIN HARRISON INTERVIEW #7100

*Calvin Harrison Toney, Cherokee.*

*Texanna, Oklahoma.*

*August 11, 1937.*

*Indian-Pioneer History.*

*Jas. S. Buchanan, Field Worker.*

*The following, including genealogy of descent from Sequoyah, is compiled from authentic information and through the cooperation of Calvin Toney and his mother, Susan (Fields) Toney, she being the grand-daughter of Teasey Guess, the son of Sequoyah.*

*Sequoyah was born about 1770, in the old Cherokee country, within one of the present states of Tennessee, Georgia or Alabama; the exact location is unknown.*

*His father was a German peddler by the name of Gist, who, like many wandering traders of those days, came among the Indians to ply his trade, and during his stay among the Cherokees he chose a wife from among the Indians, He, being an obscure wanderer, a part of the adventurous flotsam of the border of civilization, eventually deserted his wife.*

*Sequoyah was born soon after his father had deserted his mother, and he grew to manhood among the Cherokees and as his mother spoke only the Cherokee language, Sequoyah grew up without learning the English language. His knowledge of English was gained in later years of his life, Sequoyah, from his father's name, Gist, acquired the name George Guess.*

*During his boyhood he was afflicted with what is commonly called "white swelling" in a knee joint which caused a lameness that remained with him the remainder of his life. Sequoyah was about five feet and nine inches in height, slender in form, a light sallow complexion and grey eyes. In his dress he clung to the customs of his people, wearing a*

167

turban, hunting shirt, leggings and moccasins. The Turban was a strip of cloth or a small shawl twisted about his head. The hunting shirt was a loose sack coat made of buck skin or home spun woolen cloth that was made by the Cherokee women. The moccasins were made from tanned buckskin.

The first vocation to which he adapted himself in early life was that of a blacksmith, later that of a silversmith.

Sequoyah's first wife was Sallie of the Bird clan and his second wife was U-ti-yu of the Savanah clan.

His four children by his first wife were:

Tessey Guess, who married U-ti-yu and Rebecca Bowl. He was born in 1789 and died September 17th, 1867. His second wife, Rebecca Bowl was the daughter of Bowl, who was the leader of the band of Cherokees that emigrated from Mussel Shoals, on Tennessee River, to the St. Francis River country (now southeast Missouri) in 1794; moved to Petit Jean Creek on the south side of the Arkansas River in the winter of 1811-1812, finally removed to Texas in 1822 and became the leader of the Texas Cherokees. While with Teesey Guess, resisting expulsion from Texas, Bowl was killed July 16th, 1839.

Sequoyahs's second child by Sallie was George Guess, who lived to be grown but died without descent. Richard or Chusaleta, the fourth child and third son, also lived to be grown and died without descent.

Sequoyah's third child by Sallie was his daughter Polly who married Flying and Thomas Brewer. She only had one child, Annie, who married Joseph Griffin and was the mother of Ti-du-gi-yo-sti.

Sequoyah had three children by his second wife, U-ti-yu, the eldest of whom was A-yo-gu Guess, who married George Starr and they were the parents of one son, Joseph Starr, who was born December 25th, 1873, and died without issue inn 1895.

Sequoyah's second child by U-ti-yu was Oo-loo-tea, a daughter, who left no descent.

Sequoyah's third child by his second wife was Gu-u-ne-ki, who married Tsu-du-li-tee-hee or Sixkiller and had one daughter, Araminta Sixkiller.

Sequoyah's eldest son, Teesey, had three children by his first wife and three by his second wife. His oldest child by his first wife, U-ti-yu, was George Guess, who married a Girty and they were the parents of two children, the elder of whom was Mary Guess, who married George Mitchell and Andrew Russell, and by the latter was the mother of one child only, George W. Russell, who was born on July 18th, 1880, and married Minnie Holston.

*Teesey Guess's second and third children by his first wife were respectively Richard and Joseph Guess, both of whom lived to be grown but died without issue.*

*Teesey Guess's children by Rebecca, his second wife, were first, Sallie, who married William Fields, whose Cherokee name was Tu-noo-ie. They had one daughter, Susan Fields, who married Levi Toney and they were the parents of consecutively: Calvin Harrison Toney, Cicero Davis Toney, Margaret Toney and the twins, Catherine and Sallie Tooney.*

*Teesey Guess's second child by Rebecca was a son, Joseph Guess, who lived to be grown but died without issue.*

*Teesey Guess's third child by Rebecca was Catherine Guess. she was born in 1851 and married on March 11th, 1867, Joseph Downing. they were the parents of six Children as follows:*

> *Nannie Downing, born February 1st, 1878.*
> *Loucile Downing, born July 28th, 1881*
> *Joseph Edward Downing, born march 22, 1883*
> *Teesey Downing, born _____*
> *Maud Downing, born February 13, 1890*

*At the time of this writing (1937), Susan (Fields) Toney, her son, Calvin Harrison Toney and his wife, who was Leona Davis, the daughter of Jug Davis, whom he married in 1906 and their five children, Lucy, Ellis, Susie, Surphronia and Sanders are all living on the original allotment of Susan (Fields) Toney, two and one half miles southeast of Texanna.*

*Joseph Edward Downing is living in Texanna*

## Notes by Don Sticher, January 2009:

*The origins of Sequoyah as presented here appear to come from an 1870 Harper's Magazine article by William A. Phillips and the also from the work of Dr. Emmett Starr, the Cherokee historian, who stated after much painstaking research:*

*"His father is reputed to have been a Suabian peddler. His name, when it was recalled years afterward, so as to bestow it on his son, sounded something like Gist. He was an obscure wanderer, a part of the adventurous flotsam of the border of civilization."*

*The exact same words were used in the above article describing the origins of Sequoyah.*

Vance's note: Those words are also found in Foster's book, "Sequoyah, The American Cadmus . . ." Foster's book was first written in 1885. Starr's book was written 1921. So it appears as though the Phillips article for Harper's Magazine dated 1870 was first article mentioning the German peddler. Unfortunately, as was the custom of many writers of that time frame, Phillips lists no sources at all to justify his claims. We are left to take his word for it. This alone is enough to raise an eye brow. As with many things concerning the early Cherokee, some things we will just never know. I suspect a second Nathaniel Gist (not the man of that name usually called his father, but his first cousin) was Sequoyah's father.

# Appendix 5 - Gess's Station Camp, established around 1775 in Wayne County, KY

Note: In 1805, Colonel Thomas Young had a survey made to establish the original trace or path from Price's Landing to the starting corner of his (Young's) property. Ten depositions of early hunters and settlers were introduced to help the surveyor identify the various landmarks referred to through the years. One of these deponents was Nathaniel Buchannon, who was part of the original company with Benjamin Price on the first trip.

Please note the mention of "Guesses Station Camp". Notice he mentions Price's Camp and Gesses Station Camp as though they were contemporary with each other, and he mentions being at Price's Camp in 1775.

## Wayne County, KY Deed Book A, Page 213-216 (LDS Film #590703)

*The deposition of Nathaniel Buckhannon of lawful age and first sworn deposeth that some time in the year 1795 this Dept. in company with Benjamin Price & others launched a canoe above the mouth of this Creek to __?__ meadow Creek and cross the river and ever after the place was called and known by the name of Prices landing because Price was considered by us the head of the Company.*

*Question by Young - - Was there not at that time a trace leading from this place to Prices meadows?*

*Ans. - - Yes there was and generally travelled at that time*

*Question by Mills - - Was there not another trace leading from or near Prices landing to the meadows made sometime since your acquaintance with the first trace?*

*Ans. - - Yes there was*

*Quest. by same - - By whom was the last trace spoken of made?*

*Ans. - - By this Dept. I marked it myself in the year 1779 leading from a Salt Petre Cave between this and the great meadows. Also to intersect the old trace some distance beyond the top of the River Cleft.*

*Quest. by same - - After the new trace was marked out by you was discovered was not the old one neglected in a great manner and the new one the most travelled?*

*Ans. - - Yes because it was then the most plain, our company travelled it the most.*

*Quest. by same - - Was there any company in the these woods at that time besides yours?*

*Ans. - - I do not know of any who were hunting in these woods but ours at that time but Mr. Michael Stoner, Green & others came to be at the great meadows.*

*Question by same - - How long after marking the new trace spoken of did your company travel it before your departure from the meadows?*

*Ans. - - From February until the July following*

*Ques. by same - - What was your Companies motive for preferring the travelling the new trace to the old one?*

*Ans. - - Because we thought it was nearest from the landing to the meadows and because we had encamped in the salt petre cave six or eight weeks and by that means the new trace became more plain than the old one.*

*Question by Young - - Was there not another trace besides the two above spoken of leading from Cumberland River to Prices Meadows?*

**Yes, from Gesses Station Camp near the big Cotton to Prices meadows.**

**Ques. by Mills - - How far was Gesses Station Camp from the mouth of Pitmans Creek?**

**Answer - - Opposite on the contrary side of the River.**

*Question by Young - - Was not the trace last spoken of very much travelled?*

*Ans. - - It was our general crossing place when we came to or returned from Prices meadows.*

*Question by same - - Was not the trace leading by the salt petre cave generally called the salt petre cave trace?*

*Ans. - - Yes it was.*

*Quest. by same - - By whom was it called the salt petre cave trace?*

*Ans. - - Our Company called it the trace leading by the salt petre cave.*

*Question by Young - - Are you certain the trace you shewed the Surveyor this morning is Prices Old Trace leading from the landing to his improvement?*

*Ans. - - I am certain it is a s far as from the River to the Rush Glade and divers places this side of that.*

*Question by same - - Are you certain this spot is Prices old improvement?*

*Ans. - - I was here with Price in 1775 and assisted in building this Cabin and the Glade facing the Camp nearly a North Eastwardly course was at that time bare of timber and not more than 70 or 80 yards from the Camp and the meadow ground as this Dept. thinks extended somewhere about a quarter and half a quarter of a mile across.*

*Question by same - - Was there not a pond somewhere not far from here?*

*Ans. - - There was.*

*Question by same - - What was the name of that pond & what course was it from here?*

*Ans. - - a Northwardly course.*

*Quest. - - What size was that pond?*

*Ans. - - a very large one an hundred yards or thereabouts across and am not certain as to its length. And further the Dept. Saith Not.*

*Nathaniel Buckhannon*

## Wayne County, KY Deed Book A, Page 220-221 (LDS Film #590703)

*We do hereby certify that the foregoing Depositions were taken at the respective specialties referred to in them and that the several witnesses were duly sworn & subscribed each his own Deposition. We do moreover certify that Col. Thos. Young produced to us three different advertisements continued in the Kentucky Herald purposing notice of his intentions to Perpetuate Testimony and that the annexed platt of the distance from his Beginning Corner to Prices Landing was executed in our presence by the Deputy Surveyor of Wayne County & that said Young also presented an acknowledged Notice executed by John Mills, Sr. and that there were marks made by Jesse Wright & Wm. Brown disinterested bystanders on a white oak tree said to be near Young's Beginning. Given under our hands and seals this 29th day of August 1805; Anthony Gholson, Isaac West*

## Wayne County, KY Deed Book A, Page 222 (LDS Film #590703)

*The Plat (or Map) referred to regarding the 29 August 1805 survey of Prices Old Trace, for Thomas Young.*

## Wayne County, KY Deed Book A, Page 223 (LDS Film #590703)

*No date given for this entry. Presumed to be 28-29 August 1805 based on depositions given in the preceding pages that relate to this survey. Surveyed Price's old trace for Thomas Young Beginning at Prices Canoe Landing at Letter A and running then S.20.W. 18p. thence S.19 E. 22p. thence 45.E.10p. thence S.36.E. 68p. thence S. 62 E. 28p. to the ʄ of the trace where one lead to the Salt Peter Cave and the other to Prices Meadows then courses supposed to be N.37.E.420p. to the salt petre Cave by Capt. Buckhannon and M John McLuer then continuing S.62.E. line 52p. thence S.36.E.140p then S.52.E.24p. t a small white oak thence S.70.E.180 poles then S.55.E.210p. to Prices Old Improveme then from Prices Old Improvement to the salt petre Cave is supposed to be N.13.W. 3.*

173

*thence to Young's Beginning corner is S.20.E. 408p  thence N.40.W. 450p  a straight line to the beginning.*

*A.  J. Jones  D.S., Chanes C. C., James Hutchenson, Robert Hutchenson*

# Appendix 6 - The Cut Throat Gap Massacre

The Writing on the Historical Marker (below) says:

*The Cut Throat Massacre site is approximately 2.5 miles east of this marker.*

*In the early summer of 1833, the summer before "the stars fell" an Osage War Party attacked an undefended Kiowa camp.*

*The camp of Islandman, Principle Chief of the Kiowa's, consisted of women and children, the elderly, and a few warriors. Most of the warriors were on a raid against the Utes while others were hunting buffalo.*

*The Osage tracked Islandman's band from Saddle Mountain through the mountains to the campsite. Early one morning the Osage raiders struck the camp. The Kiowa's, surprised and outnumbered, were unable to organize a defense. The few warriors tried to hold the Osage back to allow the women, children and elderly a chance to flee. It has been estimated that 150 Kiowa's were killed.*

*Kiowa warriors found the camp destroyed and decapitated bodies lying where they had fallen. Before leaving the Osage put the heads of their victims in camp cooking pots. They took the sacred Tai-Me medicine bundle. Two captives, a boy named Thunder and a girl named White Weasel, and many horses were taken. Thunder died during captivity. White Weasel was returned to her family in 1834 by the first Dragoon Expedition [Vance's note: this is the same expedition that I have written about earlier in this report].*

*For allowing the camp to be surprised Islandman was removed as principle chief. To-Hau-San was chosen to replace Islandman and served as Principle Chief from 1833 to 1866.*

*Little Bear recorded the massacre on his calendar. It was known to the Kiowa as "the Summer they cut off their heads." The sight of the massacre later became known as "Cut Throat Gap."*

*Later Chief To-Hau-San, with the assistance of the United States Indian Agents, negotiated with the Osage tribe for the return of the Tai-Me medicine bundle.*

*While Ta-Hau-San was Chief the Kiowa resisted all efforts by the United States to pacify them and it is said that he never lost a battle he fought with the United States Cavalry.*

*Oklahoma Historical Society*

*Kiowa Historical Society*

The above event, the Cutthroat Gap Massacre, was one reason for the Dragoon Expedition that My Wayland's participated in while serving at Fort Gibson, Indian Territory, in the 1830s. Many tribes were about to be settled in Indian Territory and the government knew this would cause tension between the Indians who already were living in Indian Territory (Oklahoma), those called the Indigenous Tribes (Quapaw, Osage, Caddo and associated bands, Wichita and associated bands, Kiowa, Comanche, Tonkawa, and others) and those called Emigrant Tribes (Cherokee, Creek, Choctaw, Chickasaw, Seminole, Delaware, Shawnee, Miama, Sac and Fox, and others).

So the government sent troops to meet the Southern Plains tribes and secure a treaty with them. Two Cherokee signed that treaty, Captain Dutch, supposed to be Sequoyah's half-brother. David Melton, of the Cherokee Melton's from Melton's Bluff in Northern Alabama, also signed it. Melton's Bluff is just a few miles from the second Brown's Ferry, the same place I suspect my Brown's came from. This same David Melton with his brother, Lewis, were two of many who signed the Cherokee "Articles of Union", a document unifying the Cherokee Old Settlers, Ross's faction, and the Treaty Party.

# Appendix 7 - CHISHOLM, JESSE (ca. 1805-1868)

I noticed there was a Chisholm Ranch mentioned with respect to Tarleton Bull in Denton County, Texas. I thought I needed to discover more about him. I am providing excerpts and a photo from the article found here: http://digital.library.okstate.edu/encyclopedia/entries/C/CH067.html

It says:

*Of Scottish and Cherokee descent, plainsman Jesse Chisholm is best remembered today by the Chisholm Trail, the famous route of cattle drives across Indian Territory (present Oklahoma) from Texas to Kansas. He was, however, far more historically significant as a frontier trader who first worked among the Plains Indians and served as a mediator in their dealings with the Cherokee Nation, the Republic of Texas, and the United States.*

*Chisholm first emerged into historical notice as a member of a gold-searching party that explored up the Arkansas River to the site of present Wichita, Kansas, in 1826. Four years later he helped blaze a trail from Fort Gibson to Fort Towson, and in 1834 he was a member of the Dodge-Leavenworth Expedition, which made the first official contact with the Comanche, Kiowa, and Wichita near the Wichita Mountains in southwestern Oklahoma . . .*

So Jesse Chisholm was also along on the same expedition as Cherokees David Melton and Captain Dutch. They must be three of the eight Cherokee mentioned as being on this expedition. My Jarrett and James Wayland were also present. They were first cousins to my great-great-grandma. Also present was a "Melton" Welborne as a member of Bean's Rangers. I do not know if he was related to the Cherokee Melton's.

http://www.dentoncounty.com/historicalmarkers/default.asp

Found at the link above is a Texas historic marker discussing the origins of the name of the town of Bolivar, Denton County, Texas. It says:

*Named indirectly for Simon Bolivar, South American statesman, general and patriot. It might have been called "New Prospect," but for a mug of rum. When town was founded in 1852, a man who had settled here from Bolivar, Tenn., wanted to name the community in honor of his hometown. But a preacher-doctor insisted that it be named New Prospect. An election was called to settle the matter and the Tennessean exchanged mugs of rum for votes, Bolivar won. During the 1800s, Bolivar was the westernmost fort in Denton County and the first settlement west of Collin County. Two stagecoach lines changed horses here. The town thrived and could count three hotels, several stores, a gin, a flour mill, a sawmill, a blacksmith shop, a saloon, a church and a school. It was here that the Texas cattle trail joined the Jesse Chisholm Trail, but it was John Chisum, Texas cattle baron, who had herds here and furnished beef to the Confederacy during the Civil War. Bolivar and the surrounding area were havens for Sam Bass and his men. Two Bolivar men were jailed in 1890 for harboring notorious marauders. Many early settlers (whose descendants still live here) played important roles in development of county.*

It turns out the Chisholm Cattle trail started in Denton County, Texas, where my family lived in the early 1880s. It's just to the North of the Dallas/Fort Worth area. Several cattle trails in Texas met up there, became one, and continued on through Indian Territory and on to Kansas. The trail went right through what is now Duncan, Oklahoma, which is where my great grand-parents leased land in the Chickasaw Nation once they left Denton County, by the way. We lived there before Duncan was founded. Those cattle leases showed my great grandpa leased out land for cattle grazing on Kiowa lands. We probably didn't know Jesse, but might have seen or heard of him passing through and might have known of his fame.

But there was a big cattleman in Denton County also named John Chisum. After further research, it seems the ranch mentioned with respect to Tarleton Bull was his, not

178

Jessse's. However since Jesse was along on the 1834 Dragoon Expedition to the Comanche, Kiowa, and Wichita, as were two of my Wayland's, I am including this little tidbit. Chisholm and Chisum are not known to have been related.

# Appendix 8 – The Hanging Judge

My great uncle wrote in Indian Pioneer Papers, when discussing their time living in Indian Territory near Fort Smith, saying; *I remember very clearly hearing my mother say that the territory was like a wilderness and that they had to go back to Fort Smith for everything they had to buy and that when they needed protection all the officers of the law had to come from Fort Smith.* He also wrote in the same document; *Mother never ceased to tell us children of an experience, which she had while living at that place. Two White men and Two Negroes committed some kind of a crime in the Indian Territory, were taken to Fort Smith tried and convicted and were sentenced to be hanged.* After talking about attending the hanging, Great Uncle Oscar said; *Mother watched the hanging and it was so horrible to her that she regretted attending such a thing all the remainder of her life.*

There was a hanging in Fort Smith in the early 1770s.

There is also that document about Alph Brown being wanted in the 'Indian Country, Western District of Arkansas' for 'assault with intent to kill' that got my attention, especially since my great grandparents, Jeff Richey and Josephine Brown, were married in the hope of 'Alph Brown', who was Josey's uncle. Hmmm . . . this got my interest. Were these two 'Alph Brown's' one and the same? I don't know, but I recalled the hangings, and recalled a judge there in Fort Smith called 'The Hanging Judge'.

Judge Parker might not be allowed to be a judge today. The following is from "Hanging Judge" by Fred H. Harrington, University of Oklahoma Press. He quotes Parker as saying (p. 129-134); *"teach the bad and vicious among them, that as sure as they violate the law, so will punishment overtake them."* Harington states that; *In murder cases, the Judge talked for a long time, often for three hours.* He speaks of defense attorney's mentioning a reasonable doubt as to guilt. Judge Parker would say "Hold on!" adding "The jury should vote conviction unless there was a real substantial doubt of guilt, and not the mere possibility of innocence." Parker would quote the Bible, Hebrews 11:1 speaks of 'evidence not seen.' The Judge would say, "Have you ever seen your brain? . . . your heart? . . .the Maker of us all? Well, why no accept in court 'evidence of things not seen'? Harrington quotes the judge often, and his admissions to the jury seemed biased. Harrington continues, *"These words of course, tended to prejudice the jury against the defendant."* He told them they could accept the arguments of the defense attorney, then add with emphasis, But if the prosecution is correct, *"He is guilty of murder and nothing else!"*

One condemned prisoner complained, *"[Judge Parker] did not seem to think that I was a human being . . .for the jury was instructed in a most bitter, passionate and biased manner . . ."* However this man made a complete confession of the crime before he was hanged.

Judge Parker served on the Bench from 1875 to 1896. He was judge from Western Arkansas and Indian Territory. He hanged 88 men in 21 years.

Parker often quoted the Bible. But I have to think about what my great grandma said when she and great grandpa Richey attended that hanging. She said to my great uncle (her son), and probably to grandma as well, that she regretted attending such a spectacle the rest of her life. She died in 1932, so that was at last 50 years of regret.

# References

1. History of Tillman County, Oklahoma, vol. 2
2. The University of Oklahoma, Western History Collection, Indian Pioneer Papers Collection http://digital.libraries.ou.edu/whc/pioneer/
3. Denton Record Chronicle, Wednesday, January 3, 2007, Nita Thurman
4. Genealogy of the Jackson Family, © 1890, Hugh Park Jackson, Hugh Hogue Thompson, and James R. Jackson
5. Sketches of Texas pioneers published in the magazine "Frontier Times" which was published monthly at Bandera, Texas by J. Marvin Hunter. December 1923, Vol. 1, No. 3
6. Photo taken from "A Study in Tolerance with Genealogy," by William Lee McCormick, the author being in the photo as well, on the far right, wearing a bow tie and his hands behind his back. The newspaper clipping wasdated the 29th of August, 1929 That is probably when the photo was taken.
7. From "Pioneers and Makers of Arkansas", p 339-342 by Josiah H. Shinn, A. M :
8. "The History of Methodism in Arkansas," p 29-36
9. The Story of Methodism in Oklahoma" as being compiled by J. Y. Bryce, of the East Oklahoma Conference and S. H. Babcock, of the West Oklahoma Conference.
10. Chronicles of Oklahoma; Volume 7, No. 4, December, 1929, BEGINNING OF METHODISM IN INDIAN TERRITORY, J. Y. Bryce
11. "Lawrence County, Arkansas Historical Journal", Summer 1982 - Volume 4 - Number 3, History of Methodism in Walnut Ridge:
12. "Lawrence County, Arkansas Historical Journal", Summer 1982 - Volume 4 - Number 3, History of Methodism in Walnut Ridge:
13. http://www.rootsweb.com/~okgs/roster_of_beans_rangers.htm; Ft. Gibson, Oklahoma; August 25 – October 31, 1832; From Oklahoma Genealogical Society Quarterly Vol. 24, No. 1, 1979; Transcribed to Electronic form by Jo White; From Appendix II – of Western Journals of Washington Irving; Edited and Annotated by John Francis McDermott; Published by University of Oklahoma Press, 1944. Reprinted here by permission. Submitted by Mrs. Joyce A. Rex.
14. http://firstdragoons.org/unit_history.htm
15. I can no longer find this website.
16. "Arkansas Mexican War Soldiers Historical Highlights" by Jay Brent Tipton.
17. The Arkansas Gazette, June 25, 1846
18. The Wayland Files, Frances Davey
19. Most of the documents in this section can be found here – http://www.rootsweb.ancestry.com/~varussel/
20. Excellent source material on the Melungeons: *Melungeons and other Pioneer*

*Families* by Jack H. Goins; *Who's Your People? . . . a Dissertation . . .* submitted to Michigan State University 2003 by [now] Dr. Richard Allen Carlson, Jr.; *Melungeons, Examining an Appalachian Legend* by Pat Spurlock Elder; . . . *Piedmont Catawba . . .* compiled by Richard Haithcock. Goins mentions the minutes of the Stoney Creek Primitive Baptist Church, a church attended by my Wayland's. Carlson and Haithcock show direct genealogical links between the Saponi (and other) Eastern Siouan Indian, known Melungeon families, and people in Ohio called the "Carmel Indians". Elder shows direct lines from the Piedmont Catawba, composed of several bands of the Catawba (Eastern Siouan Peoples) and those known as "Melungians."

21. "Catawba Indians of South Carolina" by H. Lewis Scaife
22. http://digital.library.okstate.edu/kappler/vol2/toc.htm — all treaties between the United States government at the various tribes came be found here
23. As you can see from the above (22) link – there has never been a treaty between the Catawba and the United states government. There were treaties with the United Kingdom and South Carolina, but never with the United States government. Even though the Catawba sided with the United States during the Revolutionary War, the Catawba were considered of little consequence, and were brushed aside. The following books are excellent sources of material on the Catawba. *The Catawba Indians, the People of the River*, by Douglas Summers Brown; *Catawba Nation, Treasures in History*, by Dr. Thomas J. Brown; *History of the Old Cheraws*, by Alexander Gregg; *A Guide to the Indian Tribes of Oklahoma*, by Muriel H. Wright. That's right, she even has a section on the Catawba. Others are, *Monacans and Minors* by Samuel R. Cook; *Red Carolinians* by chapman J. Milling; *The Last Trek of the Indians* and *The Five Civilized Tribes*, both by Grant Foreman.
24. The Fort Smith Elevator; http://newspaperarchive.com/fort-smith-elevator/
25. The Vinita Indian Chieftain; http://chroniclingamerica.loc.gov/lccn/sn83025010/
26. http://web.mst.edu/~whmcinfo/shelf2/r043/shelf.html ; http://www.mst.edu/ The Missouri University of Science and Technology at Rolla contains a collection of papers donated by the Smith family, descendants of David Smith, son-in-law of James Havens.
27. *Christopher Gist of Maryland and Some of His Descendants 1679-1957*; by Jean Muir Dorsey and Maxwell Jay Dorsey.
28. http://ncgenweb.us/cumberland/cumberland.htm. Much of the information about these Gist's and Smith's can be found at the above link.
29. *Colonel Return Jonathan Meigs Day Book Numbr 2*, compiled by James L. Douthat
30. *Davey Crockett, His Own Story by Davey Crockett*
31. The following books tell of Cherokee families in Northern Alabama; *Warrior Mountain Folklore* and *Doublehead*, both by Ricky Butch Walker
32. *Footsteps of the Cherokees, A Guide to the Eastern Homelands of the Cherokee*

*Nation* by Vicki Rozema.

33. *South Fork Country* by Samuel D. Walker mentions some mixed race families that moved into Southern Kentucky.

34. More books about Sequoyah: *The Mysteries of Sequoyah* by C. W. "Dub" West; *Sequoyah* by Grant Foreman; and *Se-Qou-Yah, The American Cadmus and Modern Moses: A Complete Biography of the Greatest of Redmen* (1885) by George Everett Foster.

# INDEX

185

Denton County, Texas, 11, 18, 19, 23, 30, 31, 54, 55, 177, 178
Denton Creek, 23
Denton Record-Chronicle, 18
Denton, Captain John B., 23
Denton, James, 39
Derveer, J. S. Van, 46
Desdemona, 19, 20, 21, 22
Desdemona, Eastland County, 19
Deskins, John, 96
Dickerson, Humphrey, 95
Dickinson, Townsend, 39
Dillard, John, 44
District 96, 58, 60
Dodge, Colonel Henry, 45, 46, 47
Donelson, Stockley, 104
Dotson, Lambert, 65
Doublehead, 24, 125, 126, 127, 136, 153, 154, 156, 183
Doublehead, Chief, 24, 125, 126, 127
Downing, George, 166
Downing, Joseph Edward, 166, 169
Downing, Kate Gist, 166
Downing, Loucile, 169
Downing, Maud, 169
Downing, Maude, 166
Downing, Nannie, 169
Downing, Teesey, 166, 169
Downtain, Dr. L. C., 21
Dragoon Expedition, 43, 47, 154, 175, 176, 179
Drew, John, 155
Driskil, Mahal, 62
Dudley, William, 44
Dull, Page, iii
Duncan, Stephens County, 11, 12, 13, 46, 178
Dupuy, David, 44
Duublajies, W.H., 142, 143
Dwight Mission, 40, 55

# E

Eagan, Thomas, 23
Eastland, 19, 20, 21, 22
Eastland County, Texas, 21
Eaves, William, 24
Edwards, A. G., 46

Egner, J., 39
Einstein, Albert, 164
Elder, Pat Spurlock, 61, 183
Elders, Young, 155
Elk Creek, 15, 22
Elk Horne, 19
Elms, David M., 44
Elms, Garrett, 44
Elms, James, 44
England, John, 44
Erwin, Ananias, 40
Erwin, Annanias, 44
Eustis, William, 46
Everett, Caroline, 17
Ewing, Sam., 63, 64

# F

F. S. Ranch, 15
Fairbanks, Jonathan, 89
Fannin County, 30
Ferguson, Jack, 102, 118
Ficklin, J. S., 50
Fields, Sallie, 167
Fields, Sallie (Gist), 165
Fields, Susan, 165
Fields, William, 165, 166, 169
Flahery, Isaac, 40
Flannery, Jacob, 35
Flat Creek, 42, 43
Ford, Lemuel, 46
Foreman, Grant, 10, 128, 129, 183, 184
Foreman, Stephen, 155
Foreman, Thomas, 134, 155
Fort Gibson, 43, 44, 45, 46, 47, 48, 50, 55, 56, 71, 176, 177
Fort Sill, 28
Fort Smith, ii, iii, 10, 11, 15, 33, 34, 50, 54, 55, 74, 75, 76, 77, 78, 90, 183
Fortenberry, Jacob, 36
Fortenberry, James S., 40
Foster, George Everett, 128, 161, 184
Foster, Ruth, 31
Frazier, Elizabeth, 84, 85, 86
Frenches, 23

Price, Aaron, 155
Price, Benjamin, 102, 171
Price, Emma, 4, 10, 12, 14, 31
Price, Jacob, 44
Price, Looney, 155
Pulaski County, Kentucky, 14, 103, 118, 119, 120
Purcell, Oklahoma, 48

# R

Rains, Jonathan, 107, 108
Rainwater, Hugh, 33, 42
Randolph, J. E., 83, 84
Raney, Bettie A., 53
Raney, David J., 44
Raney, Elvina, 53
Raney, Nancy, 81
Raper, Eliza, 150
Ray, Georgia, 17
Rea/Rhea, Ann, 56
Rea/Rhea, Anne, 56
Read, John, 39
Red River War, 27
Red River, Hempstead County, 41
Redmon, J., 39
Reed, Andrew, 104
Rice, Hannah, 138
Richardson, Rubin, 36
Richey, 35
Richey, Alfred H., 49
Richey, Beatrice Pearl, 3, 7, 8
Richey, Charlotte, 3, 4, 87, 88, 90, 91
Richey, David L., 50
Richey, Etta, 54
Richey, Etta E., 3, 4, 5, 6, 8, 13, 27, 28, 148
Richey, Ettie Elizabeth, 3
Richey, Hamilton, 48
Richey, Jeff, 30, 50
Richey, Jeffrey H., 4, 33
Richey, Jeffrey Hotten, 1, 2, 3, 4, 7, 27, 33, 49, 54
Richey, John, 48, 49
Richey, Joseph David, 3, 4, 35, 36, 49, 50, 65, 95, 108, 117, 118, 119, 168, 169
Richey, Josephine, 54
Richey, Josephine [Brown], 1, 34, 54

Richey, Josey Feen, 4
Richey, Lona (Loney) Clementine, 1, 3, 4, 5, 54, 105
Richey, Oscar Taylor, 3, 4, 10, 12, 13, 14, 40
Richey, Otho Ewell, 1, 2, 3, 4, 7
Richey, Swaney, 54
Richey, Swaney Adow, 4
Richey, Swany Adow, 3, 4, 7, 8
Richey, William, 4
Richey, William Franklin, 3, 7
Ridenhour, Crea, 105
Ridenhour, G. L., 105
Ridenour, G. L., 104, 110, 163
Ridge, John, 134
Riley, Looney, 155
Ritchie, Samuel, 62
Robins, William, 137
Robinson, William, 97
Rock Island Railroad, 11
Roebuck's Regiment, 58, 61
Roll, 23
Roney, Lewis, 111, 112
Roney, Nancy, 80, 111
Roseberry, James W., 90
Ross, John, 73, 144, 145, 155
Ross, Lewis, 155
Rozema, Vicki, 110, 153, 184
Ruddell, Abraham, 36, 37, 38, 39, 40
Ruddle, Stephen, 40
Russell County, 61, 62, 93, 96
Russell, Samuel, 44
Russian, Ruthie, 141
Ryan, John, 44
Ryan, William, 44

# S

S. A. Venters, 23
Saline River, 19
Sanders, Jim, iii, 116
Sands, Anderson M., 149
Saunders, James E., 88
Sawyers, Aaron M., 32
Sawyers, William, 44
Scaife, H. Lewis, 68, 183
Scott County, Virginia, 36, 61, 62

# T

Wayne County Kentucky, 100, 114, 116, 118, 119, 120, 121, 122, 123, 126, 171, 173
Wayne County, Kentucky, 14
Wayne, Anthony, 38
Weland, Keziah, 63, 64
Welborne, Melton, 45
Welch, Mary, 40
Welch, Michael, 159
Welders, 23
West, C. W. "Dub", 128, 184
West, Dub, 161
West, Isaac, 173
Western Lawrence County, 42
Whartenburg, Sevier, 24
Wharton, Clifton, 46
Wheelock, T. B., 46
White River, 35, 36, 41, 42, 55
White Weasel, 175
Whitley County Kentucky, 117, 120, 121, 122
Whitley County, Kentucky, 14
Whittaker, Jane, 102
Wichita, 43, 45, 46, 47, 154, 176, 177, 179
Will, Tobacco, 133, 155
Williams, Daniel, 40
Williams, Geo. E., 77
Williams, Silas, Junior, 109
Williamson, G. W., 76
Willis, Owen, 107, 108
Willson, Robert, 96
Wilson, Absolom, 44
Wilson, Daniel, 45

Wilson, Edward, 45
Wilson, John S., 44
Wilson, Joseph, 45
Wilson, William, 45
Wise County, 23
Wofford, 58, 60
Wolf, David, 137
Wolf, Gibson, 137
Wolfe, Young, 155
Wood, J.M., 143
Woods, Polly, 48
Works Progress Administration, 10, 106
Wright, Jesse, 173
Wright, Muriel Hazel, 74
Wu-te-he, 133, 134
Wut-tee, 129, 134
Wyatt, Joseph S., 45

# Y

Yell, Mordecai, 148
Yockhomises, 23
Young Puppy, 155
Young, Harvey K., 45
Young, Thomas, 171, 173

# Z

Zant, Martin Van, 40
Zeachsa, Burr H, 45

Bluewater Publications is a multi-faceted publishing company capable of meeting all of your reading and publishing needs. Our two-fold aim is to:

1) Provide the market with educationally enlightening and inspiring research and reading materials.
2) Make the opportunity of being published available to any author and or researcher who desire to be published.

We are passionate about preserving history; whether through the re-publishing of an out-of-print classic, or by publishing the research of historians and genealogists. Bluewater Publications is the *Peoples' Choice Publisher*.

For company information or information about how you can be published through Bluewater Publications, please visit:

**www.BluewaterPublications.com**

Also check Amazon.com to purchase any of the books that we publish.

***Confidently Preserving Our Past,***
Bluewater Publications.com

CPSIA information can be obtained
at www.ICGtesting.com
Printed in the USA
FFOW01n1627260314
4457FF